# SURV

**Part III of The Stephen...**

By

## James Christie

To Venice
loo [signature]

# MAGE PUBLISHING

1

# MAGE PUBLISHING
www.magepublishing.co.uk

Published in Great Britain and France by
Mage Publishing 2006
Copyright © James Christie and Stephen Holbrook

## ISBN: 978 09527109 6 7

"Survival" can be ordered through all major book shops by quoting the above ISBN code in association with Mage Publishing and the author's name, or alternatively by mail order direct from the publishers at the recommended retail price of £11.99 + £1 p&p . For details of future and current publications under the Mage banner please visit the Mage Publishing website at www.magepublishing.co.uk and for details of Stephen Holbrook's demonstrations please check out www.steveholbrook.co.uk

Printed by TJ International Ltd. Padstow, Cornwall

*This book is dedicated to*
**ROBBIE HOLBROOK**
*Following in the footsteps of the father*

When you can fly
as I can fly
then talk to me of clouds.
When you can sing
As I can sing
then talk to me of music.
When you can touch spirit
as I have touched spirit,
then talk to me of dreams
and when you can dream
as I have known dreams
then talk to me of angels.
When you have learned silence
as I have learned silence,
then be silent.

## Acknowledgements

Mage publishing would like to thank Martin Steers for IT support, Allan Potts and Jan Seddon for their expertise in genealogy, and the many other people, too countless to mention, who gave freely of their time and their memories to make this book possible. Our special thanks to Bill Williams, Kelly Rendall, Alice Sandler, Alice Egerton and Alvis Ormady... and, of course, to Florence who helped us so much in our search for Archie May. Kisses to Dave Baker and a couple of bottles of Optrex.

**Chapter One:**     *Contents*

He had changed a lot in the seven years I'd known him. Sure everyone changes, but usually it's a gradual process, the years touching a grey hair here and a laughter line there, and because it is so gradual we don't notice the subtle differences in appearance – either in the people close to us or indeed in ourselves – until one day we look in the mirror and get an unexpected shock!

I found myself looking at Steve Holbrook now and comparing him to the slightly over the top effervescent guy I'd met way back in 1999, and yes he'd got seven years older and seventy years wiser – slimmer, fitter, and an awful lot tougher. And it seemed to have happened in just half a dozen months rather than three quarters a decade! Maybe it had just crept up and none of us had noticed, not even Stephen himself until he had been presented with the fait accompli, and it wasn't just that he had changed on a physical level, he'd changed on the inside as well; in his head, his mind and in many of his attitudes.

His clairvoyance had also gone through a process of evolution and revolution. Back in 1999 he'd paced up and down the stage like a caged lion, delivering his messages from the world of spirit like a machine gun spraying bullets into the auditorium with such force that one message had hardly finished before another had begun; frequently there had been a mêlée while he'd had to pause and sort out who was getting what and from where. Now, at the beginning of 2006 that style of delivery had become a thing of the past. These days he was slower, more relaxed and occasionally a damn sight more aggressive than he had been when I'd first met him. He was also a lot more precise and had swapped his machine gun for a sniper's rifle. Every bullet went home (usually right between the eyes or straight to the heart) and every message got delivered with unprecedented accuracy. He stayed longer with individual links than he had ever done in the early days of his vocation and yet at the same time always seemed to generate between fifteen to twenty connections in the space of an evening – and that, as any working medium will tell you, certainly takes some doing, especially when you're doing it night after night with little time for leisure or pleasure or the fruits of the family tree.

Another thing which, without any kind of homework or preparation, had gradually come on line was Stephen's healing gift. In the beginning and during the early days it had seemed sufficient for Stephen to give messages to people in the audience from their loved ones who had passed over to the other side, but now, along with the messages, it seemed that a unique healing energy was passing from the medium to the recipient and while in many cases it could be said that Stephen's gifts healed in an emotional and a psychological way, there were increasing manifestations of physical healing as well. The lady in Huddersfield whose hearing had been restored after fifteen years of deafness... The gentleman from Southampton who had suffered with sciatica for many months who, on receiving a message from his departed mother, walked out of the demonstration with no symptoms of the complaint. In their respective cases of three years for the Huddersfield lady and nine months for the Southampton gentleman, the symptoms of deafness and sciatica have not returned.

If this sounds mysterious, marvellous and melodramatic then blame this author, for in truth this

6

healing phenomena was a quiet and subtle thing and not something that Stephen was prepared to talk about in any great depth... He didn't know what was happening or how it was happening – in his own words... *"James, I just felt the energy go out of me..."* but the recipients of this energy certainly knew something was happening and were more than willing to talk about their experiences, to their friends, to the press, and fortunately, also to me!

It was a beautiful early spring afternoon, unseasonably warm, and with the exciting energy of new growth tingling on the breeze. We stood on the balcony of our hotel room feasting our eyes on the quintessential English landscape that stretched out before us. Meadows, forests, in the near distance an enthusiastic river and way over on the horizon the skeletal finger of a lonely church spire. Facing west, the low April sunshine shone in our eyes and bathed the small terrace with its gorgeous golden light.

There were three of us present – four if you count the bottle of Pinot Grigio. Stephen and I leaned against the timber railing while in the background Rob Green, Stephen's newly appointed manager and the latest member of the team, was trying to make a discreet telephone call.

Nominally this gathering had been arranged to discuss a project very close to my heart – namely the writing of this book – but somehow the agenda had got shanghaied and instead we'd found ourselves talking about a subject very close to Stephen's heart, which was the quality of the wine he was drinking

Some fifteen months earlier he had gone through the traumatic and humiliating experience of drinking a bottle of Bardolino that had been badly corked and he'd been a very sick parrot for a few days. It hadn't scarred him for life exactly, but he had become more careful about what he drank and where he got it from. He had been impressing upon Rob and myself the advantage of paying 20% extra for a bottle to get a 100% better quality of contents but as soon as he realised he was preaching to the converted the conversation drifted into amiable banalities about the weather and how fortunate we were to be staying in such a well appointed hotel... Which was all very nice, but me being me, I wanted to talk about the book so in my usual tactless way I steered the conversation round to the subject in hand.

'You know, with this new book we can't just do a regurgitation of books one and two,' I said firmly to my audience of two.

'James, there's nothing wrong with either of those books,' Stephen said defensively.

'No, there's nothing wrong with them – as far as they go,' I agreed. 'But that's the problem. They don't go far enough and with this new project we've got to give people a bit more than some case histories and a handful of anecdotes from your personal life.'

'But people actually *like* the case histories' Stephen interrupted.

'Yeah, I know they do,' I agreed, 'and of course we'll have *some* case histories in the book, but we've got to have more than that. Basically, if I've done my market research right, people want a lot more detail about how everything works...'

Stephen did the Holbrook Twitch – this is where the nose wrinkles up to the left and his lips purse up to the right. You see it happen a lot when he's under any kind

8

of pressure or feels that he's being backed into a corner that he can't get out of.

'What exactly do you mean when you say "how everything works"?' he asked suspiciously. 'You know, we've had this conversation before James, and if you're going to hit me with a whole load of questions that I don't know the answers to, then you might as well not bother!'

There was no animosity in his voice, just a note of pleading that begged to be let off the hook. But now I'd got him on that hook, I wasn't going to let him off it lightly.

'Steve, I know that you haven't got all the answers to all the questions – you've been up front about that since day one – but look at it this way... There *are* people out there asking questions, and even if you haven't got the answers, you must at least have some theories or gut feelings. And even if you haven't...' I took a deep breath and lit the blue touch paper, 'you're one of the best clairvoyants in the country and so you're in a helluva sight stronger position than anyone else I can think of to ask a few questions yourself and see what you come up with.'

Before he could explode, I carried on quickly denying him the chance to interrupt. 'Look, you don't have to write anything in tablets of stone. It's quite sufficient to say something along the lines of "I've thought about this or that question, and in my opinion the answer *could* be XY or Z, and when I think about it a bit more, I'm inclined to think that it *might* be Z, but hey, ladies and gentlemen, I'm not a hundred percent sure about it, and what I'm giving you here is just my opinion!" That way, you're being totally honest, but at least you'll be giving the rest of us something to think about, and who knows, while you're going through this process you might find that you *are* actually discovering a few of the answers!'

'What are the questions that you've got in mind?' he muttered, looking desperately over my shoulder to see if there might be any help forthcoming from Rob.

There wasn't, and that was good – for me, if not for Steve!

I was mindful that the previous year I'd given him a list of 20 key questions to consider, but felt that it might not be a good idea to remind him of that fact just then. I knew he would be daunted by the prospect of coming up with the answers to 20 questions, so I figured I'd be on safe ground if I mentioned just two or three.

'Well,' I said vaguely and casually, mentally referring to my well rehearsed script. 'There's the question of infant mortality and what happens to a child's spirit when it passes over prematurely? Then the one we get asked a lot, of course, is can you have sex in heaven?' He laughed at that and I laughed with him, but nevertheless pointed out that it *was* a serious question for a lot of people.

'I'd want to have some conversations with you about reincarnation,' I told him, warming to my theme. 'I know you didn't think much of this when I asked you about it back in 1999 but,' and I nodded in Rob Green's direction, 'I know you've had good cause to change your mind on that subject during the last year or so.'

'Ummm, that's true,' he conceded.

'I'd want to quiz you a lot more about your spirit guides, Archie May in particular and, for goodness sake, you must have a few tips for people who are trying to develop their own psychic abilities! Also, there's this whole business about ghosts and hauntings, and I know we covered that to some extent in one of the other books, but since then, as you well know,' I looked at him meaningfully, 'a few things have *happened* since then that makes this subject worthy of a much deeper degree of investigation. And then, of course, take the lady who's had three husbands, all of whom have pre-deceased her – so who does she end up being married to on the other side? And then...'

'James, James, enough, enough!' Stephen's eyes were slightly glazed and I realised I might have gone just a little bit overboard in selling my pitch.

'Look,' he said. 'Make out another list of questions, and let's bring Rob in on this, and I promise I will try to come up with some sensible answers before you have to start putting pen to paper... Is that okay for now? I hope it is because I need a refill.' He waggled his empty wine glass in front of my nose and I beamed genially. So far, this meeting was going very nicely, thank you!

We refilled our glasses and joined Rob at the balcony table. Not wanting to lose the momentum, I asked both of them what they thought might be appropriate to include in the book. Rob felt that it would be a good idea if we could address the subject of poltergeists and evil spirits and was keen that we should concentrate some of our research energies into Stephen's burgeoning healing abilities. In both cases our favourite clairvoyant didn't seem very keen, but by then we were ganging up on him and, to give him his due, he let us prattle on for ten or fifteen minutes without too much opposition... But there was a look in his eyes (a look that I'd come to recognise over the years) that told me he'd more or less mentally moved on from this conversation and was thinking of something entirely different. Yep, Mr Holbrook had left the building!

Pouring the last dregs of the Pinot into his glass he looked at us thoughtfully. 'We're talking a lot about what's going to go into this new book,' he said, 'but now I want to talk a bit about what's *not* going into it!'

And with that remark he had my undivided attention! Stephen has different tones of voice for different situations… There is one naughty jokey tone when he's narrating a funny story, there's a suggestive tone for when he's putting ideas forward and needs some feedback, there's a dismissive tone that he'll use when he's fed-up with a subject or is dealing with some of his sillier critics, there is a gentle quiet tone that will be heard when he's trying to help somebody and, of course, there are various tones of voice that he will use when he is addressing the general public from the demonstration platform. Then there is another tone he'll use when he's giving a thoughtful opinion about something – one that says he has made his mind up and there isn't any room for discussion. And *that* was the tone of voice I was hearing now.

'Okay…' I reached for my pipe. 'What's on your mind?'

'Just this, James – in books one and two you wrote a whole load of stuff about my personal life, you know, my family background and bits about my wife and kids and all my daily routines, and when you wrote it, it was all very relevant, but since then, there have been a few changes and I really do feel I've given away as much stuff as I need to about my private life, so in this new book I think we need to give all the private stuff a miss and just concentrate on the professional side of things –

12

you know, my work rather than me myself... In any case, do people really want to know how many times I washed my hair this week and how many times I've over stuffed my face in a Chinese restaurant?'

He kept it light, but what he was doing was offering a deal, and at the same time imposing some terms and conditions. He would try to find the answers to some of the questions that had been bugging me for the past six or seven years, but as his biographer, I was to keep my pen (or word processor) out of his personal life and private affairs. On the face of it, it was a good compromise, but there was one point that I had to have clarified.

And so I asked him about that.

He thought about it, then shrugged his shoulders. 'Yes,' he said, 'I can see how you have to write about that, so I'll trust you to use your own words, but do me a favour James, keep it brief and to the point, okay?'

'Fine by me,' I agreed.

'Er, hem...' Rob coughed politely. 'Er, before we close this meeting, and we've got to in a minute because we've got the cars to unload and the audience is going to start arriving in less than an hour, can I just ask... Has this book got a title yet?'

I was about to present my marvellous idea of what the book should be called but Stephen got there a heart beat before me.

'Yes,' he said. 'We're going to call this new book "Survival".'

# Chapter Two:     *Survival*

When Stephen came up with "Survival" as the title for this book it created an immediate resonance in my psyche for although the word could obviously be applied to the survival of the spirit after death it could equally, but less obviously, be applied to our survival of the earthplane struggles that we all have to do battle with on our journeys through life from the cradle to the grave.

While no one has a monopoly on struggles and battles – we all have our challenges to face and our fights to fight – it is nevertheless an odd fact that everyone I have ever met who works in the field of the paranormal, from vicars and priests at one end of the spectrum to fakirs and fortune tellers at the other, all seem to have far more than their fair share of disaster and calamity littered along their life pathways than does your average Mr Man in the street.

Sometimes it is the crisis of extreme adversity that pushes the individual into the arms of spiritualism and spiritual exploration and then again, in many cases, it may just be that the clairvoyance and psychic awareness that dwells within the spiritual journeyman leaves him (or her) wide open to the slings and arrows of outrageous fortune that are thrown at him (or her) from the dirty tricks department of life's bottom drawer. From my own psychic world I have never known of a reader who hasn't had a damn sight more problems than the clients they are trying to help and I am ever mindful of some of the obstacles that have stood in the way of even the world's greatest mediums.

Ozzie Rae's battle with his alter ego may have been the very thing that made him the medium that he was, but it doesn't alter the fact that this was his life long fight, and he fought the fight well right to the very end of the road. Edith Schiff, arguably (at the time of writing) the world's most convincing living medium, may never have realised her own potential without first having survived three indescribable years in a German concentration camp at the height of the holocaust. My old mentor Harry Andrews, one of America's top psychics, was once an Anglican priest – then on the day that he lost his wife and three children in a horrendous hotel fire, he also lost his Anglican faith and turned to spiritualism to find his answers. A gifted one-to-one reader that I know is a quirky rough diamond Geordie called Mick – who finally found his way into the spiritualist church after a history of drug abuse and homelessness and a decade of severely chronic child abuse in half a dozen different children's homes during the formative years of his turbulent life. Welsh mystic Stephen O'Brien's early years were plagued by poverty and ill-health, and of course Doris Stokes' battle with cancer was well publicised at the time.

Maybe this has all got something to do with the theory that you cannot really help the suffering until you have first suffered yourself. There's a guy on the bridge at midnight. He's about to jump. You try to talk him down. You tell him that you've been there and you know what he's going through. He looks you hard in the eye and if you're telling the truth he'll see it and believe you, and then you might have a chance. If you're lying he'll see that too and will probably jump – and there goes the cure for cancer or the solution to the common cold or the seed that gives life to the next Albert Einstein. Certainly, based on my own experience, this is a theory that I am willing to embrace.

15

So where and how, you may ask, does Steve Holbrook fit into this pantheon of pain? At first it is not glaringly obvious and even after one searches for it and subsequently finds it, it doesn't seem quite so dramatic as the circumstances befalling Ozzie Rae, Edith Schiff, Harry Andrews and all the other long suffering souls who have dedicated their lives to the world of spirit. However Stephen's story does bear some telling and against what you might regard as being "normal" consider this…

Take an average twelve year old child going through the anguish of puberty whilst at the same time trying to keep up with the ever present bombardment of the educational regime. For most kids, especially these days, this is more than enough pressure to bring on panic attacks and pre-adult stress disorders. Now in Steve's case, let's add nocturnal visitiations from visiting spirits seeking earthplane connections, all causing interrupted sleep patterns that take the edge off any prowess of concentration in the boy's working hours. Let's face it, even though Stephen may have been sensitive enough to deal with this situation with a degree of stoicism, it really is the stuff of nightmares!

Stephen's first experience involved a much discussed visit from his Grandfather very late at night… Stephen awoke to find this gentleman standing by the side of his bed, who instructed him to go and wake his mother and to "Tell her I've gone!". Not knowing what the blazes was going on, he did as he was told, and went to wake his mother with the message. Margaret Holbrook handled this situation with aplomb and put the young Stephen back to bed, suggesting that he'd been dreaming, because as she, and indeed the whole Holbrook family knew, Stephen's grandfather was fighting for his life in the local hospital. However, the following morning Margaret received the sad news from the hospital to say that John Clifford Sykes had died quietly in his sleep at 3.55 a.m. The exact time that Stephen had woken her with the message!

This seems to have acted as a catalyst that opened a portal between the two worlds. Although he does not speak of it in any great depth – it is as though the story about his Grandfather is a good enough example and the rest he's kept to himself – few were the nights when Steve wasn't awoken in the early hours by some discarnate identity wanting to use him as a channel to make contact with a loved one down here on the earthplane. *"Could you go round to Alice Smith who lives just around the corner at number 46 and tell her that although I died in the crash I'm all right now, and tell her this is Peter and that I love her very much."*

Even the most highly trained mediums with a plethora of experience would find this tiresome. Your average Mr Man in the street would be hard pressed to cope without thinking that he was cracking up, and a good few souls would very possibly find themselves running for help to the nearest church or mental hospital. How then should we expect a twelve year old boy to deal with these strange and disturbing events?

Add to this the increasing cacophony of babbling voices that began to reverberate through Stephen's head during his waking hours… A jumble of sounds – some of which he could recognise as words, most of which he could not – that inhibited his ability to hear what was being said to him by members of his family, his school friends and, more importantly, by his teachers. Imagine a chronic case of tinnitus and then multiply by ten!

17

Sadly, if this symptom had been tinnitus some allopathic medical help could have been applied and had these events been occurring in 2006 rather than the early 1980's he may have been diagnosed as a child with learning difficulties. As it was, some of his more kindly critics thought he was just a bit slow while other less sensitive critics just thought he was thick. Again, he doesn't speak of it overmuch, but one gets the clear impression of ostracism and no small degree of bullying through the critical years of his early teens.

Stephen's family, and in particular his extremely caring and very astute mother, were not unaware of this situation. A number of consultations with their local GP's threw no clear light on Stephen's condition other than to clarify that there was no medical problem with his hearing and that whatever was causing the noises in his head, it certainly wasn't tinnitus. Steve's mother Margaret, acting either on instinct or out of desperation, finally plucked up the courage to take her son, then sixteen years old, to see a private specialist, and this was when I suspect there was some divine spiritual intervention. Stephen's doctor said that he didn't think that there was anything physically wrong with Margaret's son, but he thought it might be a good idea if she took him down to the local spiritualist church and see if there was anything they could do – only, and he'd regard this as a great favour, please don't tell anyone that he'd given them this advice.

While this was undoubtedly a major turning point in Stephen's life it is hardly the stuff of normality. Most young teenage boys are out there playing football, chatting up girls, learning to play guitars or studying for colleges and universities, and yet while his peers availed themselves of these opportunities, Stephen was being educated and trained by the spiritualist church under the guiding hands of people like Una Pierce and Janet Fergusen (Jane McDonald's grand mother!) who were the doyens of the spiritualist movement in the North of England at that time. This training brought confidence, control and understanding but arguably did not do much for either his social skills or his academic education. And so even in these early formative years Stephen was travelling the road of the shaman and the seer, ever set apart from the crowd by his extraordinary gifts and talents, that were sometimes seen as a blessing but which could also quite frequently be regarded as a curse.

In the circumstances it is not entirely surprising that Stephen married at quite a young age: Caroline was his first serious girl friend, and in finding her he looked no further to find his life partner. They were ideally suited – both young and beautiful, both working in the hairdressing industry and both with a very convenient similarity in tastes and values. Although no relationship is ever perfect, their love for each other was strong and enduring, and Caroline brought Stephen a much needed platform of stability and security. Two junior hairdressers didn't have much spare cash and there wasn't any room for luxuries: a night out for dinner meant fish and chips from the corner shop and a holiday meant a long weekend in a leaking caravan in Scarborough. (Maybe this is something which has created a deep abiding love in Stephen's psyche for cramped holidays in leaking caravans when, at this stage in his life, he could just as easily cart everyone off for a fortnight's break in Tenerife in a four star hotel!)

Stephen describes his early years with Caroline as being *"the most normal years of my life and therefore in some ways, the very happiest years of my life..."*

If you have a destiny to follow and if that destiny is in any way involved with spirit, you do not always get to call the shots in your own life. I think that Steve would have been perfectly happy living with his beautiful young wife and working away at his career as a hairdresser... I think that he would have been perfectly happy siring and subsequently doting on his three gorgeous children... I think he would have been perfectly happy working in his garden, and maybe going to the movies once a week and having some good nights out at his local Chinese with his family and friends... But when spirit has got a job for you to do it seldom asks if you'd *like* to do it, but rather just puts you in the position whereby you've little choice other than to get on with it and get it done. We may feel, through our human arrogance, that it was we who made this or that choice, and spirit says nothing but quietly laughs all the way to the heavens.

Stephen's early training in the spiritualist church had centred around sitting in development circles, attending church services and doing one to one readings on demand for various members of the congregation – which was something he hated doing then and hates doing just as much today, so much so that he just won't do them, full stop. Regardless of this aversion he soon acquired the reputation of being a very accurate reader and his services were always much in demand. However he felt compelled to march to a different drum and after having sat through countless demonstrations of clairvoyance thinking *"I could do better than that"* or *"no, this message isn't for that person, it's for the bloke over there in the corner"* he was finally pushed to put his money where his mouth was.

In the autumn of 1985 he reserved a small village hall on the outskirts of Leeds and put a tiny advert in the local free paper advertising an evening of clairvoyance with "Stephen – Yorkshire's Youngest Clairvoyant". All of thirteen people turned up, but as far as Steve was concerned it was a fair test. These thirteen people had each paid a couple of quid to come and see him and they were all strangers to him; there were no links with his friends at Peterson Road and this was an objective, and potentially hostile audience.

Stephen: "I didn't do this out of ego or to make any money. I just felt compelled to do it, just to see if I could do it, and although my palms were sweating and my knees were trembling and my voice was croaking, I did manage to bring about half a dozen messages through that seemed to impress the crowd and at the end of the night, although I was shattered and a quivering wreck of nerves, I knew that this was the sort of thing I was supposed to be doing. I didn't see much point in preaching to the converted. I wanted to be with people who wouldn't normally go within a mile of the spiritualist church. I wasn't evangelical and I wasn't looking for converts, I just wanted to bring some comfort to people who needed some comfort. It was a bit like thinking if the mountain won't come to Mohammed, I'd better do something to take Mohammed to the mountain..."

Stephen was just nineteen years old when he embarked upon his mission – although I don't suppose he intellectualised it in such dramatic terms. He was just doing what he felt he should be doing, and if

21

nothing else, it got him out of having to do those dreaded one-to-ones down at Peterson Road.

And from small acorns large oak trees do grow.

It did not happen all at once… Rather it emerged and evolved gradually over a dozen years or more until by the late 1990's Stephen was working full time as a hairdresser in the City of Leeds and then driving half way across the North of England to fulfil his commitments as a demonstrating medium. While this did provide a modicum of security for Caroline and his steadily increasing family, it was exhausting work that denied him access to the normal family life most young married couples can expect to enjoy.

Stephen: "The alarm clock would go off at half past five, I'd be up and getting ready to drive to work by half past six, I'd be in the salon doing my first appointment by eight o'clock, I'd work right the way through until half past five and then get in the car and drive sixty miles to God knows where to do a demonstration of clairvoyance – I'd finish at around half past nine and then drive the sixty odd miles back to Wakefield, and finally sit down for a bite of supper with Caroline at around 11 pm… Then I'd have to do the cashing up and I'd rarely get to bed much before one o'clock in the morning."

No, not much of a family life, and this became the pattern, twenty five days out of thirty, year out, year in. To be sure, the free time spent with Caroline and the children was quality time and Stephen readily admits that he couldn't have followed his vocation without having Caroline to back him up, doing an absolutely first rate job in bringing up the children, not exactly like a single parent, but certainly as a wife whose husband was in absentia for much of the time.

In all fairness, the bond of family love was more than strong enough to cope with this imposition, and to all intents and purposes his children are growing up well with great love and good humour. Their love for their father does not appear to have been damaged by his phenomenal work load, and I guess that the truth of the matter is that when he is with them at weekends, days off, school holidays, etc, he overcompensates like mad, not because he feels he *has* to but because he genuinely wants to.

The point I am trying to make here, albeit somewhat long windedly, is that in Stephen Holbrook we find a loving husband and doting father who has sacrificed a very great deal of unrepeatable quality time in pursuit of his spiritual vocation.

Yes, we could all point the finger and say well, he should have made more time for his family, but it is a very glib and easy thing to say without any understanding of the other agenda that for so many years has been pressed upon this man's shoulders.

"James, you've got no idea how many times I've felt like saying sod it, I'm going to cancel this or that demonstration and I'm going to have a night in with the kids or a night out with my wife, but every time I contemplated it I get hit by this enormous wave of conscience. What happens if I don't show up at a demonstration and there's just one person there whose very life depends on getting a message through from their mum or their dad or their son or their daughter? I'd be letting them down, I'd be letting spirit down, and in a way, I'd be letting myself down too. Any time with my wife and kids would be spoiled because I'd just feel *so* guilty, and that isn't to say that I don't feel guilty about leaving my family on their own for so many hours every day, because I really do. It just feels like I'm between the rock and the hard place because whatever I do is going to be wrong. I'm nothing special, there's nothing special about me at all, but my gift is special and I owe it to whoever or whatever gave me this gift to do the right thing by it. If everyone else had the same gift then maybe I could take a bit more time off ."

This is not a diatribe designed to solicit sympathy for my poor hard done by mate Stephen Holbrook, but more of an attempt to paint a side of the coin that very few people are likely to see when they peep into the life of one of the nation's most dedicated mediums. And there are, it has to be admitted, some very profound compensations.

A few years ago Steve's wife Caroline was diagnosed with cancer of the lymphoma – the doctors were quite adamant, and there was no chance of a misdiagnosis. This illness had come out of the blue with no warning – and by sod's law, it had come at the height of Stephen's touring season when he was all over the country for dozens of consecutive nights in a row. Stephen didn't miss a demonstration, but what he did do (and with a lot of help from spiritualist friends all over the UK) was to send out a massive prayer to spirit for some divine intervention, and within six weeks all the symptoms of Caroline's cancer had disappeared. Her medical team couldn't believe it then, and they still can't believe it now, but it happened, nevertheless.

In the face of these human dramas Stephen's reaction has been to keep his fears very much to himself, to have faith in spirit and, as always, to get on with the job. He is not a man to bleat and moan, and while he will share his laughter and good humour with all and sundry, his private terrors and his nightmares are quintessentially his own and not to be shared. *"Bloody hell James, people don't want to hear about my problems. They've got enough of their own!"* But if Stephen thought that he'd had to deal with a few problems from time to time, nothing that had gone before was to prepare him for what came next... And what did come next is extremely sad, and true to my promise, I'll keep it brief and simple.

In the spring of 2005 Stephen and Caroline realised that their marriage had run out of steam, and with profound love and deep regret, they elected to go their separate ways... At least as man and wife. To this day, however, they still have a fantastic relationship. They see each other two or three times a week, take the children on holiday together and the kids spend almost as much time with their dad as they do with their mum. Their marriage may have come to an end, but their love and friendship carries on unabated, and while each may have lost a husband and a wife, both have found a brother and a sister.

Let no one imagine this transition was easy for either of them! Let all be thankful that they survived this emotional ordeal, and that with spirit's help, their love and respect for each other remains intact.

## Chapter Three: *Telephone Exchange*

On those rare occasions when Stephen really opens up and talks about his work with spirit, he describes himself as a telephone exchange between this world and the next. In his own words:

"Imagine you're on holiday in Spain in the time before mobile phones. There's one public kiosk on the sea front with 200 or so people waiting to phone home to tell their mums and their dads that they've arrived safely, the hotel isn't too bad and the weather is lovely. Then imagine there's 200 or so people back in England waiting to hear from their relatives, to make sure that that they've arrived and that everything is okay. Right, got the picture? Well, now imagine that the 200 people in Spain are up there in the spirit world, the 200 hundred people in England are my audience sitting in a demonstration and, as for me, I'm just the telephone exchange operator trying to get 200 calls through in the space of a couple of hours. It can't be done – at best I'll be able to connect 20 calls – and then I'm shattered for the night and another operator – or if you like, another medium – comes on duty manning another line, and then maybe a dozen others all over the world, until it's my shift again."

As far as it goes, this is an accurate if somewhat simple analogy and although in essence we can grasp what Stephen is trying to say, it still does not provide us either with the mechanism or the detail of what Stephen is actually doing when he opens up that telephone exchange of his. When I have (frequently) pushed him on this point he squirms with frustration. He has told us in his own words *what* is happening but he does not know *how* it is happening.

Dr Adam Wallace, author and highly experienced parapsychologist has an intriguing theory. He believes that many aspects of the spirit world are a reflection of life here on the earthplane, and vice versa! This is not a new idea – in fact it is as old as the hills – and is the stimuli within the framework of many religions that is responsible for the "As Above, So Below" school of thought. But it is within the development of the Wallace theory that we do get the glimmerings of some possible explanation.

He believes that long before Stephen Holbrook (or any other good medium for that matter) actually walks out onto the public platform a subliminal and superconscious psychic signal is emitted from that medium *which is picked up by another medium on the other side* who in turn organises a gathering of souls in the spirit world who are anxious to make contact with their loved ones down here on the earthplane.

So, when Stephen Holbrook walks out onto the stage, say at the Hilton Hotel in St Helens, another medium in the world of spirit walks out onto *his* stage in the spirit world's equivalent of the St Helens Hilton, and thus the connection is facilitated.

Wallace's theory is exactly that... just a theory. But when I read his papers on the subject I did warm to the idea of a celestial demonstration of clairvoyance attended by an audience of spirits with a medium who stood up in front of the crowd and said something like "Good evening ladies and gentlemen, and welcome to the Heavenly Hilton – everyone all right? – lovely! Well what we're going to do tonight is to try and make contact with the living, so if you think the message might be for you just stick your hand up and give me a loud yes or no..."

27

Making light of it in this way is not intended to belittle Dr Wallace's body of research. Wallace is a serious academic with many years of study and experimentation to his credit and reading some of his work has stimulated my own imagination and stretched the borders of my comprehension.

As much as anything else, Wallace has reminded me of the "As Above, So Below" theory, which I have always found fascinating, and if one is seeking the answer to the key question "what is life like in the spirit world?" the expansion and extrapolation of the theory is of paramount importance.

When I have asked Stephen for his vision of heaven and an AA road map to Paradise he has laughed in my face... "How the heck should I know?" he once reposted, "I haven't been there yet!"

It was a good line, but when I persisted and pointed out the fact that although he might not have been there himself he'd talked to thousands of people who had, he did sober up and take the point seriously.

Now we have covered "Visions of Heaven" in Steve's other books so there is no point in a lengthy regurgitation here. Suffice to say that Stephen does not have a vision of heaven other than it "being a place of great peace and calm and tranquillity... A place of great healing and learning and spiritual growth..." and while this may be a clichéd perspective, I am happy enough to accept it in part for at the end of the day a cliché becomes a cliché because it says something so succinctly and I'd rather have Holbrook's vague honesty than a load of new age fiction made up by false gurus looking to make a quick buck in the publishing industry.

Nevertheless, I want to know exactly what happens after death and exactly what it is like in the spirit world and so too, I suspect, do a whole load of other people out there.

Oh yes, I have questions – I've always had questions – and when I met Stephen Holbrook in 1999 I was hopeful he would have the answers for me. And if those answers were not forthcoming then – well, that was then and this is now, and things have changed a fair old bit over the last six or seven years.... And this brings me back to the Holbrook Telephone Exchange. Telephone exchanges are supposed to *exchange* messages, aren't they? You know, a *two* way dialogue, not just an answer machine message from another dimension? Therefore, if Steve can bring a message *through* from the spirit world, can he not send one back? And if he can, as a clairaudient, hear the voices of spirit people, could they not in turn hear him should he choose to speak to them. In short, why should it always be a one way communication from the spirit world? Why can't it be two way? Given that such a telephone exchange exists, why cannot the grieving widow come to Stephen or any other medium and ask to be put in direct contact with her late husband if only to say I love you for one last time or possibly to ask where that all important insurance policy document has been hidden away?

Once, when I took Stephen to task on this subject, he admitted that he'd never pushed his luck by asking either question or favour of spirit for fear that they would think he was looking a gift horse in the mouth or imposing some conditions of service. And yet in later and more recent conversations he concedes that he is

29

asking *guidance* from spirit all the time – never on trivial issues like "should I put this plant in the sun or the shade" but certainly on major issues than cause concern or worry.

But he will do this in a subtle and simplistic way in the mode of the "give us a sign" technique... In other words, he may be desperately worried about one of his children and be undecided as to whether he should telephone the school or Caroline... He doesn't want to cause a fuss or a panic but the thought of being considered uncaring and irresponsible is anathema to him. So, the question is, does he make a phone call? Well, if he sees a red car at the next cross roads the answer is yes, he must make the call, but if he doesn't, there is no need. Panic over. He's practised this technique for more than fifteen years *"at least two or three times a week"* and it has never failed him yet.

On another level he will allow his spiritual sensitivity to guide him on a whole variety of different decisions, both professional and personal... But this is something that many of us do as a matter of course and although this could be construed as some form of spiritual communication, it is not the direct voice dialogue that I am intimating should be possible between medium and spirit.

I know of many mediums who have *claimed* to have had this degree of two way communication, but none have, thus far, been able to prove it to my satisfaction... And let me, at this point, set out my terms of reference. Yes, I do believe we can have two way communication with spirits in our dreams and I do believe that on rare occasions we can enjoy that epiphany of communication in visions, but this is *not* the same as a two way dialogue in a conscious state. Even if you're sitting in a genuine séance with a qualified medium, by virtue of the fact that it is a séance, the medium is in a light (or very heavy) trance which by any definition is *not* a consciousness as we know it.

A little while ago we were doing a demonstration of clairvoyance in Lowestoft and as we were staying overnight I took the opportunity to show Stephen and Rob the rough draft of this chapter. When Steve had finished reading through the text he scratched his head thoughtfully...

'James, I'm not quite sure what you're trying to say in all of this... I mean, er, well, it's a bit confusing, isn't it?'

Rob Green is not a clairvoyant (although I do believe he is in possession of a very potent, if latent, psychic ability) but he *does* have an incisive mind and sharply honed intellect and he got to the heart of the matter very quickly.

'All James wants to know,' he said flatly 'is why can't you have a two way conversation with the people who talk to you from the other side, and if they can contact you why can't you contact them?'

'It just doesn't work like that,' Stephen replied, 'at least, not with me it doesn't.'

'Yes, I think James understands that, but all he's doing is asking you *why* it doesn't work like that.'

Stephen shrugged helplessly. 'Dunno...' And then, a little more brightly – 'Maybe it's not supposed to work like that?' And then, gaining a little more confidence... 'I mean, as far as I know, nobody has ever had that kind of two way communication with the spirit world, have they?'

When Rob Green first came into contact with Stephen, by his own admission, he knew little or nothing about clairvoyancy or spiritualism and although he had an open mind, his view was slightly sceptical. This was a view that changed very quickly after having attended a few of Stephen's demonstrations and, once appointed to the role of being Stephen's manager, he took it upon himself to research the subject as thoroughly as he could. In the space of a dozen weeks he had read a dozen popular books on life after death and a couple of weighty tomes that would have intimidated all but the most dedicated scholar. Furthermore, he had constantly bombarded Stephen with questions (most of the time being no more successful than I in getting lucid answers) and on more than several occasions he had drained me dry of my own limited reservoir of experience and information. Thus, although a newcomer to the subject, his terms of reference were well in place and more relevantly, his knowledge was fresh in mind.

Now he looked at Stephen and I with a degree of caution. On the one hand he didn't want to be disloyal to his boss but on the other hand, just like me, he wanted some answers.

'Haven't there been some occasions...' he chose his words carefully, '...some occasions where mediums *have* been able to contact spirits from the other side?'

'Well, it's been claimed, but never proven... Or you could say it's been reported but never recorded.'

'What about that business back in 1984 with Doris Stokes?' he asked. 'I mean, wasn't she supposed to have had a conversation with George Orwell and wasn't this filmed and recorded by the BBC?'

Stephen looked at us both blankly and I looked at Rob, studying his face for any sign of artifice or guile, wondering if he was winding me up or whether this mention of Doris Stokes and George Orwell was just a flukey coincidence, for only the previous year I had done some serious research on this Stokes/Orwell incident for another book I had been writing at the time.*

Basically, the BBC had decided that it would be a hoot if the medium of the day, a lady called Doris Stokes, could summon up the spirit of George Orwell and ask him what he thought of society in 1984 and if it was close to his own vision of that year made famous in his book. In my opinion this was a seriously flawed experiment insofar as Doris knew well in advance what her brief was and therefore had plenty of time to research her subject – for heaven's sake, she even had a list of the questions the BBC wanted answering. The only account we have of this experiment is written by her own hand in one of her books and the TV footage was never broadcast. Furthermore, no one at the BBC seems to know what ever happened to it.

This by no means infers that Doris Stokes was anything less than a totally sincere medium – indeed, it is she more than anyone else who was responsible for popularising spiritualism and providing it with some dignity and respectability in the 1970's and 1980's and I do not believe for one minute that she would ever have done anything deceitful or underhand – but nevertheless the George Orwell experiment *is* flawed because the sceptic and the scientist can point to the aspects of fore-knowledge.

The George Orwell incident probably was not one of the high points in her career but Doris was an honest hard working lady without artifice and I do not think, unlike some of the mediums who have come after her, that she succumbed to the glamour and the razzmatazz of television celebrity. She was far too down to earth for that.

'I'm even more confused now than I was before,' Stephen said. 'On the one hand you want there to be two way communication, but you're rubbishing the attempts that have been made so far, so what exactly do you want me to do?'

'I want you to do it for real,' I said bluntly.

'But I've told you before, James, I can't do that!'

'Yeah well, at least I want you to try and I want to be there when you do it...'

And for the time being, that was the end of that conversation.

## Chapter Four:     *Billy & Bill*

On Sunday 19<sup>th</sup> February Stephen was the conduit for a most unusual link with the world of spirit. We were in the East Anglian town of Lowestoft and, as usual, he was demonstrating to a packed house. We'd been turning people away on the phone for several weeks and on the evening of the event there wasn't a spare chair to be had.

The first half of the evening was unremarkable (that is, if you can call channelling messages from another dimension unremarkable) but during the second half of the evening there was a bit of an odd ball message that almost went unclaimed.

Just as Stephen was walking up onto the postage stamp of a stage to start the second part of the demonstration, a small dapper man came through the double doors of the entrance. He was about sixty, maybe sixty five years old, wearing a very expensive suit and carrying with him an air of quiet confidence and authority. He looked vaguely familiar and when he asked if it would be all right if he stood and watched from the back for a while, assuming (wrongly as it turned out) that he was part of the hotel management team, I said sure, okay, that would be fine.

Steve's first message of the second half was short and to the point as he brought through a young lady who had passed over from a drugs overdose. This young lady wanted to talk to her mum who was sitting on the second row, just to say how sorry she was, and to thank her mum for looking after her baby. By the time Stephen had provided the names and the dates and many of the intimate details that only the mother could have known, there wasn't a dry eye in the house.

Then in some state of mild agitation Stephen started pacing up and down the stage as he had done in the early days when I'd first known him. He cast stabbing glances at the audience as though trying to see someone who wasn't there.

'Windmills!' he exclaimed abruptly. 'Anyone understand windmills?'

No response from the audience. More pacing and more puzzled looks.

'Definitely windmills. Someone who used to live in a windmill?'

Still no response from the audience other than a cough from the left of the room and a scraping chair to the right.

'I've got someone here who passed over from some sort of wasting disease – someone who was ill for a very long time but they didn't know just how ill they were – someone who died quite young, well before their time? Please can anyone understand any of this? Be quick or I'm going to lose it...'

No response.

'He's telling me,' Stephen groped for the information 'that he had a heart condition but that no one knew anything about it. It was a big secret...'

Still no reaction from the audience.

'This is a young man and he's telling me he's absolutely *furious* about the way in which he died and he's going on about the windmill and I know that there is someone in this room who understands all of this...'

'I think this message might be for me,' said a well modulated voice from the back of the room and when I looked around I recognised the speaker to be the smartly dressed gentleman who'd slipped into the room at the end of the interval.

'Good, sir. Can I just have your voice? You understand what I've been saying so far?'

'I do now,' said the man.

Curious, you somehow expect small men to have small or high voices, but this wasn't the case with this guy. Devoid of regional accent, he had the ability to project his voice across the room without strain or effort and unless I was much mistaken he'd obviously had some experience in public speaking.

'You understand about the windmill?' Stephen asked.

'Yes, I do.'

'And you understand about someone passing over before their time with some sort of wasting illness or chronic heart condition?'

'Yes, I do.'

'And you can understand about how *angry* they were?'

The man chuckled. 'Furious was the word I think you used earlier,' he commented conversationally...

...And this was unusual, for when someone gets a message from Stephen they are either surprised, shocked, delighted or moved to tears. This gentleman's attitude was none of those things. Instead, whilst acknowledging the correctness of Stephen's comments, he seemed determined not to give anything away and appeared to be waiting for Stephen to come up with more information. There was nothing in his tone of voice which suggested challenge but there was something there that said *I'm not going to help you Mr Holbrook – you're on the right track though, so let's see what you can do.*

'Who's Bill or William?' Stephen called out.

The man in the suit laughed. 'I'm Bill,' he said.

'Well if you're Bill there's someone connected to you whose name is William... Not your father or anything like that, not a son either, it's more of a brother link that I'm getting.'

The man inclined his head. 'I can accept that,' he said non-committally.

Stephen paused and took a sip of water. 'Sir, did you drive here tonight in a silver car?'

'Yes I did.'

'A silver BMW?'

'Yes, a silver BMW!'

Steve cocked his head to one side. 'Sir, there's something unusual about the number plate. Have you got one of those personalised plates with your intials on it or something like that?'

The man in the suit was smiling broadly. 'Yes,' he said. 'Something like that.'

'And sir, I mean, I know we're here by the sea-side, but have you got anything to do with boats, or do you own a boat?'

Mr Suit laughed. He was enjoying this a lot.

'Yes, I do own a boat.'

'And has this boat got a bit of an unusual name... I mean it's not a name like Jolly Roger or the usual boaty names that you sometimes get, it's more like...' Stephen paused looking for the right words, '...it's almost like the boat's name is some sort of song title or the name of a book or something?'

There was now a fresh note of respect in the man's voice. 'That is perfectly correct,' he confirmed

'Well, who's Norma or Norman?' Steve asked.

'I can accept both of those names,' Mr Suit said, still obviously taking care not to furnish Stephen with any information.

'And I've got someone here called Ron and Ron tells me *he* knows exactly what I'm talking about this evening.'

'He would,' said Mr Suit laconically.

I think that by now some other clairvoyants would have walked away in exasperation, suspecting that the recipient of the message was playing some sort of psychological mind game. But Stephen, now completely relaxed and perching on the edge of the stage table, wasn't in the slightest bit phased and indeed seemed to welcome Mr Suit's responses. This was something a little bit different to the run of the mill messages and, to give him his due, Stephen always welcomes new experiences in his clairvoyant work, even if he is sometimes reticent in some aspects of his personal life...

'Right,' Stephen said in a matter of fact voice. 'I've got this young man here who says he knew you were going to be here tonight, and he just wants to say thank you for remembering him the way you have done and thank you for looking after the dogs...

'He says you nearly didn't come this evening but then you changed your mind at the last minute, and when you did come you were playing some very special music in the car and that you were cross when you couldn't find the particular piece of music you were looking for... Do you understand?'

'Perfectly,' said the man at the back of the room and I noticed that his voice was softer now. The rest of us might not have had a clue with regard to what Stephen was going on about, but it was obvious that the man in the suit new exactly what the message meant.

'Ummm,' Stephen mused. 'This young man is saying something about there being a lot of jealousy and that he's always in your thoughts... He's saying that if he had lived, your life would have been different, but the way that it worked out was the best way for everybody. He's going on about the dogs again and he's also saying to thank you for being his friend when all the others had gone... Do you understand what he's saying, sir?'

From my angle of view I could see the gentleman dabbing his eyes with a white handerchief. 'Yes, I do,' he said quietly, but I'm not sure whether or not Stephen heard this response.

'I know you're Bill,' Stephen exclaimed 'but who's Billy? I've got Billy here and he's saying that you both owe a big thank you to Jack. Do you know who Jack is, sir...?'

'Yes.'

'And sir, can I ask... Have you just written a cheque for a large amount of money? Something like four thousand pounds... Not *exactly* four thousand, but maybe four thousand and a few odd pennies?'

'Yes, I have.'

'And this young man I've got with me is saying that there was a big problem about the money, but that it wasn't his fault. Can you understand what he's going on about?'

'Absolutely.'

'Harry! Who's Harry?'

'No, I don't understand Harry...'

'Harry!' Stephen repeated adamantly. 'Harry or Barry or Larry who ties in with the money situation?'

'Oh, that's Larry...'

'But....' Stephen cocked his head to one side as though listening to a discarnate voice, which I suppose, when you think about it, is exactly what he *was* doing. 'Sir, he's telling me that this was all a very long time ago... Do you understand?'

'Yes,' there was a great weight of sadness in Mr Suit's voice. Sadness and resignation. 'It was all a very long time ago.'

Then without warning he turned and walked briskly out of the room, leaving Stephen floundering up on the stage wondering what to say next...

He recovered quickly enough, saying something about how emotions could so easily get the better of all of us, then tentatively went on to the next message. Right then and there, I knew that Stephen would regard the abrupt termination of the link as unsatisfactory and unfinished business but that by the end of the evening, after having forged another half dozen links with members of the audience, it would be past and forgotten and just an unusual and flooky little incident in an otherwise routine demonstration. For my part it prayed on my mind for the rest of the night and I somehow sensed that there was another aspect to this story that neither I nor Steve Holbrook was privy to... If you like, a book minus the last chapter that had yet to be written.

The following morning, February 20th, we had quite an early start. Steve and Rob checked out of the hotel around eight thirty, and I was about half an hour behind them. I'd just settled the account and was heading for the door when the receptionist called after me...

'Excuse me Mr Christie, I've got someone on the phone here who wants to talk to Mr Holbrook or to his manager...'

As I say, Steve and Rob had already left and I was quite anxious to get off myself, and I was half inclined to ignore this call. Then good manners and gut instinct got the better of me and I went back to the reception desk and took the proffered telephone.

'Morning,' I said, maybe a little too abruptly. 'Sorry but Stephen and his manager have checked out and they're on their way back to Yorkshire. My name is James Christie, can I help at all?'

'Ah, you'll be the gentleman I spoke to last evening,' said a voice I immediately recognised. 'You were kind enough to let me in to see part of Mr Holbrook's demonstration... I'm the chap who was standing at the back for a while.'

'Oh yes sir, I remember you. What can I do for you?'

There was a short pause, and then – 'Would I be correct in thinking that you're the man who writes Stephen's books?'

'Yes, that's me,' I confirmed, not quite sure what was coming next.

'You know Stephen gave me a message last night? Well, I wondered if I could tell you about it – it's really rather important and you might want to consider it for your next book.'

I was aware of the fact that I was running on a tight schedule and I suspected that the man I was talking to might want to talk for a long time, so I politely explained my predicament, and asked him if he could just give me a rough outline of the relevant details.

In response, and he really was very nice about it, he said he didn't know where to start, and we both agreed that it would be a good idea if he put his story down on paper and sent it through to Mage Publishing. That way I could read it at my leisure and get back to him for any further details I might need when I wasn't working against the clock.

The conversation ended on an amicable note, and then, although I didn't just forget all about it, I did push it to the back of my mind. We were in the middle of a busy tour and other things were pressing.

In any given year we will receive not dozens but scores of letters from people who have received messages from Stephen. Some writers just want to say thank you, while many others ask impossible questions – some of which we will be trying to answer later on in this book. A very high percentage of people are anxious to provide the background detail of their experiences with Stephen's clairvoyance, and while some of these letters can be barely legible, written on scrappy bits of notepaper, others, like the one I received from Bill Williams on the 1$^{st}$ of March, are so neatly presented that they can be scanned in without edit. This is what I have done with Bill's letter.

When I first read it I was full of wonder because not only does Bill Williams corroborate Stephen's evidence, he also puts me in a position where I can, at least in part, corroborate certain key aspects of Bill's story.

*Dear Mr Christie*

*You may remember that I attended part of Stephen Holbrook's demonstration of clairvoyance at the Hotel Victoria in Lowestoft on Sunday 19$^{th}$ of February and* *that we had a brief telephone conversation the morning after at which time you suggested I should put pen to paper and give you some of the background details of the message that I received. This has been surprisingly more difficult than I first thought it might be and I can only say that I hope you make some sense of my efforts.*

*Basically on the evening of February 19th Stephen brought a message through from one of my dearest friends – the late Billy Fury – whose name will probably be remembered by many of your readers should you decide to publish this letter. I first met Billy when he was performing at The Windmill Theatre in Great Yarmouth, back in 1963. He was the headline act of the summer show and I was working as House Manager. We were both working for Jack Jay who owned the theatre and was the producer of the show. You may recall that Stephen's initial connection was with a windmill – well the Windmill Theatre did have a big neon windmill on its roof and of course, this was where Billy and I first became friends.*

*Now Mr Christie, I want to make it absolutely clear that that is all we were. Just friends, albeit very good ones, and our friendship lasted right the way through till Billy died. It is true that at the time we were both battling with issues of our respective sexualities which was something that gave us common ground and brought us closer together but we were not a gay couple and we did not have a homosexual relationship. Either way Billy did have a chronic heart condition that certainly was kept secret from the general public and to all intents and purposes he passed over from a long wasting sickness just as Stephen described. I don't think Billy was furious about dying – quite the reverse in fact, but I think he was telling Stephen that his name*

44

*was Billy Fury and Stephen understandably got a bit of the name muddled up. When Billy passed away he was no longer the star he had been in the 1960's but was living in South London running a dog rescue centre. When he passed over, I took on responsibility for the dogs, and in the latter days of his life, this was Billy's biggest concern. So Stephen was dead on the ball when he was talking about someone saying thank you for looking after the dogs*

*Although I am a committed spiritualist and have been lucky enough to receive many messages from spirit over the years, principally from my mother and my father who were respectively Norma and Norman, I have never had a message from Billy, and putting it bluntly, I have always wanted one. Billy's real name, by the way, was Ron, and that was another name that Stephen connected with in Lowestoft.*

*He represented one of the happiest and yet at the same time most difficult chapters in my life and had he lived then I do believe we would have remained friends right through to our later years. As it was, we were like brothers, and we were always there for each other long after that first summer season in Gt Yarmouth.*

*I loved and still love all of Billy's music but there were three records in particular that were my favourites. One was "Jealousy" and that was the tape I was looking for in the car (a silver BMW with a private plate) on the evening of February 19th and getting so angry when I couldn't find it. My second favourite was a song called "Once Upon A Dream" – and I have a small broads cruiser with that name painted on the stern. Stephen said something about Billy always being in my thoughts, which is true, and although it may be stretching things a bit, this does, I think anyway, make*

45

reference to my favourite Billy Fury song of all time which is called "In Thoughts Of You" which was his last hit record, by the way.

Before ending this long letter can I confirm a few other things Stephen said. First he was absolutely right when he said I'd been very undecided about going along to the Hotel Victoria, but then I'd heard someone, not Billy, singing "Jealousy" on the radio and I took that as a sign that I should go after all. Stephen also made mention of the sum of £4,000 pounds that I'd just written a cheque for – and only the previous week, on February 7th, I had written a cheque for almost exactly that amount to the Inland Revenue. To be precise, £4,047.44. Also, in connection with money, although it wasn't my money he was talking about, after some initial difficulty he connected with the name of Larry. Billy's manager was Larry Parnes and Billy always blamed him for mismanagement of his finances which subsequently led to Billy being declared bankrupt.

So please say a big thank you and well done to Stephen for me. I've seen hundreds of mediums over the years but none of them has been as convincing as Stephen and I owe him a special thank you for bringing through a message from the one person I have always wanted to have a message from. Please feel free to phone me if you need any more details,

Yours sincerely, Bill Williams.

If we measure the contents of Bill Williams' letter against the message Stephen gave him on the evening of February 19th every single piece of information that Stephen brought through has been confirmed and fully corroborated. If there are any grey areas, then we point

46

the finger to Harry and Barry getting in the way of Larry and we must accept Bill's interpretation of "always in your thoughts" being relevant to Billy Fury's last hit single "In Thoughts of You".

Recently some hack journalist called John Thingy accused Stephen of cold reading and said *"Anyone can throw a name into an audience of two hundred people and get some response from somebody"* and while in one sense this might be true, let us consider the fact that Stephen did not come up with just one name – he came up with eight names, all of which had special meaning to the recipient of the message. He identified a passing from a wasting illness and heart disease. He identified a silver BMW car with a personalised plate. He spoke in detail of events that had only been happening in the previous hour ie. Bill's indecision whether or not he was going to attend the evening of clairvoyance and his frustration over a piece of missing music. He mentioned a cheque that Bill had written for *"four thousand pounds and a few pennies"* – and in my opinion the actual cheque amount of £4,047.44 is close enough for jazz. Also he connected Larry (and let's face it, Harry, Barry and Larry are very close phonetically) to some long standing monetary problem. Stephen also spoke of dogs and, on Billy's behalf, thanked Bill for looking after them. This might not be all that dramatic but if Fury's principle concern in the last days of his life was for the welfare of his animals, it does give specific meaning and gravitas to this part of the message. Finally, there is the matter of the windmill, which was the initial starting point of the message. It is true that Billy Fury must have played in many theatres during his short career, but if The Windmill Theatre in Gt Yarmouth was a special place to both the giver and the recipient of the message and of sufficient importance to act as the bridge symbol that opened the conduit of communication, then it is little wonder that Stephen's initial contact with Billy Fury came through a vision of a windmill!

In my opinion – and also in the opinion of experienced spiritualist Bill Williams – this whole message is a fine example of clairvoyance at its best and it is interesting to note that this very detailed message could so easily have been lost if Bill hadn't decided to come along at the last minute. And remember what Bill said – he had decided that he wasn't going to attend until he heard the old Jealousy tango being played on the radio. You could say that this was flooky coincidence or you could say it was a message from the other side telling him to pull his socks up and get a move on because there was someone waiting to make contact.

There is one other aspect to this story that is worth telling. As I mentioned earlier in this chapter I can confirm certain aspects of Bill Williams' testimony. First of all, in 1963 Billy Fury *was* playing top of the bill at The Windmill Theatre, and I know this for a fact, because I was in the same show at the very *bottom* of the bill. The show was staged and produced by Jack Jay and being the inveterate horder that I am, I have an old programme that credits front of house management to one Bill Williams... And for what it's worth, I spent two long afternoons rummaging through suitcases in my attic to find the aforementioned programme!

For anyone interested, the other acts on the Billy Fury Show bill were Alan Smethwick, The Singing Postman *(you got a light boy?)* Chic Robini, Tony del

Monico and me and my vivacious theatre lady mum in the guise of Kit & Joyce Yorke. I was sixteen years old and at that stage in my professional life I didn't have any control over what I was called!

Facts are one thing, but memories are another, and this report of Stephen's message from Billy Fury to Bill Williams has opened a chasm of nostalgia. For what it's worth, here is my slant on the story.

The summer of 1963 is poignantly and vividly etched in my memory. I'd just left school and was experiencing my first professional taste of showbusiness. The Windmill Theatre in Great Yarmouth wasn't exactly the London Palladium, but it was quite a prestigeous summer season venue with sufficient standing to host "The Billy Fury Show". As I say, with our rather corney country and western act, my mother and I were the bottom act on the bill, while Billy, of course, was at the top! But as much as he talked to anyone, this dichotomy didn't stop him from talking to me occasionally and the over-riding impression that I got was that he was a damn sight more scared and nervous than even I was at the prospect of walking out onto a stage and strutting one's stuff in front of a couple of thousand screaming fans – not that the fans ever screamed for me, you understand!

He was a shy man, quietly spoken, who kept himself pretty much to himself. He neither drank nor smoked, although he pretended to do the latter in one part of his act. There was none of the "I'm a big star" attitude about him, and I have a clear flashback memory of him putting an elastoplast on the tea lady's finger after she'd burned herself trying to lift an overweight tea pot.

Prior to making his entrance, he'd wait nervously in the wings, a pale slight figure, looking incredibly vulnerable, and occasionally shaking with stage fright.

"Christ, I hate this business," he once said – and another time – "How the hell did I ever end up doing this?"

In all truth, he didn't have much of an act, but he didn't need one. He just walked out there and sang his string of top twenty hits, sometimes leaning against the piano for support (although he made it look incredibly casual) and wiggling his hips once or twice, either in a poor immitation of Elvis Presley or a self depreciatory send up. His voice was pleasant and accurate if not particularly strong, and to give credit where it's due, he looked bloody good in his silver lamé jacket bathed in the glow of half a dozen spotlights. I think he must have known that his was a finite talent, and I have always thought that he felt just a little bit of a fraud.

And yet, more than thirty five years later, his songs are as popular as ever, and he's probably a bigger star now than he ever was then. I can't hear "Halfway To Paradise" or "In Thoughts Of You" without the hairs rising on the back of my neck, and I am immediately catapulted back to a different time of place in the recesses of my memory.

There is the smell of candy floss and hot dogs, the ozone of the sea air interacting with the static electricity and hot metal of noisy dodgem cars and other fairground attractions. The thrill of being able to smoke legal cigarettes without worrying about getting caught, teenage kisses and foolish flirtations, falling in love for the first time at the impossible age of sweet sixteen, the ever present underbuzz of sexual tension...

1963 was my rites of passage year, and the summer of '63 was The Billy Fury summer. Perhaps because the one has always been synonymous with the other, my passing acquaintance with Billy has always remained crisp and fresh in the memory of my mind, and may go some way to explaining why I still play a lot of his music.

But it doesn't explain his popularity with an entirely different generation who were not even contemplated when he was at the top of the charts.

Certainly, the same syndrome is applicable to Presley, Orbison, The Beetles and a host of others, but with Billy I think it may be a little different.

His songs may have been simple but they were never naive. Strong narrative lyrics with emotive melodies were his foundation stones upon which he built innovative musical arrangements. With the use of a full orchestra this set a bench mark in pop and rock music which has been emulated ever since. In the process of modern musical evolution this made Billy's work extremely original even though he didn't receive the credit for it in his own time.

His "boy next door" image held up on both sides of the footlights, although we can only guess at the tortures of his private emotionional life which (like another good rocker from the 60's) he was always able to keep out of the prying eyes of the media.

I think perhaps we have a subliminal awareness of his fear and uncertainty and that it strikes a chord of disquiet in our own souls. Billy hid his fears well and put on a damn good show – so if the boy next door can do it, maybe we can do it too. It is easier for us to identify with Billy Fury than, say, Buddy Holly or half a dozen other American stars which have gone nova over the years. He was our local idol who was clever enough to do good cover material, often a lot better than its originators, and who was fortunate enough to have a dozen great original songs which have weathered well the test of time.

As I say, Billy Fury probably has a stronger fan base today than he had forty three years ago. For anyone who is unfamiliar with his music there is a marvellous treat in store for you. His official fan club website is www.billyfuryofficial.com Go give it a look and listen to "In Thoughts Of You". It'll make your emotions tingle and bring a lump to your throat.

## Chapter Five: *The Babies*

Without doubt one of the most difficult bereavements to bear is the loss of a baby or young child. If your Grandmother passes over at ninety years old you can accept this as the inevitability of a finite lifespan, but if a child passes at nine years old, or a toddler passes at nineteen months or if a baby falls victim to cot death syndrome at only nine weeks, this is a much more bitter pill to swallow and who can blame a grieving mother for crying treason and demanding some kind of answer as to *why* such a thing should happen?

To be sure, in the developing world where there is a scarcity of medicine and clean water, families have to deal with this kind of tragedy on a daily basis (which still doesn't explain it or make it right) but here in the western world where we do have good medicine and we do have a degree of hygiene, it seems so much more dreadful when a young one is taken from us long before its time and it does make the question *why?* so much more pertinent.

I do not have an answer to this question and I know that Steve Holbrook doesn't have one either, but it is reassuring to know that through Stephen's many many links with children who have passed over there is one common denominator which is that through Stephen's mediumship these spirit children are always passionately eager to let their parents know that they are growing up on the "other side" and that they are well and happy.

There are a couple of areas of potential confusion here that Stephen has asked me to comment on. One is the concept of "growing up" in the spiritual domains and the other is the method in which a baby or toddler will communicate with the medium if the infant passed over before it learned to talk.

Dealing with this latter point first, Stephen says... "First of all I get an itchy nose and this is a sure sign that the message is coming through from a child, and then I'll become aware of one of my spirit guides moving in close to me. This is a little boy called Christopher and he's always there to act as a go between when there are messages involving children. Now obviously babies don't talk properly so what I'll get is a picture image of the message that's coming through... For example if the kiddy has died in hospital I'll get the impression of hospital beds and the smell of disinfectant. If there's been a heart problem, I'll get a pain in my chest, or if the problem has been with the brain, I'll get an awful pain in my head. Obviously this degree of communication doesn't give me much detail so I usually have to grope my way through it, doing my best to convert visual images seen from a child's perspective into words that an adult can understand. Fortunately this sort of contact doesn't happen all that often, and it's only when a little one has passed over very recently that the message comes through in this form. It's much more common for the baby to be brought through by a departed relative, like a grandmother or an auntie or uncle, who will speak on the little one's behalf. Or sometimes my spirit guide Christopher will intervene and he'll give me the information directly. Sometimes, if the passing has happened some time ago, the baby or toddler, who will have grown up in the spirit world to adulthood, will pass the message themselves..."

Which brings us very nicely to this business of growing up on the other side.

It is widely accepted among spiritualists that when we pass over we do not just remain as we have been down here on the earthplane, but that we grow in spiritual strength and knowledge. Our spirits are individual and are eternal and thus we retain all our memories from our life on the earthplane – and if you believe in reincarnation, all the memories from our previous lives, however many there may have been.

And yet, as Stephen frequently points out – "If your Uncle Arthur has been a grumpy old sod during his life on earth then there'd be little point in him trying to make contact with you as the ascended spirit he may have become on the other side. You wouldn't recognise him, would you? So if he's going to come through at all, it will be in a recognisable form, namely a grumpy old sod!"

This, of course, is speaking of spiritual growth but where children are concerned there does seem to be evidence of *physical* growth as well and on a number of occasions a spirit has come through to Stephen saying, in effect, "this is how I was then but *this* is what I'm like now." As with grumpy Uncle Arthur, to make contact with loved ones on the earthplane the child must manifest itself in a way that can be recognisable. This experience is not unique to Stephen Holbrook and many other mediums, including the late Doris Stokes and Doris Collins and my own mentor Ossie Rae, share this opinion.

If we are to talk about the passing over of very young babies, including stillbirths, miscarriages and even terminations, then there are two other factors to consider which are as complex as they are complicated, but I'll do my best to explain them in very lay terms.

First we must consider the concept of spiritual retreat, which is the idea of a spirit, once having chosen to be born on the earthplane, *changes its mind* and decides to remain in or go back to the world of spirit. Crudely put, it's a bit like that two week cooling off period you get after you've signed up for a hire purchase or credit deal.

For this to make sense we need to accept the allied theory that as spirits we actually *choose* to be born and have foreknowledge of all we are going to experience in the lifespan ahead of us. We do this dispassionately in an attempt to learn and evolve.

The sceptical argument against this is that we would not, were we in our right minds, choose to live a life that might see us condemned to spend our years in a wheelchair or to suffer (or indeed cause) great physical and/or psychological pain.

Quite obviously, we would not choose this route as human beings – but we might well consider this pathway as spirits if our main concern is to acquire spiritual strength and enlightenment from our "term at school" here on the earthplane.

It must be said that not everybody subscribes to this theory but it is a very common and widely held belief that is integral to a number of faith systems (notably Buddhism) and many of the world's spiritual masters both present and past and gone, have embraced it wholeheartedly as a tablet of stone…

…And if you find this idea difficult to accept, you're going to love this next one which is even more radical! What if – and I take a big breath here – a Higher Spiritual Auhtority, call it God, Allah, Jaweh or whatever, *uses* the death of a child either in pregnancy or its early living months to teach us, the grieving parents, a lesson the Godhead thinks we need to learn?

At first glance this is an appalling theory for it questions the validity of a caring all knowing, all loving God and therefore, if accepted, it shakes the foundation stones of benign faith and religion and propels us towards a vision of a vain and angry God more at home in The Old Testament than The New and moving closer to the dark worlds of Hecate and Shiva.

Some of my Christian friends were so horrified by this line of thought that I nearly lost them as friends, but perversely it was a very committed Christian clergyman who presented me with this theory in the first place.

To be sure, he was not your average run of the mill clergyman, and to be sure, he was also a practising spiritualist who saw no conflict of interest between the two faiths, but his conclusions, based on historical rather than theological research, echo much of the early church's teachings and beliefs.

The bottom line here is that none of this offers much comfort to the grieving mother who has lost her baby. Perhaps this next report – the story of Alice Sandler from Leamington Spa who lost her twin baby girls in a car crash when they were only eighteen months old – might help just a little.

Alice was born into a middle class family somewhere between Warwick and Leamington Spa and had a somewhat conservative and restricted upbringing. Her parents were both teachers and were very traditional and Christian in their views. Her father was the headmaster of the local boys grammer school and tended to believe that sex was solely for the purpose of procreation. Her mother, quite confident in the classroom but somewhat cowed by the overbearing personality of her husband, became little more than his shadow in all family and domestic matters.

As a child Alice was not cut very much slack – she would be in serious trouble for the most minor infringement of the family rules – and the idea of her having a boyfriend, even when she'd reached the age of sixteen, was total anathema to both parents. She was bullied into going to Sunday school and church and persuaded by her father that thirty or thirty five would be a good age to marry, and only then to someone to whom she'd been engaged for a number of years and, most importantly of all, to someone of whom her parents approved.

They might have got away with this attitude in 1953 or even 1963 but we're talking here about 1993. Alice was now eighteen years old and she wasn't having any of it. Possibly to escape the tyranny of parental control or perhaps because she really did fall in love with the boy next door, she agreed to marry Peter Skelton and they got engaged on her nineteenth birthday.

Her parents didn't like it, but from their point of view, things could have been a lot worse. Peter was a presentable young man just starting out on a career in banking. Her parents knew the Skelton family and approved of their stock, and at least their son-in-law to be spoke with a nice voice and dressed smartly and didn't have tattoos or one of those dreadful modern hairstyles with all the spiky bits sticking out all over the place. In short, they convinced themselves that they were not so much losing a daughter as gaining a son... And for the first few years it all went swimmingly well.

Things started going wrong for Alice when she realised she was pregnant. This was in 1996, having been married to Peter for two years. Alice was delighted, Alice's parents were delighted, Peter's parents were delighted, but unfortunately Peter was not at all delighted. It was too soon, he said, to start a family. His career was only just getting off the ground. Babies were expensive. He did not go as far as suggesting Alice should have a termination but he did make it perfectly clear that if this was something she decided to do on her own cognisance, she would have his total support. After all, there'd be plenty of time for making babies later on.

Alice was not only dismayed by her husband's attitude she was also hurt and deeply angry. This incident caused a deep rift between them that was never to heal completely, and was the beginning of the end of her marriage, although that was something she didn't realise at the time.

In her fifth month of pregnancy she lost the baby.

Stupid how it happened really. Peter and her father had dragged her along to see a local cricket match, played on the village green outside the local pub. Alice didn't like cricket and she didn't like pubs, but the idea of a summer evening sat on soft warm grass with a bottle of wine and the trappings of a picnic was not without merit.

Half way through the match and about half way through the evening, just as the light was beginning to fail, one of the village batsmen hit a right wallop of a ball, a real sledgehammer sixer that sliced through the fielders like a red comet out of a supernova. The cricket ball hit Alice in the middle of her stomach and by the time an ambulance had arrived, it was all over.

The loss of this baby pushed Alice into a state of depression, and while Peter seemed to be very supportive, she believed that he was secretly pleased by the turn of events. Certainly his "support" didn't seem to last very long and when Alice was still feeling miserable several months later phrases like "you've got to pull yourself together, dear" and "you really must snap out of it, darling" became regular litanies along with "I know how you must be feeling, but..."

It was glaringly apparent to Alice that Peter had no idea how she was feeling, but she did manage to pull herself together – although it took the better part of a year in which to do it and by which time much of the closeness and rapport had gone from her marriage. At one point she did think of separation and divorce, but then, by her own admission, she chickened out, knowing what a ruckus it would cause with her parents... who, in Alice's estimation, were now much more on Peter's side than they were on hers.

Nevertheless she put on a brave face and tried to make the best of things and some semblance of normality began to seep back into her young life. She was still only twenty three years old, so things were bound to get better sooner or later – weren't they?

Well, if they were, it didn't seem to be happening in a hurry and Alice's life slipped into a routine of cooking breakfasts and dinners, having Sunday lunches alternate weeks with first her parents and then Peter's parents. Her evenings were consumed by TV as Peter would frequently work very late and when he didn't he would bring his work home with him, spending hours on his computer, and more or less ignoring her unless he was in the mood for sex.

Sex with Peter became a chore and a bore and then it became a real turn-off and a no-go area when she learned that he was having an affair with one of the office secretaries. At this point she did start talking divorce but her husband pleaded and begged and swore that it was a one-off aberration and nothing like this had ever happened before and nor would it ever happen again if only she would give him another chance.

Alice told me that if it hadn't been for her parents and her upbringing, she would have ended her marriage at that point, but fear of how her parents might react, actual fear of her parents, and probably a degree of fear of the unknown stayed her hand. She gave Peter his second chance, and for a while things settled down and she did manage to find a degree of contentment.

In 1998 Alice discovered she was pregnant again, and this time around her husband did seem more enthusiastic about the prospect of becoming a father. Alice wasn't sure to what extent he was putting on an act, but she was prepared to give him the benefit of the doubt. Even when she learned that she was carrying twins Peter's care and consideration didn't waiver, and Alice recalls that this was one of the happiest times in her life.

Alice and Peter Skelton became the proud parents of twin baby girls on November 5th 1998 with the sounds of fireworks going off at a nearby bonfire celebration. It seemed that the firework display was in special celebration of their special delivery. They called the girls Katie and Louise, and three days later they took them home to begin the unsupervised panic of feeding, winding, nappy changing and nappy washing – and all the other pandemonium that goes with having a new baby, and in this case *two* new babies in the house.

It took Peter Skelton about three months to realise that fatherhood wasn't for him and it took Alice six months to discover he had recommenced his illicit affair with his secretary. This time there was no going back, and Alice filed for divorce. Just as she had expected, her parents went ballistic and so, although she hadn't wanted to do so, she presented them with the evidence of Peter's infidelity. This mollified them – how could it not? – but neither parent, especially her father, could readily accept the concept of a divorce in the family and Alice came under a constant bombardment of pressure to forgive and forget and "to try again for the sake of the family's good name, dear".

Totally disgusted by her husband's behaviour and the lack of support that she was getting from her mother and her father, Alice stuck to her guns and within a couple of months she had moved out of the marital home and was renting a small cottage in the Cotswolds. Peter visited occasionally to see his children, and her parents were quite regular visitors – but the meetings with all three protagonists were always difficult with conversations cased in layers of frosty formality and a sensation of relief when her parents disappeared around the corner in their sedate old Daimler and Peter revved off angrily in his boy racer BMW.

Alice went about the business of picking up the pieces and started building a new life for herself. With the divorce settlement she was able to buy the cottage she'd been renting, and taking in work as a copy typist and proof reader she managed to feed and clothe her family unit of three and in the fullness of time she even managed to buy a little second hand car, a little red Citroen Saxo that she called Ladybird.

*"I really loved that car,"* she told me in the course of our interview. And then, *"But maybe I wouldn't*

*have loved it quite so much if I'd known it was going to get my babies killed."*

On May 19th 2000 Alice was driving quite slowly along the A46. She was a new and therefore particularly careful driver and what she lacked in experience she made up for in conscientiousness. It was ten thirty in the morning, and although there was some traffic on the road, the rush hour had long since subsided and the traffic was light. Katie and Louise were buckled into their child harness bucket seats in the back and Alice was tootling along enjoying the early summer sunshine and the wonderful sense of freedom that came from being out on the open road.

The first sign that something might be wrong came from a little red winking warning light on the dashboard. You and I might have stopped to find out what it was, but Alice motored on nervously until the red light stopped winking and came on permanently – along with a nasty smell of burning rubber wafting up from the engine. With a sigh, she indicated left, pulled over onto the hard shoulder, put on her warning lights, unclipped her seat belt and started groping in her handbag for her AA Rescue card. That was her last conscious memory of anything appertaining to the accident that followed and she woke up a fortnight later in Birmingham Royal Infirmary with a fractured skull, two broken legs, a ruptured spleen and five broken ribs.

What happened? One of those big juggernaut lorries had been on the road all night with a driver who had fallen asleep at the wheel. The forty ton monster had drifted over the lane markings onto the hard shoulder and had hit Alice's little Citroen full on in the rear. Alice had gone through the windscreen and the babies

63

had been killed outright. The only blessing is that they would have died instantly but that brought no relief to Alice when she woke up and was told what had happened. For Alice, this was where the nightmare began. This was where she started sliding into the dark void of madness and self mutilation. This was the start of her journey through hell, a journey that she would travel for six long years.

Until she met Stephen Holbrook.

**Chapter Six:**    *Alice & Stephen*

I once had a girl friend who used to slash her wrists on a fairly regular basis. She was not attempting suicide and nor was she trying to attract attention to herself. Put quite simply, cutting her wrists and allowing the blood to flow and spurt out in all directions was the only way she could find to release the build up of pressure and tension within her body and mind. Each cutting session would take place with Bon Jovi screaming away unintelligibly in the background, and she always had swathes of towels standing by to staunch the flow and clear up the mess. More often than not her wrists were bandaged – *"got scratched by the rabbit"* she would say – and when the bandages were off she always wore long sleeves to hide the mess of mutilation that scarred her forearms.

When I met Alice a couple of weeks after Steve's demonstration at Leamington Spa, the first thing I noticed were the awful criss cross markings on her wrists and I had an immediate idea of where this lady had been and also where our interview might be going. Perhaps, because I had some knowledge of SHS (self harm syndrome), I was able to be sympathetic and communicate a degree of understanding on a psychic vibration. Either way, Alice found it quite easy to talk to me and she didn't hold anything back.

**Tape one – side one**
"At first I didn't feel anything very much at all. I was flat on my back in a hospital bed doped up to the gills with half a dozen different drugs and pain killers, driifting in and out of consciousness. I'd been told that my babies were dead and that I was lucky to be alive,

but those words didn't mean anything. They hadn't sunk in. My mother and father were regular visitors, but they didn't say very much and I suppose I was a bit of an embarrassment to them. A very nice clergyman came to visit a few times and there were other visits from a grief counsellor and the social services. Peter, I think, came once, just the one time. He mumbled something about being very sorry, but he didn't stay long and after that one visit he never came again.

It took a month, maybe even five or six weeks for the enormity of what had happened to sink in. I suppose my mind had just blanked it out until I was ready to deal with it but the truth is I've never been ready to deal with it.

When I was released from the hospital I went back to live with my parents for a while and that was awful. They didn't know what to say to me and I didn't know what to say to them. The atmosphere was so thick you could have cut it with a knife and I felt that I was going to explode with all the feelings building up inside me. I lasted about two months, and then because I was physically on the mend, I went back to my own little cottage. Here I could be on my own and I didn't have to put on an act for the sake of the family. I might have been on the mend physically but I suppose I was a total wreck mentally – anyway, I started drinking and crying in equal measures and I just let myself slip into the dark place. I'd got some sleeping tablets from the doctors and he'd also put me on anti-depressants, so I just got into the habit of drinking the wine and taking the pills... Did a lot of sleeping, a bit of walking in the woods, watched a lot of awful TV and didn't bother too much about washing or cleaning. My mother came over twice a week – never my father – and did the basics for me and she kept telling me I had to pull myself together and get some help and I said that I would, but what was the point? What was there to pull myself together for? My husband had committed adultery, my babies were dead and my parents were on another planet.

It went on like this for months, at least for half a year, and the only little ray of sunshine was the visits I'd get from Stuart, the nice clergyman that I'd met in the hospital. I was one of his parishioners, so he called in to see me once a week, sometimes twice a week, and we'd talk for ages about anything and everything. He never told me off about my drinking or tablets and he never seemed to notice that the place was in a mess. He did try to explain how God works in mysterious ways, but even he couldn't tell me why God had taken my babies from me. What had I ever done to offend God so much? What had my babies done that justified such a vicious punishment?

After a while Stuart learned to leave his evangelical streak back in the vestry, and we'd talk about everything *except* for God and the children...

...I suppose that after a few months the inevitable happened. I mean, there'd only ever been one man I'd gone to bed with and that was Peter and he'd let me down, and the only person I was getting any kind of sympathy from was Stuart, and it wasn't as though he was married or was a Catholic or anything... I mean vicars can have girlfriends, right? And I started thinking that maybe Stuart liked me in some ways more than just looking out for a headcase parishioner with a bit of a drink problem. Anyway, I started building this up in my own mind, you know, started having all kinds of romantic and erotic fantasies... God, it went on for weeks, and then there was this time he came around for coffee and because I knew he was coming and I was as nervous as hell, I'd drunk a bottle of wine and had taken a double dose of tranquilisers and, anyway, the upshot of it was I made a big pass at him, told him all the things I'd been imaging us doing, told him I loved him, and of course, you can probably imagine what happened! He freaked and told me that he liked me very much as a person but that he was a member of the church just doing his job and that anything else was completely out of the question... I mean he went on about how he'd never given me any cause to think otherwise, but by then I wasn't listening, I was sort of out of my head and said all sorts of terrible things to him, and basically I threw him out of the house and then I really started drinking and I got into an awful state...

In the end I was so mad, so furious, so upset I was ready to explode, so I went over to his church and trashed the place. If there was something to be kicked over I kicked it over, if there was something to be torn down I'd tear it down. I was screaming and shouting and swearing, and then I passed out and when I woke up I was strapped to a bed in the local loony bin...

Cutting a long story short, I was kept there for a week sometimes under sedation and sometimes in a counselling session with this awful doctor who would talk to me in this  professional way but with his eyes riveted on my boobs. He was totally horrid and I hated him on sight, but I said that I was going to be a good girl from now on, promised that I'd take the tablets as prescribed, that I would get some professional help for the drinking and that I would attend an out-patients clinic once a week until I was told I didn't need to any more. Christ, I'd have promised anything to anyone, just to get out of that place...

Anyway, for a while after that I was quite a lot better. I moved to another village where nobody knew me, reverted to my maiden name so nobody could find me, took the pills, went to the clinic once a week as promised and tried to put the awful business with Stuart out of my mind – except that it wasn't easy because I could never get Katie and Louise out of my mind and every time I thought about them, I thought about what a bastard God was, and every time I thought about God I thought about churches and vicars, so it was a vicious circle.

I never did stop drinking properly – just sort of cut it down for a while, and swapped tipples. Started drinking vodka because you can have a couple of vodkas and tell yourself you've only had a couple of drinks which is better than having a couple of bottles of wine. The only thing is, of course, that if your one vodka is like a double double measure... So soon I was on a bottle a night and I was never sober and it was around about Spring of 2003 that I thought I'd be better off jacking the whole thing in, you know, better off dead rather than living in the twilight zone of a half life. So calm as a cucumber I walked into the kitchen, took a big sabatier knife out of the cupboard and slashed my wrist...

Well, I must have hit a vein or something because there was blood everywhere, shooting up and splattering the ceiling and gushing all over the kitchen floor and *it was wonderful!* There wasn't any pain, just this fantastic feeling of relief and release – all the crap and all the tension that had been fermenting away inside me for nearly three years was being vented in one gorgeous eruption. I remember sitting down at the kitchen table and laughing with delight. It was the best I'd felt since before the kids got killed...

69

I think that if I had died that night I wouldn't have been too bothered, but as it was my mother called in on her way back from a WRVS event and got me down to the local hospital with some cock and bull story about an accident in the garden with a pair of shears, or something equally unlikely and we got away with it... Although Madge, my mother, knew full well what had happened, of course, and after that she did keep a much closer eye on me, and as far as I was concerned that was fine because I'd found a way of carrying on living.... Whenever things got really bad I'd go and find somewhere quiet with a razor blade or a Stanley knife and cut just deep enough to let the blood flow, and after five or ten minutes I'd start feeling better and would wrap and dress my wounds – quite professionally after a while, I might tell you – and I suppose things could have gone on like that indefinitely. You know, vodka bottles all over the floor, sick on the carpets, crap on the bathroom when I'd missed the loo, frequent bundles of bloody red towels shoved into dustbins and plastic bags – but everything changed on the day that I stole the baby... Yes, did I tell you that I'd stolen a baby?"

**Tape one – side two**
"Yes, well I need to tell you about the baby and what happened, not that anything much did happen really. I was just walking through the village to the post office and I passed the newsagents and there was this sweet little girl in her pram looking all lovely in pink and not another soul in sight, and ten minutes later when I was walking back, the baby was still there all on her own – and I thought what the bloody hell is this child's mother doing, leaving it out on the pavement unattended for anyone to snatch and take advantage of. Hasn't the silly

70

bitch read the papers? Doesn't she listen to the news? Doesn't she know how *dangerous* it is to leave a child unattended in this day and age? And then I got really, really angry because I would never have put my children in that position, and it seemed to me that this baby's stupid mother didn't deserve to have such a lovely baby, so as I passed the newsagents I simply put my hands on the pram and started pushing it down the road. If the mother of the baby didn't care about its welfare then it could come and live with me and *I'd* look after it properly!

Believe it or not I nearly got the baby home, about a mile from the newsagents before they caught up with me... The hysterical stupid bitch of a mother and the two rather stern policemen... Anyway, they arrested me there and then and I spent the next three nights in the cells until I was transferred back to the mental hospital and that *horrid* little doctor with the breast fetish. So, I've got a criminal record, Mr Christie – bet you didn't know that, did you? – but of course, it never went to court and I was sectioned under the schedule D thing or whatever they call it, and I spent the next eleven months in the asylum – sorry, I'm supposed to call it mental hospital, aren't I?

My mother came and visited once a week. My father never came close. And as for Peter, well no, of course he never came, and that was fine because I wouldn't have wanted him to. Cutting a long story short, they told me, or rather they told my mother and then she told me, that I was suffering from chronic depression and psychopathological paranoia, and that I was probably schizophrenic as well but they wouldn't know that for certain until they'd run some tests. And they spent the next nine months doing those tests –

71

including the old electric shock treatment and you've no idea how degrading and despicable that bit of business is – and after it all they decided that I wasn't schizo or paranoid but that I was suffering from acute depression caused by the death of my children, and they gave me another load of prescriptions and finally let me go home, on condition I went and lived with my mother...

Oh, I almost forget to tell you that while I was in hospital my father died of a stroke, and after that my mother came and visited a lot more often, and she seemed quite a bit more friendly and caring after my father had gone. Me? Well I'm sorry to say I didn't grieve very much at all. My father had had his chance to be a good father but he was too damn concerned about being a good Christian and a good headmaster and you can't be good at everything, can you?

So anyway, I went home, stopped drinking, was good about taking the tablets and started feeling a bit more like a human being. My mother and I would go out together to various places; afternoon tea, the cinema, the theatre, maybe an odd art exhibition, but inside, you know deep down at the very *inside* of me, I was stone cold dead. Nothing really mattered, nothing really got through to me, nothing really interested me and I know it was probably something to do with the drugs that I was on, but even without the drugs I knew it would be the same... And so it went on, week after week, month after month, and then my mother came back from shopping one day and told me that she'd got us a couple of tickets for an evening of clairvoyance with a chap called Stephen Holbrook who was coming to the Royal Spa Centre in Leamington.

I knew a bit about spiritualism, but not very much... It was sort of a religion whereby you could make contact with the dead... and I was very surprised that Madge had got the tickets because as far as I knew she wasn't interested in anything like that. One thing's for sure, and that is there is no way she would have gone to anything like an evening of clairvoyance if my father had been alive. He'd have thought that anything like that was dealing with the devil and would have forbidden us to go on pain of death. But anyway, we went and as you know, I got a message...

The first thing I've got to say was I was surprised that so many people were there. I mean, the theatre was full and I'd thought there'd be just a few dozen of us huddled around the front rows. The second thing that surprised me was Stephen Holbrook – I mean, I'd expected him to be some old bloke in a dinner jacket and when Stephen came on stage with a really funny jacket and torn jeans, I thought that he was the warm-up act or something.

Anyway, he did an introduction and told us about his work, and then he decided it was time to start doing the clairvoyance... and I suppose by then I'd lost a bit of interest and my mind was wandering all over the place. I mean, I wasn't going to get a message, was I? There was nobody up in heaven who'd want to talk to me, except maybe my father, and I certainly didn't want to talk to *him*. By eighteen months the children had the basics of their own language and of course we communicated, but it wasn't proper words and so obviously there was no way an eighteen month old baby could come through with a message. And besides, as far as I was concerned, it was probably all a bit of a con anyway. Nobody would be giving me a message that night.

Anyway, I was brought back to earth with such a bump because Stephen was saying that he wanted to talk to someone who had lost not one but *two* children sometime in the last three years, and he was saying that they would have died in some kind of accident. Also, he was looking in my direction.

My blood was running cold and my mother was looking at me with a mixture of panic and excitement, and for a moment I thought I was going to be sick. I couldn't say a word but in the end my mother put her hand up and shouted "over here" or something like that, and then Stephen asked if he could talk to her, and when she said yes, he said that actually he didn't want to talk to her at all but to the young lady that was sat next to her, which of course, was me. God knows where I got my voice from, but I told him yes and then he started telling me things that no-one could have known. Absolutely nobody!"

**Dictaphone recording, Leamington Spa 29<sup>th</sup> March 2006**

Stephen:  'Can I talk to you, my love?'
Madge:  'Yes.'
Stephen:  'Actually I don't think it is you I want to talk to but it's the young lady sat next to you. Please can I talk to *you*, my love?'
Alice:  'Yes.'
Stephen:  'Who's Alice?'
Alice:  'I'm Alice.'
Stephen:  'And you've lost two children to the spirit world in the last three years?'
Alice:  'Yes.'

74

Stephen: 'And their passing – it was some kind of accident? Something that happened very quickly without any kind of warning?'

Alice: 'Yes.'

Stephen: 'This was some kind of car accident?'

Alice: 'Yes.'

Stephen: 'A red car?'

Alice: 'Yes.'

Stephen: 'What I'm getting here is that the children would have passed very, very quickly. There can have been no pain or suffering. Do you understand, my love.'

Alice: 'Yes.'

Stephen: 'What I'm getting here is hospitals and wires and the smell of disinfectant but I don't think that the children died in hospital or anything like that, but tell me, my love, were *you* involved in the accident and were *you* in hospital for a long time afterwards?'

Alice: 'Yes.'

Stephen: 'And I'm getting the number 46? Does 46 mean anything to you... An address or something like that?'

Alice: 'Er... No, not really... Oh God, yes!'

Stephen: 'What's 46?'

Alice: 'It's a road number, where the accident happened. It was the A46.'

Stephen: 'Who's Peter?'

Alice: 'My husband. Sorry, ex-husband.'

Stephen: 'But he's not in the spirit world, is he? He's still down here?'

Alice: 'Yes. Unfortunately.' *Laughter*

Stephen: 'Something here to do with the month of May. Why is May significant?'

Alice: 'The accident happened in May.'

75

Stephen: 'Right... Er, I've got a gentleman with me now, very tall and ramrod straight, and he's telling me that he passed over with a stroke, and this would have been in the last two years or so... Er, I don't know how to put this, but this gentleman wouldn't have had much of a sense of humour... Do you know who this is, my love?'

Alice: 'Yes, my father.'

Stephen: 'Who's Gordon?'

Alice: 'My father.'

Stephen: *long pause* 'He's telling me that he's sorry that he wasn't the father you needed him to be but that even though he never told you, he loved you very much and he's really sorry that he wasn't more help when you needed it the most. D'you understand what he's saying, my love.'

Alice: *almost inaudible* 'Yes.'

Stephen: 'And he says he's got the children with him, and that he's looking after them as best he can and he wants you to know that they're growing up really nicely, and that they're a bit of a handful, and that they spend as much time looking after him as he spends looking after them. D'you understand this, my love?'

Alice: *sobbing* 'Yes.'

Stephen: 'I've got the two little girls with me, my love... and they're telling me they're twins?'

Alice: 'Oh, Jesus Christ!'

Stephen: 'No love, just Stephen Holbrook!' *laughter* 'All right, my love, who's Kate or Katie?'

Alice: 'That's my daughter!'

Stephen: 'Well she's telling me that she's with Louise and that although Louise is cleverer than she is, she's a lot prettier.' *Laughter.* 'Also, my love, they're both

76

going on about the ladybird and they're saying that what happened to the ladybird wasn't your fault... They're really shouting it out together that it wasn't your fault and they're not going to let me go until they're sure you understand what they're saying.'

Alice:     'Yes, yes I do! I...'

Stephen:   'I'm getting the feeling that this last five or six years have been really, really hard for you and that you've been in a lot of pain.... Different *kinds* of pain, both the physical sort and the mental sort... and that you've felt so bitter and angry and you've had so many questions, but I've got these two gorgeous little girls here and they're sending you all their love and they're telling you that they're fine and that they're with their granddad, and they're sending you all their healing thoughts and they're promising you that after tonight things are going to start getting an awful lot better very quickly...'

**Recording ends.**

I'd listened to Alice's story... It had taken a couple of hours in the telling... and yet I found it quite hard to equate the story with the woman who had narrated it. She looked svelte, smartly stylish, with a sparkle of mischievious personality in a pair of quite lovely grey eyes.   Granted, there were those nasty scars on her wrists and granted maybe she looked a little bit older than her years, but even so...

When I told her what I was thinking, she smiled quietly. 'Ah James, you should have seen me four or five weeks ago,' she said. 'Then that was the old me and I've tightened up my act since then.  Everything's changed since I had my message from Stephen. Absolutely everything!'

'Can you elaborate on that?' I asked.

She shrugged. 'Only to say that I went into the Spa Centre as one person, had my message from Stephen Holbrook, and came back out of the Spa Centre as another person…'

How, I asked, did she feel now? Three weeks on.

'Free,' she said, 'free and clean. Yes, that's a very good word. I feel *clean*. For the first time in six years I feel free and clean.'

## Chapter Seven:    *Rob Green*

On average Steve Holbrook works fourteen hour days. Remember, that is on *average* which means that while some days he'll put in a ten hour stint, on other days it means seventeen or eighteen hours. Granted, Mr H is a total workaholic with incredible reserves of energy and adrenalin, but not even Superman can put in those kind of hours day after day, week after week, year after year without it exacting its inevitable toll.

Without there being anything seriously wrong, Stephen has had a few health scares during the last three years – seemingly endless colds and viruses, throat nodules, the occasional cold sweats and for ages I kept telling him that he couldn't carry on indefinitely with this kind of punishing work schedule without some professional help – he needed a minder, driver, manager, or anybody who could take the pressure off.

Frankly, it felt like I was talking to a brick wall, but then at the beginning of 2005 something must have clicked inside his own head because around about February or March he took me to one side and told me that he'd got a friend who he was thinking of taking on as his manager, and what did I think about the idea.

I told him I thought it was a bloody marvellous idea and leading on from this in the April of 2005 I met Rob Green for the first time.

Or I think it was the first time.

It was certainly the first time in *this* life.

The meeting took place in Southampton and we were scheduled to meet Rob in the hotel bar. Steve got delayed by a phone call he couldn't avoid, so I went in to meet Rob on my own.

I didn't have any difficulty in recognising him – Stephen had said "he looks a bit like me, I suppose," but the truth of the matter was that I could have been looking at Stephen's twin brother!

I sensed that Rob was a little bit shy, possibly a bit cautious and reserved, but the moment his hand came into mine some weird flash of recognition went bedoink in the back of my head and without really thinking what I was doing, I wrapped my arms around him and gave him a big hug.

Okay, I will freely admit to being a gregarious people hugger. I do it all the time when it isn't always appropriate, but I certainly don't do it to strangers that I've only just met. But this is the point. Rob didn't feel like a stranger to me at all, and although I absolutely loathe the following cliché, I sensed his psychic vibe straight away.

Psychic vibe? Did I really say that? Maybe I'd better let Rob tell you his story in his own words!

"There are many times in life when you hear people say that they've had a 'life changing' experience, and I used think to myself, nothing can have been that important surely. And then there are times when you think, if someone had said I'd be doing this, that or the other, a year ago, I would have replied, I DON'T think so. However, something happened in April 2003 that did change the way I thought about what I wanted in life, and the direction in which I wanted to go.

I guess there are many paths in life and you never really know which one you're meant to take until you take it, by which time it's too late to change if it's the wrong one. And sometimes you see many paths in front of you which all seem to be the right one, and you just simply cannot be bothered to make the effort to decide which one is the best. Then, naturally, you spend the rest of your life wishing you had been that little bit more bothered because you aren't happy.

My path in life up to April 2003 was a pretty steady affair, working as a Travel Consultant for the best part of six years, then moving onto a global swimwear company as a Retail Support Manager. A good, decent, steady job, nothing too challenging, fairly well paid - well, just enough to pay the mortgage, and have one decent holiday per year. It took me all around the country, holding training sessions and meeting lots of very different people along the way. No-one was, I guess, any more interesting than anyone else, until I met Steve Holbrook. I have read in his previous books, that people who meet Steve are immediately somehow drawn to him. They like him, but don't really know why, it's just something that happens. It's like one of those 'feel good' movies you see, or that first bit of warm sunshine you feel on your face in April when you think, 'Oh good, summer's on it's way'.

I'd gone to Portsmouth for a meeting with one of our suppliers with a colleague of mine, and we were staying at the Hilton Hotel. I'd got there before Dave and just wanted to crash out. I'd had a long drive and a hard week, and flopped on the bed. The meeting wasn't until the morning after, so I thought I'd just have a lovely long sleep. The peace was shattered when Dave rang and said he'd arranged to meet the suppliers in the bar that night, then go out for a meal. After much umming and aahhing, I agreed.

We went to the bar at about 6.30 (we were meeting the suppliers at about 7.30) thinking it would be quiet, hotel bars usually are, but this was heaving! It seemed like there were 400 women crowded around, smoking, drinking, laughing, chatting etc. I said to Dave, 'God, you come out for a quiet drink!' I noticed that some of the women were pointing at me, or nudging their friends and saying, 'He's over there, look, the one with the blond hair'. I kept looking behind me thinking it must be someone else they were talking about. No-one knew me and I'm not that spectacularly different from anyone else to stand out in a crowd. Dave said it was probably a male stripper, being 99% women etc, but I said 'Look, I know I'm not exactly like the back end of a tram smash, but stripper material? I certainly am NOT!' He did laugh a little too hard and long at this, which made me think he'd got to have been joking in the first place.

At this point, I recognised a guy I'd seen in the pool earlier that afternoon, when I went for a swim to get my senses into gear when Dave said we were going out. We'd had a brief chat about the weather as you do, talked about the job industry and what we both did. He said he was in 'publishing'. With hindsight, I realise that he really doesn't like to talk about what he does, as some can be either easily offended, or simply too interested and bombard him with questions. He was sat quietly in a corner, doing some paperwork or other, so I went up to him and asked if he knew what was going on. He said that he had no idea, but the noise was doing his head in and he was about to retire to his room to avoid the distractions. After this dead-end, I went to one of the porters and asked him. Again, no information.

I am, at times, like a dog with a bone and wouldn't let it go. I had to find out, I don't know why, but I had to. Salvation came in the shape of the receptionist, who informed me there was 'some sort of spooky spiritual thing' going on in the main function room. I told Dave, who seemed interested, and he even said 'Shall we see if we can get in?' I think my reply was something along the lines of 'In a parallel universe, its not my cup of tea!'.

How things change when you think about it! At that point, a rather imposing man emerged from the doorway to the ballroom and said, in quite possibly the loudest voice I had ever heard, 'Ladies and Gentlemen, please take your seats for Stephen Holbrook!' He wore what can only be described as an unusual get-up: leather waistcoat, fedora hat and trousers tucked into his boots. I thought Clint Eastwood had rolled into town! Eventually, they all disappeared, to my way of thinking, like lambs to the slaughter. The suppliers came, we went out and had a lovely meal, returning to the hotel at about 11pm.

Dave was shattered, so he went to his room. I was fully awake and raring to go, being a bit of a night person, so decided to get a drink at the bar. I got a HUGE big glass of white wine and sat down, lighting up a cigarette (yeah, I know, I should give up). I'd just exhaled my first puff, looked up and saw in the far corner of the bar (hidden from view where I was sat before) a poster with the 'publishing' guy on it... Stephen Holbrook, International Medium and Clairvoyant'. So he DID know something about all the crowds earlier, the swine! And then it struck me, and only then, that we did actually look fairly similar. That's why those women had been pointing and staring, they thought I was Steve!

I must have been in some sort of far away thinking place, because I was jumped back into the real world by the unimaginable... A voice even louder than the man who turned out to be James, shouting something about having a quick fag and shopping at Gunwharf Quay the morning after. Not for the first time that day I thought how loud can one person be? There was no-one else in the bar at that point, and Steve recognised me from earlier, came over and asked for a light. At that point we got chatting again and I was genuinely interested in what he did. Like I said before, you just seem to like the guy in an instant, and it did seem like we'd known each other for years, conversation was so easy. We spent the next two hours talking about our respective jobs, the ups and the downs, the highs and the lows.

It occurred to me that as we both spent most of our time travelling around, I said that if I was ever in an area where Steve was, I'd like to come and watch a demonstration, just to see if it was a load of old bunkum or not! Anyway, I got Steve's mobile number and said I'd ring him when I knew what my plans were. We bade farewell and went our separate ways. And then, I forgot all about it!

However, at work a week later, some colleagues were discussing a tv show about mediums, and not in a good light, I must admit. At one point, when the conversation really did go a little too far, my friend Linda piped up, obviously outraged we were having a laugh about it, 'Well actually, you're all wrong, there's this guy I've seen loads of times and he's absolutely fantastic! I've had messages from my mum and dad and it was so accurate, no-one else but me and my husband knew the details he gave me. He even joked about the fact that on the day we went, we'd had an argument about kippers! How would he know that, eh?' Hell hath no fury like a medium-lover scorned, so we all went quiet. Linda then produced Steve's book 'The Light In The Darkness' and I thought, 'Oh my God, it's Steve' followed immediately by, 'He looks like Crystal Carrington from Dynasty!'

I asked Linda if I could borrow the book, and although she eyed me through a thinly disguised veil of suspicion, she agreed. I took it home and read the whole thing in one go, it was so interesting. It really fleshed out the bones that Steve had talked about a week earlier in the hotel. It re-kindled my interest, and the fact that I'd said to Steve that I'd check on his website to see if I could manage to catch one of the demonstrations. Darlington seemed to be the only place where I was working in the same place at the same time, so I rang and arranged to be there.

Arms folded, brow perspiring, butterflies fluttering, I sat in my seat, not really knowing what to expect. I suspected plants in the audience, a bit of mind reading and auto-suggestion, vague generalisations etc, but I was absolutely taken aback by what I saw and heard. God, it was absolutely fantastic, all these messages from loved ones, the laughter and the tears, it was amazing. If these were plants, then they must have had years of training at RADA to be that good at acting! My enthusiasm got the better of me and I made arrangements to meet Steve again at the St Helens Hilton in a week's time.

I ended up helping on the door, taking money etc, seating people and selling books as well, as Steve's helper, Pat the Rottweiler, wasn't there due to illness. Even then, early on, people were asking if we were twins, or brothers, or at least in some way related. To see the shock when we said 'no' was hilarious. I really enjoyed myself, being amid all the action and the buzz was amazing. I said to Steve that whenever I'd done my day job, I'd pop over if I was in the area, and lend him a helping hand.

It became increasingly apparent that Steve led an extremely hectic life, it wasn't just driving to a venue, doing the evening, then off home. There was a whole world of advertising, organising, VAT returns, schedules that really was a 24 hour job. How in heavens name he managed I have no idea. A lesser man would have cracked under the pressure I'm sure. And then it struck me like a bolt out of the blue (divine intervention I like to call it now!), my life at work wasn't as fulfilling as it could be, there WERE better things to do in life, and that this could be where I could really make a difference.

Over the next few months, I took stock of my life, asking myself many soul-searching questions and eventually, after discussions with Steve, came to the conclusion that working together, would be ideal for both of us. It would release some of the pressure on him certainly, and I would at last be in a job where I could SEE the results of my labours.

During those months of endless chats about the logistics of it all, and also if Steve could afford a Manager (his Accountant and his assistant, Richard and Lyn, assured him that even if he couldn't financially (which he could), he ought to, to save his sanity!), I still helped Steve at many venues, though I didn't mention it to work, I wasn't that bold yet. There were many close calls when my work, and working with Steve, came very close together. It wasn't that I was doing anything

86

wrong, I just didn't want the two to mix until I was finally ready to say to my boss, 'We need a chat'.

Once, Steve and I were in a hotel room having a meeting. I'd arranged to meet my South East colleague in town, in preparation for a training session. However, she thought it would be a hoot if she came early to the hotel to wake me up. The knock on the door provoked panic, as Steve ran around the room, whispering (not too quietly I must admit!), 'Oh God, where can I hide?' It was a like a scene from a Carry On film, when we finally decided on the wardrobe! Steve leapt in, I shut the door and let Cassie in. I did hear a muffled yelp from inside the wardrobe, and it turns out Steve had sat on a broken wire coat hanger - ouch!

The very same day, I was giving Steve a lift to his demonstration, when I pulled up at some traffic lights. I casually looked around to my right to see who was in the flash looking car, and recognised my boss, tapping along on his wheel to some music, and the only thing I could do, without warning, was push Steve's head down sharply into the foot well to avoid being spotted! He hadn't got a clue why I was doing it, he just suffered a nasty blow to the head on the glove compartment on the way down.

Other similar incidents occurred over the weeks, and still do. Only the other day, I went into the bank for Steve, and had a full blown conversation about where I was appearing next, when was I back locally etc - the lady thought I was Steve! At Norwich once, I was sat outside the room with James and having a chat, when a lovely lady, one of Steve's regular clients called Jan Amini, came rushing in, only slightly late, and said 'Thank goodness, at least you haven't started yet!' This lady had seen Steve regularly over the last ten years or so, but still thought I was him. Nearly every night we work together, we are asked if we're brothers, it's amazing. Maybe there is some truth in James' constant suggestion that we were brothers in a previous life after all, but I'll leave that to him to explore! James also thinks that I have some sort of psychic ability, and would even go so far as to say Steve and I will be sharing the stage eventually, doing 45 minutes each! Talk about pressure!

The time finally came when I told my work that I was leaving. It was a total shock to them. I had been there for nearly 17 years for goodness sake, but I realised deep down that I had reached a dead end. I couldn't progress any further in the company, and the plateau I was on, I really didn't enjoy much any more. So officially, on January 1$^{st}$ 2006, I became Rob Green, Manager to Steve Holbrook. It took me a while to get used to the way Steve worked, and I just tried to analyse it all and see where (if possible), things could be streamlined, or modernised, or just adapted to a more efficient way of working. The first thing I had to get was a laptop, so at least we could get emails on the many tours that Steve does. The only thing is, Steve is still a technophobe who refuses to even look at the laptop, never mind use the mouse or click a button! I swear he thinks the mouse is some little furry thing that needs cheese once a day!

We'll get there eventually, every new day brings a new challenge, and a new solution. Steve once said that there are no such things as problems, only issues that will help us achieve better things. That is something I admire and hold to as much as I can.

I talked initially about how our lives change even though we don't feel we want or need them to. Life is a very complex, intriguing concept, and how we all weave together and forge friendships and relationships is often mind-blowing. My life changed for the better when I met Steve Holbrook, and I suspect many of yours have too, although for different reasons. So, that's me, Rob Green, summed up in a nutshell. I have enjoyed meeting many different people on our travels, and look forward to meeting many more in the future."

**Chapter Eight:**    *Reincarnation*

For those of you unfamiliar with the concept, reincarnation is the belief structure that rather than having just the one life, we have many lives, returning to this earthplane time and time again in different identities in an attempt to learn new lessons and to develop spiritually.

While it is a difficult concept to grasp, it is a widely held belief that crosses the barriers, albeit with subtle variations, of all the major faith systems. Buddhism, in particular, has reincarnation as a central tenet of its divine philosophy and presents the concept that we all have lives without number; the traditional Arabic faith system speaks of us having seven lives, with each "life" making us more perfect and bringing us closer to God in the process. The Hindu faith accepts reincarnation as a reality and while it does not have the concept written into its holy writings as an article of faith, perhaps the greatest recorded *evidence* for reincarnation comes from Hindu literature.

You won't find reincarnation mentioned much (if at all) within the various branches of Christianity, and in the western world reincarnation is much more the interest of the individual; opinions and beliefs are much more affected by personal appraisal and analyisis than by religious doctrine. And yet the western mind is intrigued and beguiled by the idea, and if you want hard evidence for that statement just go and count the numbers of titles dealing with the subject on the shelves of your local book shop or library.

I first met Stephen in the Spring of 1999 and during the first year of our association we collaborated in the

90

production of his first book, "The Light In The Darkness". During the research process I did ask Stephen what he thought about the idea of reincarnation and while he was not dismissive of the subject, his answer was certainly somewhat guarded.

He said that although he was open minded about it, he didn't really know too much about the subject to offer any kind of opinion. He felt, on balance, that it was an unlikely possibility and that certainly, he had never received any evidence from his spiritual work that supported or even *hinted* at the concept of reincarnation within the framework of the spiritualism faith that he had been a part of since he was sixteen years old.

But as I say, that conversation took place back in 1999 and by his own admission his viewpoint has changed a little since then, much influenced, I suspect. by his initial meeting with and subsequent friendship and business association with Rob Green.

Stephen: "When I first met Rob it was really weird. I'd talked with him for five minutes in a bar and within that five minutes it felt like I'd known him all my life... It was stranger than that really because it felt like I was meeting up with an old friend who I hadn't seen for years. I mean, on a mental level, I knew I'd never met Rob before but all the same it felt as though I knew him... And this wasn't anything like the the feelings that I get when I'm on stage doing my spiritual work. This was something really quite different."

Although this may have been a new experience for Stephen, what he is actually describing is something that happens very frequently... It's happened to me a lot and there won't be many people out there reading this who will not have had some experience similar to Stephen's at some time in their lives.

If we are looking for evidence of reincarnation then this aspect of "recognition" must be given some credibility because it is not, as the sceptic might submit, just a matter of sexual chemistry. There is *nothing* sexual in this experience, as anyone who has experienced it will attest to, and it is purely a *spiritual* phenomena. I'll grant you that the idea of reincarnation may, on occasions, have been subverted into a marvelous chat-up line – "Hello Darling, haven't I seen you somewhere else before?" but if *these* feelings and motives are present you can take it that it's a matter of libido, loneliness or ego and has nothing to do with spiritual recognition.

Stephen: "I've known Rob Green for three years and he has worked as my business partner for the past twelve months. People always seem to think that we're brothers and there have been loads of times when one of us has been mistaken for the other. The point that I want to make here, though, is that not only do we look alike, we also think alike... I'll start a sentence and Rob will finish it off for me or I could be in Manchester thinking of a problem and Rob will phone me from Leeds to say it's all been sorted out... We're friends and business partners, for heaven's sake, but in some ways we're like an old married couple that have been together for fifty years. *"*

The aspect of "familiarity" must also be taken on board as another building block of evidence. It's fine if you *are* a married couple of fifty odd years standing... You'd expect some degree of telepathy to be making its occasional presence felt in those circumstances, but surely not after only fifty odd *weeks* of a friendship and business relationship?

What, if we think about it rationally, could be an acceptable explanation for any of this? Some sort of fluke? Some twist of serendipity? To walk away from it and say it doesn't really exist at all and that it's all in the mind? Sadly these common attitudes do not offer any plausible *explanation* for the kind of recognition and familiarity that exists not just between a clairvoyant and his business manager but also many other people who have made this kind of connection during the course of their lives.

If, on the other hand, you can accept, at least in theory, the idea that Stephen Holbrook and Rob Green were brothers in a previous life, then this provides a complete and total explanation for the connection they have made in *this* life.

But to put this in perspective, this subject is far greater than just an element of recognition and familiarity between two of my best mates and business partners, and I've simply used Steve and Rob as a device, enabling me to talk a bit about a subject which is very close to my heart.


Believing in reincarnation creates the same kind of problem as does believing in an afterlife and the problem is that no one can tell us exactly what it is like over on the "other side" and your own personal view depends upon your own faith system. To be sure, many people have postulated theories based on their "visions" (notably Welsh medium Stephen O'Brien and Father Bernard, the Christian visionary who, despite writing in the 1940's when Britain stood with its back to the wall, and despite his obviously Christian interpretation, nevertheless did give us a cohesive picture of heaven complete with palm fronds, fine marble temples and pearly gates) but the truth of the matter is that nobody really *knows* for sure.

And yet here is an interesting thought... If reincarnation is a reality, then there must be a place of residence for the waiting spirits. Shall we, for want of a better word, call that heaven?

But *is* reincarnation a reality?

I personally believe that it is and I base my belief on forty years of fairly extensive research and no small degree of personal experience – but as with life after death, it is a personal belief for which (were I writing another book specifically dedicated to the subject) I could present some extremely interesting evidence but no hard proof.

One wonderful theory I came across recently is that the American President John F. Kennedy was the reincarnated soul of Abraham Lincoln – which at first sounds absurd until you start doing a bit of research into the two Presidents, at which time some *very* odd coincidences and aspects of synchronicity reach out to grab you and start screaming for some attention.

Like...

Abraham Lioncoln was elected to Congress in 1846 and JFK was elected to Congress in 1946. Lincoln was elected President in 1860 while JFK was elected President in 1960. Both Presidents were particularly involved in civil rights, and both Presidents' wives lost children while residing in The White House. President Lincoln's secretary was called Kennedy while JFK's secretary was called Lincoln...

Now it starts getting really weird.

Both Presidents were shot on a Friday. Both Presidents were shot in the head. Both were assisanted

94

by Southerners, and both Presidents were succeeded by Southerners called Johnson. Andrew Johnson who took over from Lincoln was born in 1808 while Lyndon B Johnson who stepped into JFK's shoes was born in 1908.

John Wilkes Booth, who assasinated Lincoln, was born in 1839 while Lee Harvey Oswald who assassinated Kennedy (with a little help from his friends?) was born in 1939. Both assasins were known by their three names – and both names are composed of fiteen letters. Lincoln was shot at The Ford Theatre while Kennedy was shot in a Lincoln motor car made by The Ford Motor Company. Lincoln was shot in a theatre and his assassin ran and hid in a warehouse. Kennedy was shot from a warehouse and his assassin went and hid in a theatre. Both John Wilkes Booth and Lee Harvey Oswald were assinated themselves before being brought to trial.

And as a nice little coup d'etat, a week before Lincoln was shot he was in the small town of Monroe in the state of Maryland, while a week before Kennedy was shot, he was with Marilyn Monroe.

Anyone got any explanations? If so, please send 'em off c/o Mage Publishing. Just don't bother using that word "coincidence" because I just won't buy into that theory, not with all the weight of evidence which indicates that there is something else, something much bigger and much more important going on here.

There are some obvious parallels here between reincarnation and life after death. Night after night, Stephen brings messages through to members of his audience. They are usually concise and to the point and contain a plethora of detail. The sceptic claims that there are plants in the audience because he/she cannot explain what Stephen is doing or how he is able to do it.

We categorically maintain that the information that Stephen brings through comes from a spiritual connection that he is able to facilitate between two dimensions, in crude lay terms, the realm of the living and the realm of the dead. To the people who claim that this is impossible, we issue this simple challenge... If Stephen Holbrook does *not* have the gift of channeling information between two worlds, tell us how else is he able to do what he does? The plants in the audience idea is crazy and untenable. He is not using telepathy, proven by the fact that he will frequently bring information through that is not known to the recipient at the time of the channeling. He is not using some kind of Derren Brown mind control – he neither has the training, the skill nor the discipline required to emulate this remarkably gifted gentleman and it has to be said here that what Derren does through mind control and hypnotism to create the illusion of clairvoyance, and that is all that it is, just an illusion – Stephen does it for real.

After having been "on the road" with Stephen for seven years, certainly as a friend but also as a serious researcher and biographer, the amount of evidence I have witnessed to prove that there *is* a spiritual domain that we transcend to after death of life on the earthplane is absolutely staggering. I have observed more than a thousand of Stephen's demonstrations and, more to the point, I have interviewed (in depth) scores of people who have had messages and who are only too willing to attest to the accuracy of those messages. In my personal files I have more than 150 letters from people who have had messages and are only too anxious to have their testimony published in the hope that it might bring a little light into the lives of other people who have not had messages from their friends and loved ones on the other side. In the last half year alone we have had more than 2000 hits on the website, all attesting to Stephen's accuracy... And these people are not cranks or nutters, they are ordinary people just like you and me who have attended Stephen's demonstrations and have got something really powerful and positive out of the experience..

If you can accept that there is a spiritual afterlife and can further accept that it is possible to form some bridge of communication, it provides a beautifully simple explanation for how Stephen is able to do what he does.

Extrapolate on that for a moment and apply the same generosity to the idea of reincarnation, and here we have some remarkably simple explanations for how two strangers can meet for the first time and feel that they have known each other for years... Of how you can go to an unfamiliar place that you know you've never previously visited and think "I've been here before!"... Of how you can take instant likes and dislikes to people without knowing anything at all about them, of how the same places keep cropping up in your dreams, of how you are attracted to certain things and turned off by others...

I am frightened by heights, I have a pathological loathing of being cold and I have an anoraky fascination bordering on obsession with world war two aeroplanes. Quite recently, a very advanced spiritualist who had some knowledge of reincarnation but who knew nothing of me or my life at all whatsoever, gave me, as part of a reading she was doing for me at the time, the fact that in my last life I'd been part of a bomber crew in the second world war. Her statement made a lot of sense to me, both then and now. It's flaming cold up at 20,000 feet and 20,000 feet is very high, especially when those nasty people on the ground are shooting guns at you!

I know a man who when he is stressed, speaks fluent Russian in his sleep. He has never been to Russia, has no real interest in that country, and yet when tape recordings of his nocturnal ramblings were analysed by the language department at York university a few years ago, it transpires that not only does he speak Russian but he does so with a St Petersburg accent and in a speech form more commonly used in the 18th century than in this present day. If we seek a simple explanation would it not be logical to assume that in a previous life, maybe a couple of hundred years ago, this man had lived in Russia? There may be other explanations for this strange occurance, but if so, what are they?

These are a couple of incidents that I am personally familiar with but there are thousands more recorded by eminent researchers such as Bloxham, Cayce and Montcrief, and on another level there are many more thousands of case histories in the various filing cabinets of hypnotherapists and regression therapists all across the western world. Surely, all of this evidence must provide some food for thought, for it tugs at the strands of our spiritual DNA that dictates who we are, why we are the people we are, why we think this and why we do the other. Why are some of us rich while others are poor? Why are some of free while others live their lives in captivity. Indeed, why can some of us accept the idea of life after death while others find it such a difficult concept to grasp?

**Chapter Nine:**     *A Bottle of Wine…*

Stephen is not much of a drinker. In the early days, when I first met him, all you had to do was pass a wine gum over a glass of water and he'd be tipsy. After having been associated with me for half a decade he's learned how to knock it back a bit more liberally, but even so, a bottle of wine quaffed over an evening is about his limit. Anything more than that and, depending on his mood, he's either going to fall asleep on you or he's going to start acting like a kid in a sweet factory! But there's always the odd exception to the rule…

We were on the Isle of Wight. We'd had a very successful evening and most of the messages Stephen had brought through were very bright and upbeat. There had been a few tears – there always are – but there was also an awful lot of laughter. We ate a generous supper at the local Indian restaurant and then went back to the hotel to get some sleep – except that Stephen was in a very buzzy mood – and to cut a long story short, we found ourselves sat in a couple of over stuffed armchairs in the lounge, watching the rain slash against the windows, made ever more magical and mysterious by the daubs of colour provided by the strings of fairy lights that swayed on their cables out on the terrace. Apart from the night porter, the hotel was deserted (well, it was the Isle of Wight out of season) and although we'd talked about having a couple of coffees, we ended up ordering a bottle of wine. We'd already polished off a bottle in the restaurant, but we weren't driving anywhere and the adrenalin was still racing away. It seemed that we needed a little longer to wind down. I lit my pipe and Stephen smoked one of his occasional cigarettes.

At first we talked about the demonstration, and then the conversation shifted to the up-coming schedule for the rest of the tour. At that time my old Volvo 740 had 334,000 miles on the clock and it was about time she was retired, so we started talking about cars, and then we started talking about clairvoyants and their cars and Steve reminded of the time when he still thought that the Austin Montego was the finest thing on four wheels...

'Well, I'm sorry James, but I honestly did like the old Montegos. They were always good cars for me, and I remember the time I was looking for a new one and I couldn't find one anywhere. I'd been scouring the local newspapers and the trade magazine, and there was nothing to be had... Nothing that I wanted. I knew that it had to be an automatic and it would have to be nice and clean with very low mileage, but everything I went to see was an absolute wreck...

'Anyway, there was this night that I was driving back home from a demonstration and I had Pat the Rottweiler with me. We were belting along the M62 in the pouring rain, a bit like tonight, and I suddenly had the impulse to pull off the motorway one junction ahead of my normal turn off. I mean, Pat wanted to know what I was playing at because it was a bit late and she was ready for her bed, but it was just a pure instinct thing. Even I didn't know why I'd come off early, but anyway, we were driving back along the back roads and through the villages, about half past eleven or something like that, and we passed this pub car park. Right in the middle of the car park there was this lovely Austin Montego, so I stopped the car and got out to have a look, and you'll never believe this, but there was a "for sale" notice in the back window with some bloke's name and phone number. Anyway, I phoned the next morning and went around to see the car and I had the number 54 in my mind – really clear like a beacon – and when I got to see the car it was white, had an automatic gearbox, was really clean inside and had done 54,025 miles. So I bought it there and then... Talk about spirit guiding me to the right car!'

In a way, this opened the door of opportunity to talk about other spiritual matters and I asked him if there were other ways in which spirit intervened in his daily life...

'No not really – I mean it isn't like I walk down the high street with all my spirit guides in tow and if I'm doing the washing up, then no one's looking over my shoulder trying to get my attention, but having said that, at the end of the day, if I need them to be there, then they'll be there... I mean you know all the pressure I've been getting to do this flaming television show? Well one half of me was saying yes go on, do it, and you can use the money to give everyone a really good holiday or I could have afforded the conservatory Caroline had been going on about, but in my heart of hearts I knew I didn't want to do it. I was all mixed up about what I should do for the best, and then I was out digging the garden one morning and I heard my Granddad's voice as clear as a bell in my ear.

'He said "Steve you're not in a race, lad..." and that was it. Just those few words, but I knew it was a message from spirit and I knew exactly what I was being told. There was no hurry to get onto the telly. I could afford to wait until the kids had grown up, and if by then the TV companies weren't interested any more, well that was fine by me.'

At that time in our association I was keen for Stephen to do some television work and was quite frustrated and annoyed with him when he kept saying no to all the offers that were coming his way. Since then I've had cause to change my mind and I'm heartily glad Stephen didn't take the TV bait – but we'll talk more about that later.

For the time being I poured him another glass of wine and encouraged him to carry on with the conversation. 'What about,' I asked, struggling with my pipe which wouldn't draw properly, ' – those times, especially in the early days, when you *were* prompted to give messages to people you met in the street, and that story you told me about the lady in the supermarket who'd just lost her son? Surely in those circumstances, spirit is with you in sufficient strength to make those connections?'

'Yeah, sure, I suppose so, but that's not quite the same as wandering around in a permanent trance waiting to give a message to the first person I meet. Like I always say, James, it's a natural process and other than having learned how to turn it on and off at the beginning and end of a demonstration, I don't have that much control over it.'

He sipped at the wine. It was a nice Rioja. I always buy Rioja in a gesture of solidarity towards Spain. Got to do something to aid the Spanish economy.

'Curious,' I mused. 'After all, you *are* a bit of a control freak and yet every time you go out on to the platform you're willingly giving up that control… Must be a bit scary?'

He shook his head. 'No, not really because that's what being a medium is all about. You've got to give up the control if you want spirit to use you as a channel, and I really don't have a problem with that. It isn't really scary at all because I just take it as an article of faith that when I go out on stage spirit will be waiting to make contact with their loved ones down here, and they've never let me down yet and I've been doing this work now for nineteen years.'

'Yeah, but what happens if one night you *do* walk out onto the stage and there's nothing there?'

'I'd look a bit of an idiot, wouldn't I?' he laughed. 'No, seriously that's never happened and I don't think it ever will. At least I hope it never will. But if it did, then maybe that'd be spirit's way of telling me it was time to pack it in and find a proper job. Maybe even go back to hairdressing.'

'Lord, you'd not go back to being a hairdresser, would you?'

'No, not in a million years! I was only joking. I enjoyed it while I was doing it and I met some fabulous people, but I don't think I'd ever want to go back to it.'

'So, if you weren't a medium, what would you do?'

'I could always become a stripper!' – And we both had a chuckle about that because he was making reference to something that had occurred a few months earlier when his car had broken down on the M6 and the AA mechanic who'd come out to rescue him had thought he was one of The Chippendales or something similar.

'No, come on,' I said. 'Seriously, what would you do?'

'Dunno... I mean I've always fancied running a model agency but I dare say I'd probably end up opening a tea shop somewhere.'

A pair of bright headlights swept into the carpark outside and just for a second we had a glimpse of how heavily the rain was falling. Two figures dashed from the automobile up to the hotel entrance and a moment later a bedraggled and windswept couple hurried across the foyer to the lifts. They were in their late thirties and neither of them looked very happy.

I called out a cheery "good night" but got no reaction and as the lift doors closed, shutting them from sight, I looked at Steve drily. 'Well, what do you make of that?' I asked.

'They'd just had a row,' he said. 'And she was wearing Joop.'

Stephen has this – trick? knack? ability? – to be able to identify a woman's perfume at twenty paces. I don't know how the blazes he does it but he seldom gets it wrong.

'How do you know that?' I asked with mock incredulity.

'What? That they'd had a row or that she was wearing Joop?'

He was smiling at my slyly, enjoying the tease.

'Both,' I said.

'Well, she smelled of Joop and you didn't have to be psychic to sense the mood of hostility between them, did you? Now come on, James,' his tone sobered but his eyes were still twinkling. 'Don't read more into it than there is.'

We were half way through the bottle. It was a 1999 Raimat Abadia weighing in at a full 14% and it was

104

obviously having a warming effect on my fair haired friend. He poured himself another glass, then in a gesture of defiance against authority, kicked off his shoes and propped his feet up on the coffee table.

'I'm really enjoying this wine,' he said.

'Yes, I can see you are,' I filled my own glass. Then, remembering an earlier conversation we'd had in the car driving down from Yorkshire, I changed the subject. 'You were going to tell me,' I reminded him, 'the story about the corn on the cob?'

'Oh yes, so I was, and if you want to use it in the next book that'd be fine, because if nothing else it only goes to prove how daft people can be sometimes...'

So Stephen told me the tale of the corn on the cob, and it all centred around a demonstration he'd been doing a few years ago somewhere near Lincoln. Apparently he'd been having a lovely evening and then about half way through the night he'd got locked into a rather sad message for a very elderly lady called Tilly who had lost her husband only a few months previously. This gentleman came through with lots of loving thoughts and plenty of detail... He said that he was with Alfred and Arthur, his two brothers who had predeceased him. He said that he hadn't liked all the weeks he'd spent in hospital stuck full of tubes, but that he was fine now and all the pain in his tummy had gone. He asked for his love to be passed on to Rosie, who was Tilly's life long friend and next door neighbour and who had helped Tilly through her bereavement. He *also* said that one of the best things about having passed over was the fact that he'd got his teeth back and could enjoy one of his favourite dishes which was corn on the cob.

When Stephen had talked to Tilly at the end of the demonstration she had been able to confirm all the details of the message. He had been predeceased by his two brothers Alfred and Arthur, he had been in hospital for weeks dying with stomach cancer, and they had both been close to Rosie their next door neighbour and Rosie had done a lot to help Tilly through the dark days after the funeral. Tilly confirmed that her husband's favourite dish was corn on the cob dripping with butter and that he had loved nothing better than to take the cob in his hand and gnash away at it with his teeth.

Tilly went on to say that in the last eighteen months of his life her husband had lost all of his teeth and had refused to wear dentures because they made his gums sore. He had no longer been able to gnash away at his corn cobs and it had caused him a disproportionate degree of distress and frustration. However, on a special occasion, he had made one last effort to eat his corn on the cob – and had actually choked and died in the process.

Tilly had been delighted with her message, and the thing that had clinched it for her – that proved beyond all shadow of doubt that the message had been coming from her late husband – was the business about the corn on the cob.

*However...*

In the audience that night there had been a reporter from the local press and in the revue that he wrote he said something like – *"I attended Mr Holbrook's evening of clairvoyance last Tuesday and initially I was quite impressed with some of the messages he brought through but when he started talking to a corn on the cob I started losing interest..."*

Obviously this gentleman had been half asleep or he'd missed the point of the message entirely, but one good thing came out of the tale and that was both

106

Stephen and I were having a good laugh about it now. And, of course, laughter can be infectious and I chose to remind him of the night he'd been demonstrating in Retford when he'd been trying to connect the name of Richard to someone in the audience, except that nobody was responding.

'I've definitely got a Richard here who is desperate to talk to a lady in this audience tonight,' Stephen had said. 'And if I don't make the connection soon I'm going to have to move on...'

At that point a very bosomy lady with blond hair, bright red lips and a tight leather skirt stood up and shouted out – 'I can't take a Richard, but I can take a Dick!'

The audience had rocked with laughter, and both Stephen and I guffawed out loud at the memory. That took us into remembering other innocent faux pas that Stephen had made... Like the time when he was giving a message to a lady and said something along the lines of "you're very hot in bed, my love" – meaning that she became physically hot every time her late husband came to visit her in her dreams. Needless to say, the audience took it completely the wrong way, and no matter how hard he tried, Stephen wasn't able to dig himself out of that particular hole!

And then there was the time up in Darlington when Stephen was trying to get a message over to a very shy gentleman who was sitting on the front row. This gentleman was extremely nervous and in an attempt to relax him Steve had said "Is this your first time at anything like this, sir?" The gentleman said no, and that as a matter of fact he'd attended a number of Stephen's demonstrations. At that point Steve came out with the immortal line "Ooh it's lovely to meet a man who

107

comes more than once." And I remember to this day the way he stood there with a bemused look on his face, wondering what it was that he'd said that had reduced his audience to tears of mirth.

Maybe we were making a bit too much noise because at that point the night porter shuffled over – well he was about ninety – and asked if we needed anything else.

'Er, yes please, I think we'll have another bottle of this lovely red wine – and I'm sorry if we're causing a disturbance.' This was Stephen, not me.

'No gents, you're fine. No one can hear you down here. So that's another bottle of the same coming up.'

I raised my eyebrows questioningly. This was our third bottle over the course of the evening, but if he was on a roll I wasn't going to stop him. In any case, Stephen never does relax very much, he's always hyped up with this that or the other and he's always pumped up with adrenalin. If for a few hours I could convert him from being a workaholic to an alcoholic, I didn't think it would do him any harm. I'd certainly not seen him as relaxed or as chilled out as this for ages, and of course, it had been him who'd ordered this last bottle.

The aforementioned bottle duly arrived, and giving up on my pipe, I pinched one of Stephen's cigarettes. Bad habit, of course, and no, I don't mean smoking them, I mean pinching them from other people, but I've done it all my life and I have no intention of stopping now.

'I reckon there must be a few ghosts wandering round in this place,' I observed, letting my eyes drift around some of the dimly lit dark corners. It was a lovely old hotel, very traditional and rustic, and not one of the modern steel and plastic chains.

'Apart from the night porter?' Stephen quipped, and because the Raimat was beginning to have some effect, it set us off on another fit of the giggles.

'So tell me about ghosts,' I said. 'I know you saw one once because we wrote about it in the first book we did – you know, the little old man who walked across the room and disappeared into the wall – but we never really did get to the crux of the matter, did we? I mean, the ghosts that you read about in ghost stories and the spirits you make contact with every night, they've got to be different things, right?'

'Absolutely,' he confirmed. 'I'm not exactly sure what the difference is, but I know that there is a *big* difference... but please let's not talk about ghosts. It's spooky enough in here as it is.'

A clairvoyant using words like spooky? Making it pretty clear he was a little bit nervous about ghosts and things that went bump in the night? Ummm, well, there was a story there (a couple actually) but this was obviously not the time and place to go looking for them. So I changed the subject.

'Okay,' I said. 'Come on, one last story before we hit the sack – what's the weirdest or most bizarre message you've ever brought across?'

'Oh that's an easy one,' he grinned. 'That would be Fifi, the red poodle.'

'A *red* poodle,' I echoed. 'You sure you haven't had too much *red* wine?'

'No, seriously.'

'Well which way was it going?'

'Which way was what going?'

'The message. Was it coming *from* Fifi the red poodle or going *to* Fifi the red poodle?'

Well, for God's sake, I'd had a few drinks as well.

109

'Oh. Yes. I see what you mean. Er, well, neither actually. It was *about* Fifi the red poodle, and when I think about it, it wasn't so much red as bright pink!'

'Red or pink or whatever, what's the story about Fifi?'

'Well, when I think about it really, I suppose the message was more to do with the big pan of tomato soup...'

How had we got from poodles to soup, I wondered – and then realized that my clairvoyant companion was well and truly smashed. But he was still coherent and I was still listening.

'I was giving a message to a lady, and I was getting all sorts of names and dates and stuff like that, and I was linking with her mother... Apparently, for the last eight weeks of her life, this lady's mum had only been able to eat tomato soup and it had to be Heinz tomato soup mind you, absolutely nothing else would do! But on this one occasion just before she passed over, the lady had run out of canned soup so in desperation she concocted a mixture of her own from the tomatoes in her garden and because it had come out as a browny muddy mess she'd added a good dollop of red food colouring just to brighten it up a bit. Anyway, this lady's old mum still thought it was horrible and wouldn't touch it, so not wanting to waste her labour, she fed it to Fifi the poodle, and Fifi thought it was great and ate the lot. Within an hour there'd been some sort of doggy allergenic reaction or something and Fifi went from white to tomato pink... The lady told me that the vet couldn't do anything about it, and so now Fifi's permanently plink.. No not plink. I mean *pink*... And James, if you don't mind I think I've really got to go to bed now...'

My friend stood up and swayed gently. I thought it expedient to lead him over to the lifts.

'Jamesh?'

'Yes, Steve.'

'Am I going to have a hangover in the morning?'

'Yes, Stephen, you are going to have a hangover in the morning.'

And I didn't have to be psychic to work that one out.

Stephen went to bed. It was two o'clock in the morning and it was still pouring down with rain. I put on my hat and my coat and I went for a walk along the sea front. There was a blustery wind and I got wet, but I didn't really mind. I needed just a little time and space to clear my head and I found the sound of the waves breaking on the shingle beach to be soothing and evocative. Despite the rain there was the delicious tang of ozone in the air and although I was tired enough to sleep for a week on a clothes line, I also felt stimulated and excited, especially when I re-ran the last couple of hours' of conversation through my mind.

I smiled to myself. What an odd night this had been. We'd talked on lots of subjects but I have to confess it was the image of corn cobs and pink poodles that stuck in my imagination, and I was ever mindful of the fact that it is always in these silly little details, meaningless to an audience at large but so totally *meaningful* to the individual in receipt of the message, that Stephen provides proof of post mortem survival.

I mean, I suppose anyone could stand up in front of a crowd and say 'I've got someone here who passed over with stomach problems' and be reasonably hopeful of making a connection with somebody in the audience, but who in their right mind would have the balls or imagination to whitter on about corn on the cob unless they were damn sure that corn on the cob was relevant? And pink poodles and tomato soup, for heaven's sake! All right, this might be a bit amusing, and it is also very parochial, but it is also so convincingly specific.

I remembered other messages Stephen has given over the years, and although different and disparate, they all have one thing in common. Personal detail, insignificant in some ways but so evidential in others. A mother may be given the name of her dead son, the date he died and the circumstances in which he died, but for Stephen to then go on and say "he's telling me that when he was down here there was something a bit funny about his left foot... One of his toes, the one next to his little toe was much longer than all the others and you used to joke about it, calling him the boy with toeselitis or something equally daft..." and for him to be absolutely 100% correct in this statement – well, the chances of him being right almost beggar belief and it gives the mother the very last bit of conclusive proof that she needs to know that she has indeed been in communication with her dead child.

And that, when you're grieving, lost and confused, can mean absolutely everything.

## Chapter Ten:     *Hauntings*

Rob Green has got a haunted toilet. No, don't laugh. It's serious and from Rob's point of view it's causing him an awful lot of inconvenience.

New house, new bathroom, new loo, and of course new plumbing. Third day in the new house Rob notices a small puddle of water about a eighteen inches to the left of the toilet. Thinks nothing of it. Mops it up. Two days later, same puddle of water in the same place. Again, thinks no more of it. Five days after that another puddle of water, now somewhat bigger.

Rob comes to the obvious conclusion that there must be a leak somewhere so checks everything carefully and can't find any faults – also he thinks it's a bit strange that the puddle is in the *middle* of the floor well away from any appliances that might possibly have sprung a leak. Mops it up, but now he's curious and on the lookout for any anomalies.

Two days later, another puddle in exactly the same place. Rob, ever practical and never to be put off by a challenge, gets down on his hands and knees for a closer inspection and to his horror realizes that this isn't just a puddle of water, it's a puddle of pee.

'Disgusting!' he thinks, yet again doing artistic maneuvers with his mop and bucket. Rob isn't saying much, but secretly he is now very puzzled as to what is going on. Not really concerned yet, but definitely puzzled... So much so that he starts checking the bathroom every couple of hours or so and makes a point of ensuring that his aim is spot on whenever he is using the bathroom.

For a week all is quiet, and then for three days in a row there are three more even bigger puddles. He hasn't yet twigged that there might be something supernatural going on so he does what most people would do in the circumstances. He calls in a plumber. The plumber pulls up the lino to check for subterranean leakage or seepage, everything is fine, no problems, eighty quid's worth of call out fee, and back to normal for a fortnight.

Then the hero of our tale pops into his smallest room one morning to find that although the floor is dry, there is a tiny nugget of pooh right where the puddles usually form... And *now* Rob does start getting slightly worried and worried all the more when erratically over the following few weeks there are irregular but nonetheless frequent droppings of somebody else's business standing proudly in the middle of his new lino.

'Stephen,' he says, 'I've got a haunted loo!'

Steve laughs.

'No Stephen, don't laugh, I'm being serious. I've definitely got a haunted loo. Someone, and it certainly isn't me, is piddling and poohing all over my bathroom floor.'

Stephen inspects the trouble spot.

'Any psychic vibes?' Rob asks hopefully.

'Not a flaming thing,' Stephen replies.

'Well this has got to be sorted out,' Rob is getting more and more frustrated and (if you'll pardon the pun) pissed off with this rather untenable situation. 'I've only just moved into this place and I'm not moving out just because someone or something has decided to use my loo as a toilet!'

'Dunno what to suggest,' Stephen says. And then remembering something he's read – 'I suppose you could open your bathroom window and tell whatever's in here to go away, and maybe you could put some flowers in a vase or something, light a bit of incense and say a few little prayers.'

'You're the expert, why can't you do it?' Rob wants to know.

'Because it's your loo and you're the one with the problem,' Stephen answers correctly.

So Rob opens the windows, tells whatever is in his toilet to depart and desist, buys a bunch of daffs and some sandalwood, says a couple of little prayers... and that's how things stand at the moment. The puddles and pooh still keep manifesting themselves, but now only every couple of weeks rather than every couple of days, and this is an ongoing situation so if it resolves itself or anything happens between now and me finishing this book, I'll keep you informed.

As well as Moaning Myrtle in J.K. Rowling's Harry Potter epic, ghosts do seem to be attracted to toilets. Maybe it's got something to do with running water – and I'm not being facetious here because over the years I have observed that Stephen's really outstanding nights of clairvoyance always take place when it's pouring with rain. Water is, after all, a conductor of electricity, and although it cannot (yet) be scientifically proved it does seem that all aspects of paranormal activity have some element of electricity associated with them. Certainly, at the time of writing, Rob Green isn't the only guy in Yorkshire having a problem with poltergeists in the privy.

Another much publicised haunting that has been thoroughly reported and investigated by The Yorkshire Evening Post – and it has to be said the YEP is not a frivolous tabloid but rather one of the oldest and most conservative publications in England. Perhaps the

115

involvement of the West Yorkshire Police gave the story some gravitas.

At one thirty in the early hours of Tuesday, April 25$^{th}$, Roger Froggatt, landlord of The Low Valley Arms in Barnsley was woken from his sleep by the sound of his security alarm going off. Only two hours previously he had checked the premises, turned off the three big plasma screen TV's, and primed the security system.

Now, venturing downstairs from his flat above the pub he found that the TV screens were *on*, and that although there was no sign of an intruder, the heat seeking security alarm was going hell for leather. Mr Froggatt carried out a thorough inspection. The last place he checked were the toilets and it was here that he got the shock of his life.

In front of him stood a grotesquely disfigured apparition dressed in white. Half of her face was missing from her cheekbone to her jaw.

At this point he was joined by his wife Kathryn *who also saw exactly the same apparition!* This is an important point because if there are two witnesses, one's testimony gives credibility to the other. It was also Kathryn who noticed that the toilets, which were manual units, were flushing themselves continuously.

The terrified couple did what a lot of people would have done in the circumstances. They slammed the toilet door shut and bolted. Then, because they didn't know what else to do and because they were genuinely frightened, they called the police.

Approximately ten minutes later the police arrived at the pub to find a very traumatized Mr Froggatt and it was a shaking Kathryn that led the officers into the ladies toilets. There was no sign of the white woman with half a face but the loos were still flushing away all

116

on their own and one of the officers attending clearly noted that the flush handles were moving of their own accord as though some ghostly hand was pushing them down every time the cistern tank refilled itself from the main water supply.

The police were concerned about Roger Froggatt's condition and they offered to call an ambulance, but he refused medical treatment and elected to have a stiff brandy instead.

Talking to The Yorkshire Post reporter the following day the landlord said that although he was not the kind of man to be frightened easily he had been badly shaken by the incident, and that he and his wife would now be calling on the services of a priest to perform an exorcism and rid the pub of what they describe as being an evil spirit.

Whether the spirit in question was evil or not is subjective – we must remember that Roger and Kathryn were taken by surprise and were honestly disturbed and upset by the horrendous apparition of a disfiguered old lady, who from their point of view probably looked as though she'd stepped straight out of a horror movie – but there can be no doubt that the manifestation of this apparition has caused the couple no small degree of psychological distress. This makes me mindful of some of the stories I was told when I was a child – and some of the stories I've heard time and time again ever since when the theory and belief that "ghosts can't hurt you" has been put forwards with great confidence by people who do not know nearly as much as they think they do.

Perhaps a ghost can't hurt you by swinging a punch or sticking a knife between your ribs (although that point is debateable as we shall see later on in this chapter) but a ghostly apparition can, as we have learned, damage the mind and the emotions of the unwary and the unprepared.

The Shrieves House is a beautiful old 13th century building in the middle of Stratford-upon-Avon and is leased by a pal of ours called Steve Devey. Sometimes when Stephen is demonstrating in Stratford and we're in the middle of a tour, we'll stay overnight, and it is always a lovely experience. Devey maintains that the place is haunted, and although it may well be so, I have only ever sensed the warmest and friendliest of atmospheres within this incredible building. Stephen, however, isn't so sure.

On one of our stopovers Stephen had been sleeping in the room known as The Cock Loft up on the top floor. Low ceiling, oak panels, loads of beams – I'm sure you get the picture. After a very good demonstration at The Falcon Hotel and an extremely satisfying dinner provided by Devey and his beautiful wife Kay, Stephen got to bed a little before one o'clock and fell asleep almost as soon as his head touched the pillow. However he was awoken some time later in the early hours by a voice hissing in his ear: *"Get out of my bed!"*

This was a little girl's voice, but it wasn't all sugar and spice and all things nice; it was mean and malevolent, redolent with spite and anger.

Steve sat bolt upright, startled and alarmed, and put on the bedside light. The Cock Loft was empty and there was no sense of any ghostly or spiritual presence, but Steve knew what he'd heard, and he hadn't liked it much at all!

He gets up, checks the bedroom, goes to the loo, comes back and gets back into bed and is just about to

118

turn out the light and try and settle down when the voice spits at him again *"I told you to get out of my bed!"*

Not one to argue with the paranormal Steve gets out of the bed, gets dressed, and sits in the arm chair until morning, whiling away the hours by trying to catch up on his office work and casting nervous looks over his shoulder.

This might seem like bizarre behaviour coming from one of the country's foremost clairvoyants, and yet it is not without precedent and there is an explanation to be offered.

Stephen: 'I communicate with spirits and I'm very happy with that. Any of the spiritual contacts I get are carried on a vibration of love and if there *is* something nasty out there my guides take care of it for me and make sure I'm protected at all times. When I'm on the platform doing a demonstration my principle guide is always on duty – this is a soldier called Archie May who I think got blown up towards the end of the first world war – that's the impression I get anyway, and he's a tough old sergeant and you do not want to mess with Sgt Archie when he's on guard duty... Having said that, I suppose there are times when something does filter through the screen which isn't exactly a kind or loving energy, and there are just the odd one or two occasions when something comes through which doesn't really feel like a *spiritual* entity at all. Now I don't know what came visiting last night but it certainly wasn't the kind of spirit that I make contact with on a nightly basis when I'm doing my clairvoyance. For want of a better expression I'm inclined to call this kind of entity a ghost rather than a spirit.'

We were having breakfast in Café Rouge on Sheep Street the morning after the disturbed night and I remember looking at Stephen quite shrewdly.

'That,' I said carefully, 'infers that *all* ghosts are potentially unfriendly.'

'No, not really,' he answered. 'I mean I dare say that there can be nice ghosts as well nasty ghosts, it's just that I don't have very much experience with ghosts. Plenty of experience with spirits, but at the end of the day, I think that ghosts are a different thing altogether.'

'So what's the difference between a ghost and a spirit?' I pushed.

'Dunno.' He shrugged his shoulders. 'Maybe a ghost is nothing more than a spirit that's in the wrong place. All I can tell you for sure is that, in my opinion anyway, there's one heck of a difference.'

I was mindful of another occasion when Stephen had a run in with a ghost and although it happened a number of years ago and while this particular haunting was mentioned in an earlier book "The Light In The Darkness" it's worth retelling here because of its relevance to the matter in hand.

Although many thousands of books have been written on the subjects of hauntings and ghosts no one has come up with a precise or definitive explanation of what exactly a ghost is. Theories vary from there being trace energies in the place of the haunting that cause some degree of time displacement when connected with the individual psyche of the person seeing the ghost or apparition, to the more controversial proposition of there being parallel worlds running on a different time scale of which we occasionally receive flash visions.

I suppose your belief in ghosts rather depends upon whether or not you've ever seen one and, to a lesser degree, how susceptible you might be in believing some of the stories that have been told and written. In this context, we are not talking about poltergeist activity (which has been very well researched and documented) and nor are we talking about atmospheric presences or hauntings in a purely psychological sense: what I *am* making reference to is Old Marley, The Headless Horseman and the ubiquitous Grey Lady.

It is easy to dismiss the idea of ghosts until one has actually seen one – at which point in time one's subjective appreciation of the concept usually does a faster U turn than a politician in the The Houses Of Parliament!

Here I have a confession to make. In all of my years working within the realms of the paranormal, I have *never* seen a ghost! To be sure, I have sensed presences, some of them very strong indeed, and especially in the 1980's when I was exploring the avenues of Magick, I was frequently aware of some extremely powerful forces moving around me – but never once have I come across headless horsemen or grey ladies and the like – although I have talked to any number of people who say that *they* have!

Stephen has, on one occasion, encountered a ghost and it is interesting to note his reaction to it. The first thing that becomes glaringly apparent in Stephen's assessment of the phenomenon is the fact that the "ghost" was a totally different entity than a "spirit" and carried with it an entirely different energy.

When you are known as a spiritualist, or indeed as anyone who works within the fields of the paranormal, it's quite amazing how people will phone you up at all hours of the day wanting an instant fix to their problems. You become a lifeline and a crutch, and even though *you* might know that there isn't too much you can do for anyone over the 'phone other than to offer a few words of encouragement and advice, the message seldom sinks in with the person who is making the call. I had a client called Hank who used to phone me quite regularly from the United States, and always around tea-time. The trouble was that it was *his* tea-time, which for me was around two o'clock in the flaming morning! I'm sure that Hank was working for the CIA or some such organisation, (either that or he was a crook) and he'd always telephone just before some sort of operation – *Hi James, I'm just calling because I've got a very tricky job on tonight and I wondered if things were going to work out OK* – and even though he never paid me for it, I'd turn over a tarot card on the bedside table and suggest that (a) he either stayed at home or (b) that he had a good night out.

Stephen had an acquaintance called Paul who would frequently call him up when he was faced with a problem and Stephen, being Stephen, would always do what he could to help. Paul was on thin ice though, when he called Stephen up at one o'clock in the morning, saying *"Steve, you've got to come round straight away because there's a ghost walking round my living room and its scaring me half to death!"*

As you can imagine, Stephen was not amused. He didn't exactly tell Paul to get lost, but he did make it clear that he had no intention of getting out of bed and driving half way across Wakefield in the middle of the night. Whatever the problem was, it could be sorted out in the morning.

Half an hour later the telelphone rang again and this time it was a young lady called Angela on the line. Angela was a mutual friend of both Stephen and Paul, and she was ringing to assure Stephen that Paul wasn't seeing things. That there really *was* a ghost wandering around Paul's living room, she too had seen it and she really did think Stephen should come over, despite the lateness of the hour.

Much against his better judgement and against the protestations of Caroline who clearly thought he was off on a wild goose chase, Stephen climbed into a pair of jeans and a tea shirt, and drove bleary eyed to Paul's house on the other side of town.

Stephen: "When I got there I could tell straight away that something was going on. Both Paul and Angela were agitated to say the least... Anyway, we went inside and had a cup of tea, and Paul and Angela both told me how they'd seen this figure of a little old man materialise in the middle of the room, before walking across the floor and disappearing through the wall. Neither of them had ever experienced anything like this before, and it had really got to them.

So anyway, we all sat together waiting for something to happen... I remember thinking that this was a load of old cobblers, and wondering how long I'd have to wait until I could make a reasonable excuse to get off home to my bed and then, after about ten minutes, there it was... It was just standing there by the fire place, looking at the three of us, sprawled out on the settee. It was this little old man wearing nondescript and indistinct clothing that *might* have been Victorian... He simply stood there, silent but unmoving... No he wasn't the see-through sort of apparition you get in the movies, but neither was he wholly present either.

123

I was out of my seat like a shot, almost as if a five ton mouse had just scurried across the room. I must have said something stupid like 'what the hell is that?' or some such expression, and Angela said that it was their ghost. I think they were rather relieved at that moment – you know, to have their ghost confirmed by a third party, namely me, and I think that they were more than pleased that I could see it as well, because, of course, it meant that they were not having hallucinations or going off their trolleys.

For my part, I didn't like it all. When I'm with a spirit, there's this lovely warm feeling of love suffusing all around me, and I feel incredibly safe and protected. But there was nothing like that here at all. It was a cold alien presence that made my hackles rise...

Anyway, the figure walked in front of the fireplace and then did a right turn at the wall, and then walked over towards the other side of the room, and then when this little old character suddenly reached forward and grabbed at my leg I nearly jumped out of my skin. I can remember yelling 'It's got my leg! It's got my leg!' – then just as quickly as it had materialised, it disappeared. I never saw it again, and for that matter neither did Angela and Paul, but I have to confess that I did *not* like this experience! It wasn't nice at all – and whatever or whoever the little old man was, he wasn't a spirit in the mould of those spirits who come and talk to me when I'm giving a demonstration. And yet, here's the funny thing, I'm quite sure he knew I was there, and when he grabbed my leg, I actually felt his fingers wrap themselves around my knee. It wasn't anything that you'd call evil, just cold and alien and like I said before, not very nice. Even when I think about it now it gives me a fit of the shudders."

So what *are* we to make of all this? Despite Stephen's words I'm certainly not an expert on ghosts, although obviously I have had more than my fair share of paranormal experiences. Perhaps we need to detach ourselves from the subjective and look at some hard facts.

First of all, ghosts and their kin (hauntings and apparitions) have been recorded in the writings of all cultures since the beginning of history. One can take the scientific stance of this being hysteria and over active imagination, but one can just as easily say "there ain't no smoke without fire", and surely not every ghostly sighting can be attributed to an unstable mind. Moreover, some very *objective* minds made a point of studying in depth these phenomena in the $19^{th}$ and $20^{th}$ centuries (everyone from Elifas Levi to our own Colin Wilson) and concluded that although the "ghost" was inexplicable it was nonetheless very real, even if only insofar as it was a real experience for the person encountering such an entity. We cannot see the wind but we know when it is blowing. We cannot explain the power of electricity but we know that it works.

Secondly, Stephen Holbrook had his first contact with a spirit when he was only thirteen years old. Since he was sixteen (almost 27 years ago at the time of writing) he has had meaningful contact and dialogue with literally thousands of spirits who have proved the veracity and validity of their existence by the linking information which has been so very applicable and uniquely relevant to their loved ones left behind. Stephen is clairvoyantly and clairaudiently tuned to the world of spirit – in his own words *"I've got to sit down with a spirit right up in front of my eyes and have dinner with it before I'll believe it's really there"* – and

125

if therefore he says that whatever it was that he encountered in his friend's home was something entirely different to what he understands to be a spirit – a warm, loving intelligent energy functioning with personality and individuality, albeit in a different dimension – then he more than anyone should be able to tell the difference and who can gainsay him? I for one am prepared to take his words at their face value.

This incident seems to be of some specific relevance because it breaks with the long held tradition of belief that says there can be no interaction between Man and Ghost. Indeed, as far as I know (lurid ghost stories apart) it is without precedent and it opens up a whole new strand of investigation.

Stephen not only *saw* the apparition in Paul's house, he also physically *felt* it when it grabbed at his leg. Of course one could put this down to Stephen's shock and to his imagination. Pardon the pun, but there is no doubt that he was 'spooked' by the incident, and in one sense it must be acknowledged that anyone who does what Stephen does for a living must have some heightened degree of imagination. But in another sense this argument falls apart, for it is through having faith in these very same qualities, the reality of his imagination and his powers of creative visualisation, that helps him to communicate with the spirit world in the first place!

What is obvious is that Paul and Angela's Little Old Man reacted to Stephen in a different way in which it reacted (or didn't react) to them, and the fact that it reacted at all makes one wonder whether it was a ghost in the accepted sense of the word. But, if not a ghost and if not a spirit, what else could it have been? …And of equal importance, where might it have come from?

Back to the Café Rouge in Stratford and an attempt to open the envelope.

'What about...' and I chose my words carefully. 'What about *evil* spirits?'

'No, I don't really think there are evil spirits.' Stephen answered. 'Lots of evil people yes, but evil spirits no, and that's because when we pass over to the other side there's this great balancing and sorting out process. If you've done some wrong things down here, then you've got to spend some time putting those things right. If you're an Adolf Hitler or a Fred West, then maybe you've got to spend a *lot* of time making up for the mess you've made and the hurt you've caused, and bearing in mind that time works on the other side a bit differently to the way it does down here, I don't know if we're talking about years, decades or centuries... Maybe in Hitler's case it could take thousands of years to put right. The only thing I feel for certain is that at the end of the day it *does* get sorted out.'

'No evil spirits then?'

'No evil spirits.'

I took a slurp of my cappuccino and kept my thoughts to myself. I love Steve to death, and to give credit where it is due, I have learned a great deal from him over the years. This does not, however, mean that I agree with *everything* he says, and this evil spirit business is a point in question. I'd like to think that Steve is right, but my own experience suggests that on this one he might be a bit wrong.

'What about that business with the garage up in Darlington?' I asked. 'I remember you telling me about that, and I did the research and I got the impression that there was something *very* wrong about that particular incident.'

127

'Ummm, no,' he admitted. 'I didn't like that situation at all…'

Joe and Betty Quarmby run a small car dealership in the middle of the Stockton-Darlington conurbation. In Joe's own words, it's nothing flash – a dozen second hand cars on the forecourt all around the three to six thousand pound mark, with a client bank of regular customers who bring their motors in for servicing and repairs. He stocks a few tyres and exhausts for the most popular models and although he knows he can't compete with the likes of Kwik Fit and ATS, he offers the tyre and exhaust service as a convenience rather than a profit maker. Behind the display forecourt there is an office, and behind the office there is the work shop with a couple of hydraulic lifts and all the other things you would expect to find in a motor car workshop.

Stephen's only link with Joe and Betty is that over the years he has bought a couple of cars from them, and on one occasion Joe fitted an emergency tyre when Steve had a blow out on the A19. Having said that, Steve does have a very high profile in this neck of the woods and Betty had recognized him after having attended a couple of his demonstrations.

Therefore, when some very strange things started happening in their garage, it was Betty who suggested that she and Joe should give Steve a call and see if he could do anything to help.

It began on an ordinary Sunday morning in May. Joe arrived, parked on the forecourt, opened the office, made a cup of coffee and went through into the workshop to raise the steel shutters.

He turned on the lights, walked over to the shutters, pressed the electric button on the electric mechanism that raised them automatically, and as they rolled upwards he took a sip of his coffee and thought what a nice morning it was.

As he turned to walk back into the work shop he stopped in amazement because a tyre was bowling towards him out of the shadows and before he had time to react it caught him right between the legs in that most delicate of male places. Ooomph! He went down in agony and the coffee went up and all over the place! Not a nice way to start a day's trading.

Assuming that the tyre had somehow become dislodged from the rack at the back of the workshop, when he was able to, he wheeled it back into place and went through to the office to do what he could about the coffee stains. Betty, arriving half an hour later was not slow in giving him a telling off.

At four o'clock in the afternoon, with Betty by his side, Joe went about the business of shutting up the garage. He turned off all the lights, and they went out – and then immediately came on again. So Joe turned them off and the lights went out, and as he was turning to depart, on they came again!

'What are you playing at?' Betty wanted to know.

'I'm not playing at anything,' Joe said, a bit nervously. 'I turned the lights off, and they've come on again. On their own. Twice.'

'Oh come here,' Betty said in exasperation, and she herself flicked the lights off. Off they went and on they came again.

'Leave the bloody things and I'll get an electrician to sort it out in the morning. Must be a short circuit somewhere.'

Betty wasn't so sure, but that's how it was left. The following morning an electrician came and did quite a

129

thorough check and found nothing obviously wrong with the wiring. The lights responded to the switch just as they should and Joe and Betty put it down to a glitch in the system that had sorted itself out.

That Monday evening when they left the garage they turned off the lights and the lights stayed turned off. However, when they returned the following morning, all the lights in the workshop were on again.

Betty was now getting a bit spooked and over the following three days (during which time nothing else happened) she nevertheless refused to go into the workshop on her own. Betty and Joe's son Darren worked in the garage as a mechanic and he thought the whole thing was a huge joke, telling his mum that she was watching too many scary movies and going to too many of those "psychic thingies" at the town hall.

Having said that Darren was not amused to walk into the workshop on the Friday morning to find all his tools scattered across the workshop floor. And he was even less amused when in the process of picking them all up a tyre "jumped" off the rack and hit him in the small of the back, sending him sprawling among the screwdrivers and spanners.

The Quarmbys held a council of war that Friday evening. Although Darren, the latest victim of spectral assault was the least convinced, both Betty and Joe felt sure that their garage workshop had acquired a ghost, and from the way it was behaving, it wasn't a very nice ghost either.

'I'm going to give Stephen Holbrook a ring,' Betty announced. 'He'll know what to do!'

'You'll do no such thing,' her husband warned her. 'We hardly know the bloke, and this is something we should be able to sort out ourselves.'

'Oh yes,' Betty shot back. 'Do you mind telling me how?'

'Well I don't know,' said her husband, now on the defensive, 'but for the time being let's just keep our wits about us and our eyes open, and see what happens next.'

As a matter of fact nothing at all happened for a whole ten days and the Quarmbys thought that the ghostly goings on were all over. Then on May 19$^{th}$ the haunting began again with a vengeance and it was Darren who was to be on the receiving end of the first attack.

He had a car up on the ramp and was trying to loosen a rusted exhaust bracket. Realising that he needed a heavier spanner, he ducked out from beneath the car and walked across towards the bench where he kept his tools. A full ten feet from the bench he stopped in horror as he watched a heavy spanner lift itself into the air as though held by an invisible hand, and then he instinctively ducked as the spanner came hurtling directly towards him. It missed his head by a hair's breadth and smashed through the plate glass window between the workshop and the office. When Joe and Betty came running to see what was going on, they found their son kneeling down in a daze, not able to believe what he'd just seen and experienced.

'Are you *sure* that's what happened, Darren?' his father asked, and even before Darren could formulate a coherent answer a tyre came sailing towards them from the tyre rack, flying through the air as though suspended on an invisible wire.

131

It crashed to their feet, to be followed by two others within the following three heart beats, one flying off to the left and bouncing off the workshop wall while the other bounced straight out onto the forecourt and was only brought to a halt when it banged into the side of a Transit van.

'That's it!' Betty wailed. 'I'm calling Stephen Holbrook *right now!*'

This time she got no argument from her husband and her son.

Unfortunately at this time Stephen was on tour in the west country and it would be a full week before he was due back in Yorkshire. He listened to Betty's story and promised that he'd come over as soon as he got home, unless things had sorted themselves out by then. In the intervening week, things did not sort themselves out at all, and if anything they got a damn sight worse.

The workshop lights started playing up again, Darren's tools were constantly being moved and messed with, neatly stacked tyres were found higgledy piggledy all over the place, small objects like spanners and screwdrivers, and on one occasion quite a hefty wing mirror assembly were being thrown all over the place... And then there was this really quite awful smell that began to waft around the premises – Joe described it as rotting flesh, Betty called it a bad toilet smell, and Darren used much stronger language that I cannot possibly repeat on these pages.

In the end, they simply closed the garage and walked away from the place. This was on the Thursday. Stephen Holbrook arrived on the Monday and after he'd been briefed, was not at all keen to get involved, but knowing that he couldn't just leave the Quarmbys in the lurch, felt that the least he had to do was go and have a look at this haunted workshop.

So, while the Quarmbys waited nervously on the garage forecourt, Stephen went and had a look inside.

Stephen: "No, I wasn't happy with this situation and for quite a few reasons really. First of all, I'm not an exorcist or anything like that. I'm just a medium who brings messages of love and support from their loved ones who have passed over, so with this situation I was way out of my depth. It'd have been far better if Joe and Betty had contacted their local spiritualist church because then they'd have probably found someone far better qualified than me to help them, but by then Betty had convinced herself that it *had* to be me, so I knew I had to do what I could.

Anyway, when I first walked into Joe's workshop it didn't seem anything out of the ordinary. The lights were on and there was loads of natural daylight flooding through from the entrance. I'd been told about the flying objects and I thought if anything comes flying at me I'm going to be out of here like a shot – but nothing did, and I just walked around for five minutes or so, asking whatever was there to go away and leave this family in peace...

And this was a totally conscious thing because I wasn't getting anything at all on a clairvoyant level. Anyway, I was just thinking that there wasn't anything else that I could do, when I started getting this very, very sad and heavy feeling... Oh it was absolutely awful, so much sadness and so much despair, and I got a horrible picture of someone who had killed themselves by hanging themselves from some sort of beam or rafter, and they were just dangling there, turning round and round on this old chain that was wrapped around their neck. It was a man, maybe middle aged with thinning hair, and wearing a brown overcoat or overall.

Quite honestly, I wanted to get out there as fast as I could, but I just repeated my little prayer asking this spirit to go away and leave Mr and Mrs Quarmby alone and then when the picture faded from my mind, I went back out into the sunshine.

I asked Joe and Betty if they knew of a man who had committed suicide by hanging himself..."

...And at that point Joe and Betty went into a state of mild shock because they both knew of a man who had committed suicide, and only very recently.

Before Darren had come on board as the garage mechanic, they'd had another chap working for them for quite a short while.

He'd lasted about three months before Joe had had to fire him for dipping his fingers into the till and falsifying some of the customer accounts.

This gentleman, who was probably not sound of mind in the first place, had gone home feeling very embittered, and because being sacked from the job had been the straw that had finally broken the camel's back, he'd hung himself with a rusty chain in his garden shed. It was something that had been in all the papers at the time, but neither Joe nor Betty had made the connection with the angry spirit activity they'd been experiencing in their workshop.

Once Stephen mentioned suicide and described what he'd seen in his psychic vision, everything fell into place for the Quarmbys. After Stephen had driven off back down the A19 Joe and Betty said a few prayers of their own, and since that time all the poltergeist activity has stopped.

I report this story with a disturbing thought in the back of my mind. Had that flying spanner actually hit Darren's head it could quite easily have killed him. So who says ghosts can't hurt you...?

When Stephen read this chapter in its proof form, he wasn't very happy about it at all. 'James, I can't have you frightening people like this!'

In my defence I pointed out that I wasn't trying to frighten anybody and that what I *was* trying to do was detrivialise this whole business of lost spirits, ghosts and hauntings.

Over the decades the film industry has presented us with all manner of things that go bump in the night and in the last twenty years or so I think of Ghostbusters to Moaning Myrtle and Nearly Headless Nick.

As with violence and sex on the cinema screen (plus TV and video) we have become numbed to the truth and the reality of what we are seeing because it is presented to us in such a commercial and formulaic way. The film industry's version of a ghost or haunting is what many of us have come to accept as being the real thing, when in truth, the reality of the event is frequently very different indeed.

If you want a parallel, you'd be surprised at how often William Shakespeare's version of history is taught in our schools not as English literature, but as history! You think I'm joking? Come to York and investigate the *true* story of Richard III... Hunch back and withered arm? I don't think so! And as for murdering those two little princes in the tower – well what a load of old rubbish. It simply didn't happen, but it suited Will Shakespeare, writing under the patronage of the Tudor court, to *say* that it did, and that's the version of history that so frequently gets handed down.

All I'm saying is that in the same way that the historical truth is different to the perceived truth, so the truth about ghosts and hauntings is just as different to the version of the reality that we are fed by Mr Hollywood and his friends.

Please bear this in mind should you see a spanner flying in your direction.

**Chapter Eleven:** *Lowestoft Revisited*

When I first met Stephen he was very well known in the North of England and also down in the far west country. It was my job to promote him in areas where no one had ever heard of him and over the last seven years we have opened up venues in Scotland, Middle England, East Anglia and the South Coast. Whether to go to this town or that town was a very arbitrary decision based on wherever took my fancy and I started off by arranging demonstrations in all of those places that I liked and had happy memories of. Sometimes this worked – but a lot of times it didn't!

For example, both Glasgow and Liverpool *should* have been perfect areas but in both cases it was like rolling a snowball uphill. Given their demographics, Cambridge and Bournemouth *should* have been a piece of cake, but getting a decent audience together in either of those places was like trying to plait fog!

Two "personal choice" locations have worked very well for us however, one being Stratford-Upon-Avon (thank you Stratford and The Falcon Hotel) the other being Lowestoft on the Suffolk coast.

In all fairness, our first visit to Lowestoft was a total disaster. The hotel we had arranged the demonstration at managed to get us double booked with a wedding, and as they were not prepared to cancel their much more lucrative wedding contract we were left with the choice of either canceling the event, which we were loathe to do as we'd already sold more than a hundred tickets, or staging the demonstration in the hotel's tiny dining room.

We went for the dining room option and with people sitting on cushions on the floor and stainless steel work surfaces, we managed to cram our hundred bodies into a space fit for half that number. We turned as many people away on the door and instead of getting any courtesy and sympathy from the hotel whose cock-up it had been in the first place, all we got was hassle from the management and snide remarks from the staff about the "the spook show" and if we'd been any kind of clairvoyants we'd have known that the hotel had a wedding on that night so we should have gone somewhere else in the first place.

This attitude did not help and although looking back on it now one can find some amusing aspects of the disaster, at the time it was both stressful and distressing. To add insult to injury we had to drive back to North Yorkshire after the demonstration in thick pea soup fog that didn't clear until we were passing Peterborough and I think we finally collapsed into our beds around breakfast time.

After that experience we may have been forgiven if we'd elected to give Lowestoft a miss – it's a bloody long journey from anywhere and the hotel at Carlton Coalville had a lot to answer for – but the response we got from the people of Lowestoft was quite phenomenal and the after event feedback convinced us that we had an audience there if only we could find the right venue.

At this point in time The Hotel Victoria came to our rescue and we were more than happy to relocate to this beautiful and very professionally run hotel on Lowestoft's sea front. The bedrooms are large and spacious, the public rooms are clean and tidy with attractive décor, the building is on the beach with incredible sea views, their restaurant is superb and most important of all, the staff is fantastic... Young keen and enthusiastic, nothing ever being too much trouble. The turnover of personnel in the hotel industry is always remarkably high, but the Hotel Victoria hangs on to its people; we always see the same faces at the hotel and have become first name mates with many of their team. Little wonder then that we visit Lowestoft twice a year and always look forward to our visits.

I also regard it as one of my few personal victories because Lowestoft is one of those places from the past that has had an ongoing if subtle influence over the whole of my life, but space permitting, I'll speak of that a bit later. In the meantime, let me tell you the story of Ted and Barbara.

Admittedly there are always more ladies in Stephen's audiences than there are gentlemen, and it has to be admitted that quite a percentage of those gentlemen are there under some kind of sufferance; either to keep their wives or girl friends happy or to provide transport to and from the venue. However we have noticed over the last two and a half years that there is an increasing number of men, and young single men at that, who are not present under sufferance but rather are there of their own volition out of genuine curiosity and a desire to assess the evidence for post mortem survival themselves.

Certainly Ted Lightfoot of Lowestoft was a frequent and enthusiastic member of Steve's audience. He never missed a demonstration, was always one of the first people to phone in his reservation when we opened the booking lines, and he truly believed that Stephen was the bees knees. He had always been convinced that there was life after death and was quite evangelical about Stephen's gifts, saying that as far as he was

139

concerned Stephen provided the absolute proof of his own beliefs.

Ted died suddenly after a short illness on Wednesday 16th November. This came as a great shock to the family because although they knew that Ted was quite poorly they had been told by the doctors that Ted was getting better. Ted's wife Barbara found it incredibly difficult to adjust – after all she and Ted had been married for 51 years!

On the 4th of May 2006 Stephen was demonstrating in Lowestoft. Barbara Lightfoot and her family were in the audience and I'll quote from Barbara's letter, and let her tell you what happened in her own words.

*"On May 4th of this year, myself and two of my daughters, my son-in-law and three friends went to see Stephen Holbrook as we always do whenever he comes to Lowestoft. The second message of the night started with Steve asking who had recently lost their husband to a heart related illness and I put my hand up straight away, because I knew the message was for me. Ted had died of volvulus which is some kind of chronic heart disease, and when Steve told me that Ted had passed over at one o'clock in the morning I knew there couldn't be any doubt that this was Ted coming through for me because, of course, that's exactly the time Ted died!*

*Steve said that Ted hadn't wanted to die the way in which he did and that he loved me very much indeed. He also said that Ted wanted to thank me for the fifty one years we'd been together and also thank me for holding his hand the night that he died. I held Ted's hand for nearly four hours before he passed over and Steve said that Ted would be there holding my hand when it was my turn to go – although that wouldn't be for years yet.*

140

*Steve said that Ted had a yappy little dog with him that had always barked a lot especially when Ted was trying to watch the TV and he went on to mention how Ted always liked to be in charge of the television, and that made us all laugh because it was so true. Steve then wanted to know who John was and I told him that I had a son-in-law called John and also a grandson called John. Steve spoke of my grandson's 21$^{st}$ birthday party which had taken place the previous October – Ted always loved parties and this was the last one that he was at. Steve also said that the month of July was very significant because of a very important anniversary and in July of 2004 Ted and I had our golden wedding anniversary and had renewed our marriage vows in front of all our family and friends ..."*

There was a wealth of other information concerning the welfare of children, erratic tyre pressures, names, dates, marques of cars and confirmation of the fact that Ted was extremely proud of the way in which his family was coping and "getting on with it." At the end of the demonstration Barbara and her daughter Janice came over to say thank you and we all marveled at the way in which Ted Lightfoot had been determined not to miss one of Stephen's demonstrations. He had attended many such events in the flesh, and now he'd attended one in spirit. All of us involved think this is a pretty fantastic achievement, so thank you Barbara for letting us use this evidence, and well done Ted for making it happen.

After the demonstration we went out for a meal at our favourite Italian restaurant up at the north end of the town. Lorenzo's is small, intimate, very personal, and because it was late we more or less had the place to ourselves. Ted and Barbara Lightfoot cropped up in our conversation more than once and we paid homage to their achievement. They might not have been rich or famous, they'd never made the national headlines, neither of them had written best selling novels, but what they *had* done was make a good marriage work for 51 years and had built a firm and unshakable foundation stone for their children, grandchildren and great grandchildren. If the rest of us could do half as much as that, this world would be a better place and that's for sure.

One subject leads to another and I found myself reminding Stephen of a conversation I'd had with a lovely Lowestoft lady called Sylvia Collette on one of our earlier visits to the town.

Mrs Collette was a sprightly eighty year old with merry eyes and an agility that belied her age. She walked with a stick but most of the time didn't seem to need it, using it more as a theatrical prop than a walking aid. She had a penchant for Gordons gin and smoked unfiltered Piccadilly cigarettes through a long Dunhill cigarette holder. A characterful lady of wit and intelligence and when I found myself talking to her prior to one of Stephen's demonstrations I found myself enjoying her company enormously. She was a knowledgeable woman with a secure grounding in the basic principles of spiritualism but she had a problem – a question really – that was playing on her mind and causing some genuine psychological distress.

Sylvia had recently been diagnosed with lung cancer and had been told that if she gave up the cigarettes and the gin she might have three or four more years to play around with, but if she *didn't* quit the booze and fags she might have as little as twelve or eighteen months.

I presumed this was the cause of her distress and wondered if she was going to be strong and go over to drinking shandy and chewing gum. This made her laugh out loud causing the other customers in the Hotel Victoria bar to cast curious glances in our direction as we sat at the counter on high stools drinking one of the hotel's lethal cocktails.

'Good Lord, Mr Christie, I have *no* intention of giving up my cigarettes or my gin. I'm eighty years old and there are not that many pleasures left in life when you get to my age. Maybe if I felt really ill or sick I might change my mind, but despite what the doctors have told me I feel reasonably well thank you, and I'll die when I'm good and ready to die not when some holier than thou whipper snapper of a medic in a white coat tells me I'm going to die!'

I joined in with her laughter, but wondered what it was she wanted to talk to me about.

'Ummm,' she mused, 'I rather wanted to ask Mr Holbrook a question and get his opinion on something. I know he's busy and I don't want to take up any of his time, so you can ask on my behalf, if you like, and have a word with me later.'

'Sure,' I said. 'Fire away with the question.'

'I've been married three times,' she informed me, 'and I've had the greatest good fortune to have been married to the three most marvellous husbands any woman could hope to find. I had nine wonderful years with my first husband Tom, sixteen years with my second husband Lionel, and twenty three years with my late husband Dickie. All of them had their problems because, let's face it, there's no such thing as the *perfect* man, is there?' She looked at me disarmingly, daring me to disagree with her. ' – but nevertheless I loved all

143

three of them to distraction, and now I'm faced with a bit of a dilemma, aren't I?'

'Er, what's that?' I asked dimly while she fitted another Piccadilly into the black and silver holder.

'Well, if those idiots of doctors are right and I only have a year or so left to me, obviously my time down here on this mortal coil is running out and I shall soon be following my lovely gentlemen into the realms of the Great Beyond. I'm assuming all three of them will be there to meet me when I arrive, and I have to tell you I shall be very cross if they're not, but the question is, who will I be married to in Heaven? Tom, Lionel or Dickie?'

On one level this seemed to be a very superficial question but when I thought about it from her point of view I realized that it wasn't superficial at all. Given her background and upbringing, traditional conservative English Christian, there were none of the nuances and belief structures that one might find in other cultures and faiths that might make the question irrelevant; there were no shades of grey and Sylvia wanted a Christian English answer.

'I'll talk to Stephen after the demonstration,' I promised, 'and if you give me your address and phone number, I'll get back to you as soon as I can and let you know what he says...'

And I did ask Stephen and he didn't give me an answer, not then anyway, and Sylvia Collette pricked my conscience to such an extent that this "marriage in heaven" issue has constantly been a thorn in Steve's side because I've constantly reminded him about it... Just as I was doing yet again in the safe garlicky haven of Lorenzo's.

Stephen sighed in mock exasperation. 'You're just not going to let this one go, are you James?'

'No,' I grinned. 'I'm not. It's an issue. An important question that a lot of people out there are asking. And they're waiting for an answer.'

'What makes you think I've got the right answer?'

'Maybe it isn't the right answer, but I'll bet you the price of this dinner that there's a load of folk out there who want to know what you think on the subject anyway.'

'You buy the dinner if I answer the question?'

'Yep!'

'All right, let me think for a minute...'

We'd finished eating and were doing the coffee brandy smoky thing. Steve lit a Marlboro and sipped alternately at the last dregs from his wine glass and then the first dribbles of Lorenzo's fine old cognac.

'It's this marriage thing that's the problem, isn't it?' he said abruptly. 'I mean "marriage" is just a word on a bit of paper and at the end of the day it's the connection made between two people that's the really important thing. I mean I'm not married to Caroline any more but for heaven's sake I still love her... I'm not married to my mother but I love *her*... I'm not married to you and Jo but I love both of you... You're not married to your son Nick, but I know that you love him... Jesus wasn't married to Mary Magdalen* and his twelve disciples, but the bible tells us he still loved all of them...

'Sure, I know it's different when we *fall in love* with someone and they become our partners and unfortunately, because life is what life is like, some of those partners are taken from us far too soon into the spirit world – or at least, that's how it seems to us lot left down here, and of course it's only right that we shed

145

our tears and do our grieving. But at the end of the day, we're still alive and we've got a responsibility both to ourselves and the world of spirit, to move on in whatever way possible and make the best of things.'

He puffed furiously at the cigarette. I was tempted to open my mouth, but he was on a roll so I kept it shut.

'Some people lose a partner and it hurts so much that the only way they can cope with it is to battle on year to year keeping the memory of their departed loved one alive in the mind and in their memory, and although I can understand this, I'm not so sure it's a great idea. Other people do their grieving and do what they can to heal the wounds and then, usually quite unexpectedly they find themselves falling in love with someone else... This is always a bit of a problem because they get caught in the guilt trap and feel as though they're being unfaithful to the memory of their late partner. I can understand this as well, but if you ask me, most of those partners who have passed into spirit would actively want their loved ones left behind to find some happiness and solace somewhere...

'I mean, James, after all, we human beings aren't meant to be solitary creatures are we? Well, I don't think we are anyway. I don't see why someone who has say, lost their husband, can't marry a second husband, without it being assumed that her feelings for her first husband have changed in any way. Being bereaved wasn't a situation of her own choosing, so why should she feel bad about carrying on with life as best she can? The love she might have for husband number two will be a different love than she had for husband number one because obviously we're talking about two different men here – two different partners, two different loves – and in any case I think it's quite possible to love more

146

than one person at the same time and we'll find qualities in one partner that the other didn't have, and vice versa.

'So when it comes to who we are married to in heaven I think we should disregard marriage certificates and get rid of the earthplane way of thinking. You know, I'm yours and you're mine, and at the same time get rid of the jealousies and insecurities and possessiveness, and be free to love everyone we love and have *ever* loved in a whole load of different and unique ways.

'It's the spiritual connection of love that counts so when your lady Sylvia gets to the other side I would imagine that all three of her husbands will be there to meet her with open arms and they'll have one hell of a reunion…'

Stephen saw the look in my eyes and held up a hand. 'Yes, I know what you're going to ask, but hang on a minute because now you've got me started I haven't quite finished yet. You want to know which one of the three blokes does she end up with and I think the answer is any one she fancies most, maybe all three of them or maybe none of them, and that isn't me copping out because the honest truth is that I don't think it matters. What *does* matter is that the love bond will be so strong that it transcends our earthly understanding and one thing is for sure, and that is that if there *have* been any niggles and jealousies between this lady's three partners, they'll be sorted out long before she arrives on the other side of the pearly gates!'

'The other question then,' I shot in quickly, 'that everyone wants an answer to, is what about sex in heaven? Do they have sex in heaven?'

'I blood well hope so,' he grinned. 'Otherwise I'm not going!'

**Chapter Twelve:**    *The Corton Experiment*

It was around this time that Stephen was getting some very irritating emails from a free lance journalist (previously mentioned in chapter four) who felt that Stephen was a fraud and challenged him to take part in some psychic "tests" of his own divising. Stephen declined, not because of being afraid of a challenge, but because this self styled journalist was extremely rude and aggressive and went about things completely the wrong way. We were talking about this a couple of weeks prior to our visit to Lowestoft and I asked Stephen if he might be interested in taking part not in a "test" but a psychic experiment that I was keen to set up. He readily agreed to this and thus on 4th May 2006, a couple of hours before the demonstration at The Hotel Victoria, I piled Steve and Rob into the back of my car and drove them a couple of miles out of town to the small cliff top village of Corton.

As a village Corton is a most pleasant little place – it has some nice cottagey houses, a knapped flint church with a Burn Jones window, a couple of good pubs, a newsagency-cum-giftshop, a fish and chippie – and a holiday camp.

The holiday camp that stands there now is a far cry from the one that stood there in 1962 – for one thing it's called a holiday club, for another it's got en-suite in all the beautiful stone built apartments, and for a third it has an excellent entertainments complex with a first rate theatre bar fitted with all the technical wizardry of the 21st century.

In 1962 the chalets were made of plywood, the loos were in concrete blocks at the end of the chalet lines, and the entertainment played out in a long jerry-built ballroom with a leaky corrugated iron roof.

And yet my memories of that tatty old dump from the early 60's are the most precious jewels of my mind. I lived and worked there for two and a half years and consider myself most privileged to have known that world before it disappeared beneath the onrushing bow wave of holiday clubs and chalet hotels that by the late 1960's had wiped the traditional old holiday camps off the face of the earth.

Like a bald haired old man buying himself a flashy sports car for his sixtieth birthday in a vain attempt to recapture his youth, I took Steve to Lowestoft to recapture something of my own youth – or at least, to make some connection with a vital time in my formative history.

I could write thousands of words about that time and place but you haven't bought this book to hear me nostalgically reminiscing about the good old days of my misspent adolescence. Suffice to say, those jewel memories are as hard and clear as Cartier diamonds and quite unashamedly I have used those memories as part of the framework for Stephen's first test.

I pulled the car to a halt outside The Hut Hotel. A lifetime ago it had been a proper hotel; these days it was just a nice old ramshackle pub redolent with charm but contaminated by the ubiquitous colour telly in the corner permanently tuned to some cable sports channel showing never ending sequences of football.

For God's sake, why can't we have the occasional bit of croquet or archery on our TV screens?

'Er, it's a bit early to start drinking, isn't it?' Stephen asked.

'We're not going for a drink, we're going for a walk for half an hour, and all you've got to do is see if you pick anything up on a psychic level... You can discuss any thoughts you get with Rob and I'm sure Rob won't mind taking notes.'

'Ummm,' Stephen was less happy than he'd been a minute earlier. 'What happens if I don't get anything? I probably won't, you know. I never do when I'm put under pressure.'

'For one thing you're not going to be under any pressure – we're just going for a nice little stroll through the woods – and if you don't get anything, then either I don't write the chapter, or I do write the chapter and say that on this occasion Mr Holbrook *didn't* get anything.'

'So, we're going through the woods, are we?'

'Yes.'

'Which woods?'

'These woods over here.'

To get to Corton from Lowestoft you drive out of the town along the B1385. This takes you along the top of the cliffs and eventually brings you into half a mile of heavy woodland before you emerge at the other end of a tunnel of trees into the open space of Corton village. The Hut Hotel is on your right and the playing field is on your left. The landward forest is significantly more overgrown than the sea cliff side, mainly because over the last forty years a lot of the cliffs have eroded and collapsed and a caravan site that once contained a handful of 'vans in the early 60's has quadrupled in size and has now become home base for two dozen static monsters. Even so, the area of woodland between the road and the cliff still covers a couple of hectares and there are a number of well worn pathways that wind their way beneath the bowers of trees and the profusion of rhododendron bushes. It is an old wood and although scarred and compromised by the encroachment of the modern world, it still maintains a degree of mystery and dignity.

I led Steve and Rob along the pathway past the caravans, through the first frieze of rhododendrons then into the cathedrals of trees.

'What am I supposed to be tuning into?' Stephen asked.

'Anything that crosses your mind,' I answered.

'Well, I know why you brought me here,' he said flatly. 'It's a warm afternoon but I'm all cold inside and my left arm is tingling, so there's certainly some kind of psychic energy hopping around... but I don't dislike the feeling. It's just sort of making me feel excited in an odd kind of way...'

'It's almost as though the forest is watching us and waiting for something to happen.' Rob added astutely.

'Yes, that's *exactly* the way it feels,' Stephen confirmed.

For my part I said nothing and we carried on walking for another fifty yards until I brought us to a halt beneath a huge old oak. It was ancient, barren and leafless but it's presence dominated the forest glade we had arrived at. Its higher branches thrust upwards through the springtime foliage of its neighbours, while its lower branches hung low to the ground, drooping with age. One such branch was no more than three or four feet above our heads.

'I'd like you to touch the tree,' I told Stephen. 'Just for a couple of minutes – and see what impressions you get... okay?'

151

'Okay James, but I'm not one of the tree hugging types, you know.'

'He doesn't want you to hug it,' Rob put in. 'Just to touch the flaming thing.'

'Ummm...' Stephen rested the palm of his hand against the gnarled old bowl, said nothing for half a minute, then pulled his hand away. 'Sorry James, I don't know what I'm supposed to be getting but I'm not getting anything at all, other than the fact that I don't think I like this tree very much, although I don't know why I don't like it. But I'm not getting any visions or impressions or anything like that...'

'That's fine,' I said neutrally. 'Let's move on then.'

We carried on for another hundred yards or so, at which point Rob paused in his stride. 'That's odd,' he remarked.

'What's odd?' Stephen asked.

'Listen to the birds,' Rob suggested.

'All right... I'm listening to the birds and I can hear them chirping away, er, so what?'

Rob cast me a canny glance. 'Well, they're all singing and chirping on the other side of the road, but over on *this* side of the road... well, the only thing that's making any kind of noise is us.'

'Maybe that's why the birds are quiet. We're scaring them off.'

'Maybe.' Rob cast me another glance and said no more. His look, however, told me that he wasn't convinced by Stephen's reasoning. *And good for you mate,* I thought as we pressed further into the trees, now turning away from the road, and moving into a wilder part of the woods, not so frequently visited by the casual tourist or morning walker.

152

This part of the small forest was darker and more intense. The tall oaks and chestnuts gave way to tighter clumps of thorn and wild apple whose branches created an interwoven tapestry above our heads, filtering the light and making huge dappled patches on the undergrowth beneath our feet. Another hundred yards brought us to a long line of squat concrete blocks each about four feet square. There were eight or nine of them, evenly spaced, and obviously man made. They ran across the centre of a small clearing that dipped in the middle. It created the impression of a small and very strange amphitheatre...

'What's this?' Steve wanted to know.

'What's left of some military defences, dating back to the first world war.'

'Doesn't feel very military,' he offered. 'But then, I suppose the first world war was a long time ago.'

'What *does* it feel like?' I asked.

He cocked his head to one side. 'Well, I know it sounds daft, but it's all a bit witchy and wizardy, isn't it? You can just imagine loads of people bouncing around in the nude or wearing those long druidy robes – you know, dancing around bonfires at midnight and having a bonk in the bushes.' He giggled mischievously, and rested a hand on top of one of the fat concrete blocks. 'And let's face it, these bits of concrete would make marvelous sacrificial altars!'

Rob and I joined in the chuckle, but again Rob caught my eye, raising a quizzical questioning eyebrow. I smiled quietly and imperceptibly shook my head... and led them on along a narrow path that wound its way through some thickening undergrowth towards the edge of the cliff.

'This is like something out of Lord of The Rings,' Stephen commented from behind me. 'I tell you what, I *like* this bit of pathway, it's got lots of laughter and fun attached to it…' I threw a quick look over my shoulder and saw that his face was lit up with a lovely beam. 'It's amazing how an atmosphere can change in just a few yards! I mean back there with the stones it was all a bit eerie and spooky, but this is totally different…'

We carried on along the cliff top for a couple of minutes and I brought them to a halt by an old broken railing right at the very edge of the precipice. The remains of an old pathway cut into the very earth of the cliff, led down to the beach a couple of hundred feet below. Much of it was gone and blown away, but you could still see the tracery of where it had been. From this vantage point the view was magnificent! Miles of golden sand in either direction, a deep blue sea and a pale blue sky!

'Get anything from this place?' I asked innocently.

Stephen, who by now had relaxed into my little game, nodded in the affirmative. 'Uniforms,' he said promptly. And then, with a bit more caution – '…But they're not the usual kind of uniforms… I mean, they're not military uniforms or nurses uniforms or anything like that, but definitely uniforms of some description.'

'Any sense of colour?' I asked, breaking my own rules and leading the witness.

'No, not really…'

'Right then chaps, time to move on…'

I led them away from the cliff but we'd only got a couple of dozen yards when Stephen slowed to a halt. 'I'm getting something here,' he said directly, and we all came to a halt. I don't know whether Steve or Rob were aware of it, but I noticed that Stephen's left arm had suddenly become a bit stiffer than it had been a few moments before.

'Sword fights and pirates!' Stephen exclaimed. 'Like you see on a movie set, like a scene from The Pirates of The Caribbean... And I'm getting a really funny smell...' He wrinkled his nose. 'A bit like bad eggs! Rob, what's the name of the smell you get from bad eggs?'

'Sulphur,' Rob said promptly.

'Yes, sulphur, and there's other stuff as well... Something a bit like tar...'

Stephen walked around in a small circle, kicking at the earth with the toe of his shoe. 'Something to do with barrels,' he said shortly. '...And... Urgh, that's not very nice! Something about a severed head and something being buried that everyone is looking for but nobody can find.'

He looked at me accusingly. 'I'm not enjoying this any more. Let's go back to that pub and have a drink, shall we.'

This wasn't a suggestion, it was an instruction. 'Fine,' I acquiesced. 'We're pretty well finished here anyway – and for the record, you've done very well.'

'Tell me later.'


Later turned out to be much later, back in Lorenzo's Italian restaurant. I don't know that Stephen was desperate for a dénouement, but Rob was highly intrigued to know what had gone on in the woods that afternoon. So, while I smoked several of Rob's cigarettes, I told them both what it had all been about.

'Back in 1962 and 1963 I worked at the holiday camp just up the road from where we went for our walk through the woods,' I began.

'Holiday camp? Where was I looking? I didn't see a holiday camp anywhere?' Stephen stirred in interest.

'I didn't draw your attention to it,' I admitted, 'because if I had, then knowing that you know a bit about my history you might have put two and two together, and would have pulled me into any of the links you were getting. The fact of the matter is that I actually once had a caravan in those woods we went walking through this afternoon but it fell over the edge of the cliff and into the sea years ago...

'Anyway, I just wanted to see what you might pick up and as I say you did very well, although there were a few bits that surprised me.

'First of all, do you remember that first tree I took you to, the old knackered oak that I asked you to touch? Well, I have to admit that I thought you *might* have got something from that because a bloke I knew called Tony, a really nice chap who was a bloody good piano player, committed suicide and hung himself from that big branch that was right above your head. I know that it was more than forty years ago, but I thought you might have got something...

'What you *did* get right was just about everything else. That dark little area by the stones that you associated with witches and wizardy? Yeah well, the local wiccan covens used that as their gathering place from about 1956 through till well into the early 1970's and from what I can gather, it was all the naked frolicking and bollocking that made the police crack down and the covens moved to somewhere further south and a bit more isolated near Saxmundham.

'The pathway you liked so much was where we used to lead the holiday camp ramble through every Sunday morning, and every second Friday we used to go out on a midnight ghost hunt. You've got to imagine two hundred happy campers foraging through the undergrowth, most of 'em being half or three quarters plastered, and if I tell you that it was hilarious it would be the understatement of the evening!

'That spot on top of the cliff where you picked up uniforms... Well that was where a lot of the entertainers would get together for private parties and barbecues and it was the one place where you knew you could bring a girlfriend or a boyfriend without fear of being caught by inquisitive parents or an angry camp manager. We all wore uniforms – green blazers and white trousers or skirts. Not military, just as you said, but definitely uniforms.'

I paused. 'Now we come to the heavy bit. The bit you didn't like all that much. You remember talking about sword fights and pirates? And you were getting images of barrels and a decapitated head, and something being buried...? Well, back in the 17$^{th}$ and early 18$^{th}$ century, most of the smuggling activity in this country was taking place down in Kent and Essex, but when the customs men started getting very good at stopping the contraband coming in, a lot of the smuggling moved up here to East Anglia and in the early 19$^{th}$ century this was a hot spot for stuff coming in from France, although mainly from Holland, I believe.

'One Dutch gentlemen called Henryk Van Troost was regarded as being the most prolific contraband merchant and he lead the customs and excise a merry dance for years – but anyway, to cut a long story short, the Brits set a trap for him and somewhere back around the early eighteen hundreds he walked right into it. There was a big fight on top of those cliffs where we were today between the customs guys and half a

157

regiment of soldiers and two big barges full of smugglers and barrels of rum. From what I read up on the subject it was a very bloody affair and somewhere in the affray old Henryk had his head chopped off. The customs laddies hauled his body off to be hung on public display – but they never did find his head, and ever since there's been the local legend of Headless Henryk haunting the Corton woods searching for his lost head which a few of his surviving mates were said to have buried for want of a body.

'There were lots of sightings around the turn of the century and again in the late forties and early fifties, and witnesses have spoken of seeing a headless fat bodied man with breeches and leather jerkin with a barrel under each arm... In connection with the smells of sulphur and tar, this was the medicine that was used to treat sword cuts and gunshot wounds back in those days... So you see, although you didn't like the experience much, you did pick up on something that was very specific to the ground you were standing on.'

'Ummm,' Stephen digested what I'd told him without much more response than the 'Ummm' but Rob looked a bit thoughtful.

'There's a bit of a problem though, isn't there?' he said.

'Yes there is,' I admitted readily enough.

'What's the problem?' Stephen wanted to know. 'I've lost you both.'

'People are going to say that it's all a bit circumstantial, and that anything you picked up you could have picked up through James by reading his mind.'

Rob looked at me for comfirmation and I nodded in agreement with his analysis.

'But I'm not a mind reader!' Stephen protested.

'We know you're not, but Rob's dead right. That's exactly what the the skeptics and cynics are going to come up with, but…' I waved at Mr Lorenzo indicating that we'd like to pay our bill. '…but *I'm* prepared to call the experiment a partial success in one respect and a total success in another. It's a partial success because most of what you said was relevant to the circumstances and the history of where you were and I know you well enough by now to know that you couldn't have had any foreknowledge of Corton's history either in the 19<sup>th</sup> century or in the 1950's or the 1960's…'

'And in which way was it a *total* success?'

'It was a total success mate, in the sense that you agreed to take part the experiment in the first place and as far as I know it's the very first time you've agreed to put your head on the block and have a go at anything like this!'

'Well done James!' Rob grinned.

'Not really Rob, more a case of well done Steve.'

**PAGES 1 – 12 OF PHOTOGRAPHS**

Rob, Caroline & Steve.  Three great friends!

Were these two men brothers in a previous life?

Robbie, Ellie and Bradley. Robbie is going to be a medium, Ellie is going to be an actress and Brad is going to be a model.

Margaret, Steve's Mum, who takes many of the bookings for the various venues, and is always on hand with tea and sympathy.

Steve with Jill & Roger from Prior Engagements

Karen Sommersby & Chris Nichols

Steve and Rob with Jan Amini of Norwich who arrived late one night, saw Rob, thought he was Steve and relaxed because she thought she still had some time to spare. In reality Steve had started five minutes earlier and Jan wondered who the warm up act was! Jan is a beautiful lady and she wins our Groupie of The Year contest for 2006! Love you, babe!

3

Barbara & Ted Lightfoot from Lowestoft celebrating their Golden Jubilee, a year before Ted passed away and eighteen months before Ted attended Steve's demonstration in spirit form!

Front page of NME circa 1963

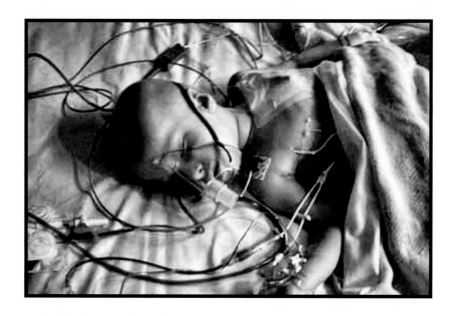

Jamie Rendall aka Jaime Beebo, left in Superhero mode, and above, fighting for his life in intensive care. In three different demonstrations Steve brought through a wealth of evidence for three different members of Jaime's family to prove post mortem survival of the spirit. Below, Jamie with his Mum, Kelly.

Is this, the guy with the moustache, Archie May? It's certainly Florence Aptree's Archie May , but is it Steve's spirit guide? Steve's not 100% sure but all the evidence points to this being the right candidate.

Below is an extract from the 1901 national census showing the entry for Archie May and registering his profession as an assistant hairdresser.

Geneologists Jan Seddon from York and Allan Potts from Corwen, both of whom did stirling work in our quest for Archie May

Steve on board MSC Opera with Clan Elliott—left to right, Emma, Wendy, Sue & Christopher

8

MSC Opera… 57,000 tonnes of opulence and luxury !

The Author with Opera's Captain Guiseppi Gallano (who Stephen told to sit down and take part or else) and, of course, the elusive but ever present Mrs Christie without whom Survival would never have been written - although you'll be hard pressed to find her in these pages!

On the left Steve Holbrook with Emma and on the right, Stephen Smallwood with his Mum, Angela.

Steve demonstrating in The Caruso Cabaret Lounge. The audiences may have been small but Steve's clairvoyance was spot on once he'd overcome his initial stage fright.

10

# London College of Dance

**Principal: Patricia Whittock**

College of
the I.S.T.D.

Under the auspices of
the University of Buckingham
the College is offering
a new B.A. (Hons) Degree in Dance
From September 1989

This degree for dancers
will have Classical Ballet
as the core discipline.
Integrated studies will include:
Music
Dance History
Drama
Choreography
Modern Dance
Repertoire

Optional Specialisms:
Music for Dance
Aesthetics of Dance
Dance in Education
and in the Community
French
Italian

This is Lisa—the beautiful and talented daughter of Jill and Roger Prior who died tragically in 1991 through carbon monoxide poisoning. It took fifteen years for Jill and Roger to get a message from Lisa, but when she did finally come through she certainly made a dramatic entrance!

11

This is Robbie Holbrook—Stephen's eldest son—to whom this book is dedicated. If ever there was a case of the son following in the footsteps of the father, this is a prime and most wonderful example. At the time of publication Robbie is just 12 years old and he's already developing his own gifts and bringing through verifiable evidence from the world of spirit.

12

## Chapter Thirteen: *Karen and Chris*

In this report I have changed the names of a couple of people. This is something I do *not* like doing in any circumstances because if anyone ever wants to check on any of the reports recorded in the Stephen Holbook trilogy, then they should be free to do so without hindrance. For heaven's sake, both Stephen and I encourage independent investigation of anything I write and anything he does. Having said that, it's something I've sometimes had to do before and I dare say it's something I'll have to do again in the future if the circumstances warrant it.

*But I don't like doing it!*

In the case of Karen Sommersby and Christopher Nichols I am faced with a dilemma. Here I have hard evidence of post mortem survival which can be corroborated and cross referenced by four independent sources – but to tell this tale I have to change a couple of names and indeed the location of the events as they took place to protect the privacy of one family involved and to comply with an ongoing legal situation which is still sub justice in the eyes of the law, both in this country and in France.

What do I do? Walk away from it and leave the story untold, or tell it and ask you, the reader, to take my words on trust?

In the end, because I think this report is so important and because I believe that there might be a time in the future when I can name the right names and put the events in their correct location, I have chosen this latter option.

And so I'm going to start this story somewhere in the middle with Stephen Holbrook having a sly cigarette

161

out by the stage door of The Assembly House in Norwich and the arrival of four unusual people in a very expensive Rolls Royce motor car.

It was raining and Stephen had a pounding headache. He had twenty minutes spare before he was due to start the demonstration, and he had nothing to do. His front of house team were on the ball and he felt like a spare part. Also, he was strangely nervous and on edge and he wasn't quite sure why. There were some niggling problems at home that he was concerned about, but those in themselves did not explain his mood of agitation. By his own admission, he was tired and in need of a break – but that was quite normal half way through a grueling thirty night tour and therefore could not really be taken into the equation.

He took a long puff on his cigarette, and knowing that he was smoking too much, vowed that he would start cutting down again just as soon as he'd finished this current packet. He was about to go back into The Assembly House when his attention was drawn to a large car pulling onto the car park. Not brilliant at motor car recognition, he nevertheless knew a Rolls Royce when he saw one and he paused in admiration as the elegant beast cruised past where he was standing and came to a gentle halt a score of yards away outside the main entrance to the venue.

He watched as four people climbed out of the vehicle and couldn't help thinking what an odd couple of couples they made. Two people, the driver and his front seat passenger, were dressed in typical English conservative attire, the gentleman in a tweed jacket and cavalry twill trousers, the lady in a formal black skirt with a short woolen stole. The other couple who

162

climbed out of the back, were significantly more casually dressed, the man in a black leather bomber jacket and jeans, his female companion wearing a gypsy style skirt with a brightly embroidered blouse and black leather waist-coat. They were all of an age – vaguely mid to late forties – but from Stephen's viewpoint they looked like four different souls that came from two different worlds.

As they entered The Assembly House Steve had a subtle impression of somebody else – someone in spirit – walking in with them, and he felt certain that one of this strange quartet was destined to have a message before the end of the evening. As it happened, all four of them were to get a message, but no one knew that at the time.

Stephen smoked another cigarette – honestly, he really would stop in the morning – then he went to the loo, and then Rob Green made an appearance to tell him that all the audience was in and seated, that the mike was live and that he could start any time he liked.

Still burdened by a feeling of agitation and aware of a different "thrum" to the psychic atmosphere and the ambience of the evening, he walked out onto the stage and went into his usual introductory speech of hello, good evening, and welcome, and this is how it all works...

This speech bored him and he knew that it bored those members of his audience who were regular attendees at his demonstrations, but this speech was essential insofar as it gave the audience time to settle down and more importantly it gave him chance to tune in to the vibration of the room.

Gazing into the sea of faces and feeling the all too familiar thrill of fear at the centre of his solar plexus, his eyes were drawn to the four people from the Rolls Royce. They were sitting over to the left, about three quarters of the way back towards the rear of the room, and although he would be the first to admit that he didn't see auras or coloured lights, there was, nevertheless, a distinct rippling of disturbed air above these peoples' heads and even at this distance he picked up tremendous waves of sorrow and despair. In his psychic mind he received the image of a fair haired young girl who had gone to the spirit world very prematurely who wanted to speak with her mother.

His introduction that evening was uncommonly short and within only three or four minutes he was striving to make his first link. He looked in the direction of the Rolls Royce quartet and said: 'I want to talk to someone who has lost a daughter in the past twelve months or so. And this young lady who I think had very blond hair, would have died very suddenly and probably...' Steve felt a sharp pain in the back of his head... 'Er, probably quite violently. Something to do with a blow to her head...'

Stephen saw two hands go up. Two people sat next to each other. The conservative couple from the Rolls. He wasn't really all that surprised.

*"Those two people are my mother and father,"* A soft but definitely feminine voice spoke into his left ear and his nostrils were assuaged with the delicate scent of a light floral perfume. *"My Dad is Gerald and my Mum is Joyce – and I'm Karen, by the way."*

Stephen has been bringing messages through for more than twenty years. Some of the voices he hears can be garbled and indistinct, others can be quite clear, if sometimes a little distant. In this case, Karen's voice was as clear as a bell, and it was as though she was

164

standing on the stage next to him not more than a foot away, and talking directly at him.

He focused on the two hands at the back of the room. He could have launched in feet first, but instead chose to feel his way carefully. 'Just give me your voices, or at least one of your voices,' he requested. 'Let me just make sure I've got it right. You've lost a daughter in the last twelve months? Just a yes or no. Please don't tell me anything else.'

It was the gentleman's clipped old school voice that echoed back at the stage. 'Yes!'

'And your daughter had fair hair and passed over suddenly?'

'Yes.'

'Who's Gerald?'

'I'm Gerald.'

'Who's Joyce?'

'That's my wife…'

'It's me! It's me!' This was the lady in the black skirt and stole calling from her husband's side. Her voice was quite shrill and she was quivering with anticipation.

*"Sorry,"* Karen said apologetically. *"My Mum always gets wound up when she's excited about something."*

'I've got your daughter with me,' Stephen said simply. 'She's telling me her name is Karen.'

'Oh my God…' This from the excited mother.

'Yes!' – A simple affirmative from the father.

*"Please tell them that what happened wasn't my fault and that I wasn't doing anything wrong and that it was all over before I knew it and that I really didn't feel anything at all…"*

Stephen repeated this message word for word.

*"Their imaginations will have been working overtime,"* Karen confided. *"And they'll have been a bit confused by the medical examiner's report, so just tell Mum and Dad that what they did to me in the back of that smelly old van didn't matter because I'd already left my body... Now this is the most important part of what I want to tell them so do please get it right..."*

Stephen was feeling physically sick at this point for along with Karen's words there were disjointed flash visions of the most depraved kind of violence and bestiality. He also remembers there was a bloody metallic taste in his mouth.

'Was there,' he coughed to clear his throat... 'Was there some kind of controversy or confusion in connection with a medical examiner's report?'

'There most certainly was!' Karen's father exclaimed with indignation. The gentleman now stood up, resting either a restraining or reassuring hand upon his wife's shoulder.

'Karen wants you both to know... Er, well, what she's telling me exactly is that there's something about being in a van, but when she was in the van she'd already left her body, and she really hopes you know what she's trying to tell you...'

*"You're making a mess of this,"* Karen tut tutted in Steve's ear. *"Look, just tell them that by the time I was in the back of the van I'd already passed over. It isn't strictly true. But at least they'll understand what you're trying to say if you put it like that."*

'Karen is telling me that by the time she was in the back of the van she had already passed over and she wants to be sure that you understand what she's going on about.'

Karen's mother had started weeping quietly. Her friend, the other lady she had arrived with, passed her a tissue. Karen's father, meanwhile, stood ram-rod straight, almost as though at attention on a military parade ground.

'Yes,' he said with formality and iron self discipline. 'We understand the message perfectly. Thank you very much.'

*"Thank goodness we've got that out of the way!"* Stephen heard Karen laugh and again he was assailed by the scent of perfume. *"Anyway, just to prove it's me, please tell Mum and Dad that I've seen Granny Ecclestone and that she doesn't bother with her wheelchair any more, oh, and please tell them that I take Buster for walks every morning and afternoon, and I suppose most important of all, please tell them that I'm with Chris and that we're still together, and would they please please please pass on that message to Jack and Melanie."*

Stephen did his best to convey the messages... Granny Ecclestone was okay and out of her wheelchair, that Karen took Buster (the dog?) for walks every morning and afternoon. However it was the last part of the message that got the greatest reaction, for when he repeated the request that her parents should let Jack and Melanie know that she was with Chris and that they were still together, the couple next to Gerald and Joyce sprang to their feet with great whoops of joy, the guy with the leather jacket pumping the air with his fist and chanting Yes! Yes! Yes! in triumph and exaltation.

As I said at the beginning of this chapter, I've started this story in the middle. So let's go back to the start of this story and let me tell you a little bit about Karen and

Chris. How they met. How they loved. And how they died.

I suppose it could be said that their relationship was destined to be difficult right from the very beginning. When they first met, Karen Sommersby was just fifteen years old and still at school while Chris Nichols was ten years older and her music teacher. I'm sure you can understand some of the problems they encountered in those early embryonic days of their friendship and I don't suppose that anyone other than Karen and Chris will know exactly how they coped. There must have been all kinds of torment, especially on the music teacher's part, for, after all, he *was* a teacher and as such bore the responsibility of his students' welfare on his young and relatively inexperienced shoulders.

One of the things he *did* do was to resign from his teaching position at Karen's school – whether this was an attempt to sever the friendship or to facilitate its progress is open to debate, but the fact of the matter is that by the time Karen was sixteen years old she was "seeing" Chris at every opportunity out of school hours and by that time the relationship had certainly gone sexual.

Her parents, and especially her mother, were aware of the fact that she had a boyfriend and because of Karen's constant refusal to bring her young man home for tea and to meet her mother and father (well, you can understand why she wouldn't want to do that, can't you?) their concerns and suspicions were aroused which led to quite a degree of friction within the Sommersby family circle. Karen was an only child and came from a well protected upper class background wherein things were supposed to be done in a certain way and with a modicum of decorum...

168

Chris Nichols' background was the antithesis and complete opposite – he came from East Anglian working class stock with a gypsy bloodline running through his ancestry. With the absolute encouragement of his parents who were both professional musicians, Chris worked very hard through school and college ending up with a modest degree, which on its own would not have gained him much of a position in the teaching profession – the fact that he was quietly charismatic and a brilliant pianist with a natural aptitude for teaching did, however, pave the way for him to secure his position at Karen's school. While Karen's parents were staunch Catholics and committed Conservatives, Chris's parents were more of the pagan persuasion and ardent socialists. Not an in-law match made in heaven even if Chris and Karen had decided to go public with their relationship!

Their relationship *did* get forced out into the open around the time of Karen's 18th birthday. She was in her last few weeks of schooling and Gerald and Joyce were pushing her towards taking up a positon with the Paris Conservatoire to follow through with her training as a professional violinist. Karen was very opposed to this idea and wanted to join the folk rock band that Chris was in the process of putting together at the time. There were some very heated family arguments that drew both sets of parents into the fray, and both the Sommersbys and the Nichols were amazed to discover that their respective children had been having an affair for the past three years! While Jack and Melanie Nichols accepted the situation with a degree of stoic bemusement, Gerald and Joyce Sommersby went ballistic with apoplexy. In short, the shit hit the fan in a major way.

Amid the accusations and condemnations, Karen finally took control and brought the matter to a head. She told her parents that she loved them very much indeed and was dreadfully sorry that they were so angry and upset – but that at the end of the day her love for Chris was not just a teenage crush, it was the real thing and that if her parents were forcing her to choose, then she would choose to be with her lover. She was not totally dismissing the idea of further studying in Paris, but that she wasn't going to be pushed into anything against her will and that for the time being, until she made up her mind about where she wanted her musical career to go in the long term, she fully intended to play fiddle in Chris's band and she'd think about the "Paris thing" a year or so up the road.

As you can imagine, this did not go down well with Mr and Mrs Sommersby and the upshot of it was that the day after her 18th Karen moved out of her family home and took up residence with Chris in a large static caravan a few miles west of Great Yarmouth. Whereas Jack and Melanie Nichols welcomed Karen into their world, Gerald and Joyce cut her off completely. Sad, but in some ways understandable. Their sense of hurt and disappointment born of their background and social expectations must have been quite profound.

Chris and Karen lived in their Yarmouth caravan for the better part of a year, they laughed and loved and worked hard at getting their musical ambitions off the ground – which turned out not to be quite so easy as either of them had imagined. Maybe there were too many folk rock bands already on the scene? Either way, to supplement their frugal income Chris started giving private piano lessons and Karen took on some part time work as a waitress.

This she did not enjoy. In fact she absolutely hated it, and although her love for Chris was undiminished, she did start thinking seriously about her long term professional prospects. Gently and insidiously the idea of doing a further course of study in Paris became more and more attractive, but initially she was loath to mention this to Chris for fear of either hurting him or upsetting him. However, when she finally did pluck up enough courage to broach the subject, Chris was very supportive and encouraged her in the idea...

....Perhaps for a number of reasons.

Firstly he saw no reason why he should not also relocate to Paris and living in the French capital with the love of his life would be no great hardship. There might not have been much scope for folk rock bands in France but he could play Tchaikovsky with his left hand and Oscar Peterson with his right, and he didn't think that there'd be much difficulty in finding work as a piano player somewhere. But more importantly he was aware of the fact that the breach between Karen and her parents was causing Karen some pain and he saw this as a possible pathway that might lead to the healing of the wounds between parents and daughter.

Tentatively they made their plans and when Karen wrote to her mother and father to inform them of her decision to resume her classical studies this did, just as Chris had hoped it would, go some way towards bringing the Sommersby family back together. Gerald and Joyce still detested the idea of their daughter being with a working class music teacher, but if she was seeing sufficient reason to carry on with her education perhaps it would only be a matter of time before she got rid of her bit of rough in favour of some nice young man with some blue blood and breeding in his veins.

171

Given the timing of the term schedules of the Paris Conservatoire, it was agreed that Karen should relocate to Paris in January and that Chris, who needed some time to sort out some loose ends in the UK, would join her in March. Chris sold anything he could sell to raise some money and along with a bank loan and some limited financial support from Jack and Melanie, he and Karen had a short holiday together in Paris some six weeks prior to her term commencing. They managed to find a small bed-sitter apartment in one of the less salubrious streets behind Gare de Nord and Chris used all his available funds to pay the deposit and the first couple of months rent. At least, this way, they would have a home to call their own, be it ever so humble.

Karen left the UK on January 3$^{rd}$. She phoned Chris twice a day for a week, then on January 10$^{th}$ the phone calls suddenly stopped. When Chris tried to phone her all he got was a blank line. His texts went unanswered, and when, tentatively, he checked with Gerald and Joyce, he was alarmed that they had not heard from their daughter since the evening of January 9$^{th}$. Intuitively knowing that something was badly wrong, he impulsively started throwing some things together, fully intending to leave for Paris the following day if he hadn't heard from Karen overnight.

He didn't hear from Karen, but later that evening, January 12$^{th}$ he did receive a telephone call from the Paris Police Department informing him that Karen Sommersby had been found dead in the back of a white van somewhere near the Bois de Bologne. Her passport had been discovered in her purse and in the back of the passport she had designated him as her next of kin.

I choose not to dwell on the events of the following few days. Suffice to say that Chris and both sets of

172

parents travelled to France to be informed by a deeply sympathetic lady police officer that on the evening of the 10<sup>th</sup> of January Karen had been the victim of an abduction by a person or persons unknown. She had been raped, mutilated and ultimately murdered by a severe blow to the back of the head by a blunt instrument, possibly a hammer or the haft of an axe.

Despite what I have been told, I cannot imagine how those five grieving people got through the next days of their lives. The devastation, the pain, the sense of anger and loss must have cut them to the core of their souls. To have had such a beautiful and talented young woman wiped off the face of the planet in such a cruel and barbaric way must have twisted in their guts like shards of hot steel and words like shock and horror do nothing to convey the depths of their anguish and their despair. And then, of course, there was the guilt... If Gerald and Joyce hadn't been so insistent of Karen carrying on with her classical training, if Chris hadn't agreed to let Karen go to Paris... If...If... If...

But no amount of self recrimination, no amount of grieving and praying was ever going to bring Karen back into the light of the world, and in the same way that a recovering alcoholic has to deal with his problem on an hour to hour, day to day basis, then so the Sommersbys and the Nichols had to deal with their loss in the same way. Gerald's stiff upper lip continually quivered. Joyce wept constantly, and Jack and Melanie were at a loss to know what to do to help their grieving son who slid into a fugue of grief and depression.

Three months after Karen's death, Chris Nichols sat in the caravan where he and Karen had shared so many happy and precious hours, and at around four pm on a

Sunday afternoon in April he blew his head off with the single barrel of a 12 bore shot gun.

Stephen felt weak at the knees and he had to sit down on the edge of the stage. He made it look casual, but if he hadn't sat down he'd have fallen down.

*"Chris wants to say sorry to his Mum and Dad,"* Karen told him. *"He knows that what he did must have hurt them, but he just couldn't take it any more. He couldn't bear it for another minute."* Karen's spirit voice sounded sad and choked with emotion and Stephen had the mental impression of looking into the barrel of the gun that had transported Chris Nichols from one world to the next. *"It wasn't an accident,"* Karen's voice said, a little more distantly than before. *"I wish he'd have stayed where he was because there were so many wonderful things he could have done with his life... But he's with me now and I've got him safe and we'll be doing what we can to look after our Mums and Dads... Just tell them that we're here and we're fine and that we love them all so very very much..."*

Stephen couldn't see properly because there were tears in his eyes. He also found it difficult to speak because of the lump in his throat.

'Er, Chris is telling me that he's so sorry for the hurt he must have caused,' Stephen began, fumbling for the right words to pass on Karen's message as accurately as he could. 'And I'm being shown some sort of a gun, and there's something to do with a caravan and something that happened on a Sunday afternoon... D'you understand any of this, my loves?'

There was an almost inaudible response but it was enough to encourage Steve to continue with the rest of the message. 'Karen's telling me that she's got Chris

174

safe and that they're together, that they love you all very much and they're doing all that they can to help you...'

Karen's voice was now little more than a distant whisper. *"And just tell them that we're so pleased to see the four of them here together and that we're so pleased that they've become friends at last..."*

'And Karen wants you to know that she's so pleased that the four of you are here together and that you've all become friends.'

Karen departed from an exhausted clairvoyant who was still only at the beginning of a two hour demonstration. She left two fathers, both mute with emotion, and two openly sobbing mothers. She has also left this writer secure in the knowledge that there is no spiritual recrimination against those who choose to end their own lives and also reinforces the deep belief that true love is the most powerful force in the universe, so powerful, in fact, that it actually transcends death itself.

If there is any silver lining aspect to this most awful tragedy, it is that two disparate couples have come together – all class divisions and prejudices have been dismissed as these four people have consoled each other in their darkest and most dreadful of days – and together they have gone in search of evidence of their children's post mortem survival.

At The Assembly House in Norwich on May 6th I believe that they got that evidence from Stephen Holbrook.

## Chapter Fourteen:    *'What dreams may come...'*

Some time later when I was speaking to Stephen about the message he had channeled through from Karen, he didn't really remember much about it, which considering the volume of spiritual traffic he facilitates is hardly surprising. And yet, he clearly remembers the night in question and remembers that this was a particularly taxing and exhausting demonstration and that on more than a few occasions it became intensely emotional. I recall that on the night drive journey from Norwich to North Yorkshire, he slept like a baby in the back of the car and that for the following few days he seemed very tired and just little bit spaced out.

In some ways I found his back seat somnambulance frustrating because I had spoken at some length with both the Sommersbys and the Nichols and I was eager to get Stephen's slant on the experience. Furthermore, it has to be pointed out that it is on these long car journeys from one end of the country to the other that I get a lot of my feed back and information from Steve on a whole host of different subjects.

For example on one such journey from Dumfries in Scotland to Stamford in Lincolnshire we found ourselves discussing the potency and the meaning of dreams and Stephen was eager to point out that it is through the process of dreaming that the spirit world is often able to make contact with us down here on the earthplane.

Consciously we may not be aware of that contact, but subconsciously the message will have been delivered. Indeed, some of us might actually be aware of contact having been made and I suppose it depends upon our own levels of spirituality and our individual ability to be able to remember – and interpret – the dreams we have experienced.

In some cases the connections are obvious. We dream of a departed relative, and to be sure it could be said that we are simply dreaming of that person, but on the other hand it seems perfectly logical to me (and to Steve) that we have, albeit in our dreams, been visited by that person and what they may have said to us, or what we have acted out with them, will have much to do with the message they have been seeking to impart.

For example, a number of years ago a friend of mine had a dream whereby he was with his dead father and they were on some sort of cruise ship or pleasure boat that was sinking rapidly with water flooding in all over the place amid an atmosphere of horrific panic and impending doom.

My friend remembers his father saying to him, in quite an unflustered and casual voice – "I told you that you should have taken the bloody aeroplane!" – and that was it. End of dream.

Although the dream was quite a vivid dream it made little sense to my friend and he forgot all about it until fully a year later when he was planning a family holiday in Europe. He was actually in the process of booking four tickets on the Zebrugge ferry when his dream flashed back to him in all its immediacy and vividness, and he walked out of the travel agency with four package tour tickets courtesy of Intasun and Air Europe.

And on the day that he, his wife and their two kids were flying at 35,000 feet heading off to sunny Spain, the Zebrugge RoRo ferry capsized and sank like a stone in Zebrugge harbour with tragic and fatal consequences. Needless to say, this was the very ship that my friend and his family *would* have been aboard had he not remembered the dream and the "I told you so" message from his late father.

Stories such as these are legion and one could fill a book with examples of dream messages such as the one I have just spoken of... The point is, however, that all of us have these dreams while only some of us remember the dreams and even fewer of us pay any valid attention to the dreams.

Stephen, who dreams in 3D and Technicolor, is very good at remembering his dreams – even if he doesn't always understand them – and over the years he has learned how to discriminate between what is a personal visitation from the spirit world and what is a precognitive dream of prophesy. For example, a departed friend walking through long dark corridors and telling him not to worry about "those silly people down at the newspaper" was clearly indicative of some of the problems Steve was having with a local newspaper's advertising department a number of years ago, and was uniquely personal to a situation Steve was directly involved with. On the other hand, for three nights in a row immediately prior to 9/11 he was dreaming of some horrific terrorist attack on something called "the center" and because this did not involve him directly he had no understanding of the dream's meaning until that fateful and dreadful morning of September 11th.

It's a flaming long way from Dumfries to Stamford – a good four and a half hours if you don't exceed the legal speed limit – and that's a lot of time for talking. Stephen can sometimes be very reticent about giving opinions and it can, as I have found over the years, be difficult to draw him out on a subject that he's not totally sure about. On the other hand there are times when he can warm to a theme and you just can't shut the man up. So it was with this long conversation about dreams.

Stephen: "I actually think that our loved ones and friends in the spirit world are just as eager to contact us as we are to contact them, and in some ways it's much harder for them to make contact and in other ways it's much easier.

"I mean, if you're in the middle of a really exciting football match, or you're half way through a cliff hanger movie, or you're as busy as hell in your place of work, or you're looking after half a dozen kids, or you're worrying about your husband or your wife or your boyfriend or your girlfriend, or you're in a lot of physical pain, then quite frankly you haven't got time to tune into the spirit world and even if your late Uncle Arthur was yelling a message in your ear you probably wouldn't hear him over the noise from the telly or the sound of the machines down at the factory.

"But, when you're asleep things are a bit different, aren't they? You're in your own private space and your mind works on a different level. Spiritually, you're still awake, and in fact you're more awake spiritually when you're asleep than you are when you're not, if you see what I mean?

"Anyway, it's when you're asleep that spirit will find it much easier to make contact with you than they would when you're yelling and shouting and racing around like a blue arsed fly. I mean, I'm not sure about this next bit, but it's what I've been told and it's more or less what I believe, but I think that because spirits exist in another dimension where their vibrations are a lot higher, then to make contact with us lot down here they've got to work very hard to lower their vibrations… A bit like descending through some thick and really mucky water before they can get to the sand on the sea bed. And it's just the same with us, because at the end of the day if we want to make contact with spirit from down here, what we try to do when we have a séance or a spiritualist church service, or even when we hold our demonstrations, is to lift the level of our vibrations so we can meet the spirit world half way.

"Anyway, I'm sure it's easier for spirit to make contact when we're asleep and I think that they do make contact night after night, but to us, when we wake up, it's just like a dream and, as with all dreams, we remember some of them and forget others. But that's only mentally. Subliminally we remember and register everything…

"And there's a load of other stuff in connection with this, isn't there? I mean, imagine that you're in hospital and that you're in a deep coma… Your body is still alive, but mentally, you're out for the count. Where's your spirit at a time like this? Well, I reckon that for the most part you're already there in the spirit world, and if you're not, then at least you're in direct contact and communication. If you're in a coma for only three days, well it would be like having a long weekend away from home. If your coma lasts for three years or ten years or you never wake up from it, then your spirit has gone on in advance so to speak and maybe, just maybe, your comatised body has had to languish in the hospital bed for a while to play a vital part in someone else's life plan down here on the earthplane.

"I always get asked loads of questions and most of them I can't answer properly because I'm never sure of the answers, and in any case the answer I might have for one person might not be the right answer for another. I mean, one of the questions I always get asked is 'how can I get to be like you' and I always think you really wouldn't *want* to be me or anything like me, but I understand what they're asking. Basically people want to know how they can enhance their own clairvoyance and have some sort of direct link with their loved ones in the spirit world without having to attend demonstrations of clairvoyance conducted by a third party like me...

"And I suppose that if there is a stock answer, it would be to raise your vibration, and you can do that in lots of different ways, starting off by being nicer to other people. Going to a spiritualist church will help a lot of folk out there and other people might find some kind of short cut through meditation – although I've got to be honest and say that's never really worked for me. Certainly you can achieve more by listening rather than always being the one who is doing to the talking, and also, to get back to what we were talking about originally, it would be really good if you could do something to remember your dreams, because at the end of the day, your dreams are really very, very important.

"Also, of course, it's got to be said that anyone asking how they can tune more easily into the spirit world or who is looking for the gift of clairvoyance is probably vibrating on a bit of a higher wavelength than your Joe Average man in the street anyway. The very fact that they are asking these questions suggests that they're already in some kind of atunement, but it works on a thousand different levels because your own personal vibration is unique, a bit like a psychic finger print, and people develop in their own way in their own time depending on their individual personalities...

"And can we stop at the next service station, please James, because I'm bursting for a pee."

You see what I mean about not being able to shut him up?

Well anyway, we stopped at Scotch Corner and paid an extraordinary price for a very ordinary lunch (come back The Greasy Spoon Transport Caff – all is forgiven!) and then resumed our journey south through tidal waves of road spray and torrential rain. The A1 was crowded with monolithic juggernauts and idiots in BMW's and for a while it became something of a white knuckle ride. Stephen fell asleep somewhere near Thirsk leaving me to concentrate on my driving and to dwell on a few thoughts of my own.

I'm of the opinion that Stephen is absolutely correct in his assessment of dreams and of how important they are to us – and also how important they are to our loved ones in that other dimension, the realm of spirit. However I have a suspicion that our dreams play an even more vital role in our lives than we could possibly imagine and this is something which goes beyond the facilitation of communication between the world of the living and the world of the dead.

By all means, I'm sure we receive dreamstate visitations from our loved ones, but I also think that it is through our dreams that greater spiritual entities also attempt to make contact with us – some of them beautiful and bright and some of them rather more dark and negative. Just as our conscience does battle with our desire in our waking state, then I believe that there is a more powerful reflection of this ongoing battle in our subconscious which, of course, comes very much to the fore while we are in our dreamstate. If it is given that Man is born with free will, then, putting it into Biblical terms, I suspect that there may be a bit of a contest going on for control of that free will – the powers of light versus the powers of darkness, or again using Biblical terminology, our angels versus our demons. It might be suggested that when the demons are winning we are on the receiving end of our nightmares! When our angels are on top this is when we receive our flashes of knowledge, our guidance and our inspiration. Many of us have dreams wherein we are in states of great tension, and although we may not remember them, we wake feeling depressed and unrefreshed – or as one colleague of mine put it "as though we've just come through a war zone"!

It is from the dreamstate that the artist finds his muse, the thinker finds his ideas, the searcher finds his pathway. On very rare occasions it is in the dreamstate that we are touched by the finger of whatever God we worship and are invited to do His bidding.

The scientist will confess that we still know very little about sleep. Rapid Eye Movement (REM) can be measured to indicate that we are dreaming, but pure science has little or no understanding of what our dreams might be. The psychologist will expound the theory (presenting it as hard fact) that our dreams are no more than mental clearing houses in which we process the detritus of our conscious experiences enabling us to start each day afresh with a clean slate. The psychiatrist, whether coming from the Freudian or Jungian schools of study, will have us believe that our dreams are a reflection of our hopes and fears based on our actual life experiences, usually in the very early years of our lives. Indeed, Sigmund Freud suggested that *all* of our dreams were connected with our deep

183

rooted desire to have sexual intercourse with our parents in a vain attempt to return to the womb from whence we came.

Scientists and psychologists and psychiatrists have their careers and reputations to protect and ninety nine times out of a hundred anything that falls outside their own remit of experience will be rejected and rubbished out of hand. Therefore, suggest to your friendly neighbourhood scientist that in our dreamstates we frequently have visions of and even have cause to visit Other Worlds, and you'll be regarded as some nutty New Ager to be derided, and in no circumstances to be taken seriously.

And yet... And yet... I am most certainly *not* a nutty New Ager, but I nevertheless believe that in our dreamstates we do make contact with Other Worlds that are tangibly more than just alternative states of consciousness. Within this pantheon of worlds we are in effect making contact with parallel universes and dimensions, and as such it seems perfectly logical that somewhere within this framework of reality we are able to visit and make contact with that place that Man calls Heaven.

In my own dreams I have visited many places on more than just a single occasion – so frequently in fact that some of those "places" have become very familiar. I do *not* know if any of those places have been Heaven, but I *do* know that some of those places have been purely spiritual realms, and I also know that some of the places of which I speak are not of *this* world. "In My Father's House there are many mansions..." and we are all entitled to interpret that statement any way we damn well like!

Stephen and I both accept the fact that each and every person will have their own concept of Heaven and that in all probability each of us will transcend to a Heaven that fits in with our own preconceptions and expectations. In fact, after quite a bit of pushing on my part, Steve did put pen to paper the other week, and this is what he wrote:

"Every single person has his or her own concept of what it would be like, or even if the thing exists at all. Who's right and who's wrong can never be proved. Who am I to say what heaven is like or if it exists? All I can do is give you my thoughts on what I perceive it to be. We'll all find out one day I suppose and whether we're proven right or wrong is anyone's guess until we get there!

We all have a different take on our current earthly life, how we run our lives, who we interact with etc, so each individual's vision of heaven will be dependent on many factors, taking into account the decisions we make (both right and wrong) and how those decisions affect other people in our lives. As the saying goes, "no-one's perfect". As we sow,so shall we reap, so it is important in this life that we take into consideration not only what is best for us, but those around us.

Belinda Carlisle once sang 'Heaven is a place on earth'. To some this may be true, it all depends on how we run our lives and how difficult or easy it is. To some, living from day to day is some sort of earthly based Utopia, flitting from one day to the next without problems or stress. However, I believe that we need to have gone through some sort of suffering or encounter problems in order to grow emotionally and spiritually. How can we appreciate other people's problems when we've had no experience ourselves? Of course, there will always be those people who really couldn't give a hoot abut other people's problems and those are people who I pity. Other people exist in a living hell, suffering daily issues and long standing problems and their only thought of release would be dying and hoping to have a better life in heaven.

Each and every one of us has daily stress and worries, it's all part of life's great tapestry. Whether these are real issues or just in our minds, they can be financial, emotional or otherwise. Sometimes people suffering from depression are given a technique to 'escape' from reality, at least for just a short time. Imagine being in your favourite place, with no commitments to pile the pressure on, no problems awaiting you each morning at work, no worry, no pain or illness, no time constraints or daily routines. You are now in your own little version of heaven. People use the word heaven loosely on occasion, eg 'this meal is heaven' or 'this hotel is absolute heaven' – all it means is that to them that particular moment is perfect. Heaven must be a place where everything is perfect and just-so.

Needless to say, your heaven will be very much different to mine and that of your partner or family members, and also dependent on your current lifestyle and the things you do and don't like. In a nutshell, the powers that be will make the decisions, starting from the day you're born when the first piece of your own personal spiritual jigsaw is put on the map, leading right up until the day you die when the final piece fits in. Only then can the full picture be seen and the decision made on how your heaven will be, based on how we've run our lives and the original 'master plan'."

So we have Steve's version of heaven…

Now, going back to the original subject of dreams, if you're up for a little experiment of your own, start going to bed with a note pad and a pen under your pillow on on the bedside table. Immediately upon waking from a dream scribble as much of it as you can remember down on the pad. Sometimes just a couple of key words will do – *Sean Connery on The Orient Express* – and over a few weeks you'll be surprised at how much more of your dreams you start to remember. Maintain this discipline until it becomes a natural habit and you'll be amazed at what doors will start opening for you. After a dozen months or so try taking this experiment to the next stage and decide *before you go to sleep* where you want to go in your dreams and who you'd like to go with – and then sit back and let's see what dreams may come!

In part, I accept that the scientific community is right when it states that our dreams are a clearing house for our anxieties and the detritus of our everyday life, but that is such a small part of the overall picture and, in my opinion, to believe otherwise would be incredibly naïve. Our dreams enable us to live out some of our fantasies – you have no idea how many times I have dreamed of being in bed with Angelina Jolie – and they facilitate an insight into our own subconscious levels of thought. They permit us to have contact with friends and loved ones who are still on *this* side of the great divide and, more importantly, they create a bridge between this world and the next, enabling us to have contact with our loved ones in the world of spirit.

If you're in any doubt, put my little experiment to the test and see how you get on.   Feedback please to www.magepublishing.co.uk

## Chapter Fifteen:    *Bad Day... Bad Night*

There are some mornings when you wake up and instinctively know that you should just pull the covers over your head and stay in bed.

And so it was with Stephen one particular morning in March. He'd got to bed around two a.m. after driving half way across the country from one of his demonstrations and, knowing that he had a busy day ahead of him, had set the alarm for a seven o'clock call.

He was awakened not by the alarm but by the telephone shrilling away on the bedside table. Time 5.45 am. He'd been asleep for less than four hours.

The telephone call was from a friend – not really a close friend, just someone Steve knew socially – who had woken up in bed to find that his wife had passed away in the night and he had been sleeping next to her corpse.

This is a totally distressing scenario and indeed somewhat macabre and one can sympathise with and fully understand the state of mind in which this poor man found himself. It is interesting to note, however, that he did not call the doctor, the ambulance or the police – he called Stephen Holbrook!

It took Stephen the better part of half an hour to sort this situation out as best he could, and of course by then any further sleep was out of the question. By the time the alarm clock went off he was bathed and dressed and located in his office – deeply saddened by the dramatic news of the death which he had just received and trying, through his yawns, to get the rest of his day's schedule into some kind of order.

At 8.30 he took another telephone call, this time from his wife Caroline, who was not well pleased. He was supposed to be taking the children to school, and where the blazes was he? Had he forgotten or something?

Truth to tell Stephen *had* completely forgotten that he was scheduled to take his kids to school, and he flew out of the house to go and get them, dropped them off at the school gates and then had returned home to find he'd left the kitchen tap running and there was a mini-flood all over the kitchen floor.

Even as he was mopping up the mess the phone was ringing away, this time with a call from Rob, telling him that a whole series of advertisements that had been placed in a local newspaper had failed to appear. Although this was neither Rob nor Steve's fault, it led to an angry argument between the two friends that went on to cause an atmosphere of angst and hostility between them for the rest of the morning.

When Steve opened his mail around half past ten he was horrified to discover (a) a last minute warning invoice from an account he'd settled weeks previously and (b) a bank statement which indicated he had far less money in his current account that he should have had. Another intense twenty minutes on the telephone got it sorted out but not before he'd lost his temper with the ineffectual bank official that he'd been talking to and finally got an admission that the bank had made a "small clerical error".

By twelve noon Stephen had a serious headache and a sore throat and he was sneezing. He went out to the local shop to buy some man-sized tissues and some Lemsips, and only when he was in the process of getting back into the car, came to realize that some kind soul had scored the nearside passenger door with a key or some other sharp instrument. It was a new car (well, newish) and Stephen was not well pleased. His day was going from bad to worse and it wasn't even half over yet.

Stephen and Rob left Castleford at around two pm heading towards Chester where Stephen was demonstrating that evening. They deliberately left early in an attempt to beat the notorious traffic delays that occur daily on the M62 but they hadn't got more than half a dozen miles beyond Huddersfield when they ran into gridlock. It doesn't take much to screw up the M62 – a single lane closure, a lorry that's jettisoned its load – it's all a recipe for chaos and disaster. What should have been a two hour journey turned into a four hour journey and Steve and Rob finally limped into Chester at six pm by which time Steve's nose was streaming with the serious onset of a bad cold. Also, although the thought of eating anything made him feel nauseous, he hadn't eaten anything all day and he was hungry.

Having made up a little of the lost time Steve and Rob parked their car in the small car park adjacent to The Guild Hall, then grabbing their gear from the boot they dashed around the corner to The Guild Hall's main entrance and almost ran into a riot.

On one side of the street Stephen's audience of around 200 people were queuing to get into the building while on the other side of the street, carrying banners and placards, there was a group of about a dozen born again Christians haranging the crowd.

'Look, here he is!' screeched one skinny lady whose banner said *"Jesus is the ONLY way to God"* and then running over to him, she shouted full in Stephen's face – 'Stephen Holbrook you should be ashamed of yourself, leading all these poor innocent people astray!'

191

'Oh shut up you silly cow!'

This was *not* Stephen's reply but a scornful cat call from a member of the waiting audience on the other side of the street who had been on the receiving end of the Christian tirade for fully half an hour before Steve and Rob had arrived. Cheshire folk are usually easy going souls, but they don't suffer fools gladly and they don't like being told what they should and should do or where they should and should not go.

A bearded boy wonder whose banner said *"The Holy spirit is the ONLY spirit"* yelled back across the tarmac, 'You're damned! You're all damned!'

A large lady in a blue coat marched across the road and took a swing at the bearded boy wonder with her rather copious hand bag. 'I'm damned if I'm going to be damned by some snivelling little toe rag like you,' she said flatly. 'Now why don't you just piss off out of it and leave us alone!'

Stephen gritted his teeth. 'I'm not in the mood for this,' he said to Rob. 'Let's just get inside as quickly as we can and get our audience in, and maybe this other lot will just go away.'

The two men pushed their way towards the entrance amid encouraging calls of recognition from the people up at the front of the queue and then one big burly chap with a red face and a dog collar grabbed hold of Stephen by the shoulder and spun him around.

'Repent thee thy sins,' he yelled into Stephen's face, spraying him with spittle and the stale smell of cheap wine. 'For I am telling you that the only way to spirit is through our Lord Jesus Christ and not through fakirs and fortune tellers and hairdressers from hell.'

And indeed this guy was waving a placard that said *"Beware of the hairdresser from hell!"*

192

Stephen removed the offending hand from his shoulder. 'I haven't been a hairdresser for three years,' he said quietly, 'and as for the rest, you're misinformed. I'm not from hell, I'm from Castleford.'

At that point another Christian lady, mistaking Rob for Steve, hit Rob over the head with her placard. 'Satan's spawn!' she shouted joyfully.

'Oh do me a favour dear,' Rob muttered under his breath and finally managed to get Stephen into the sanctuary of the Guild Hall.

Stephen went straight to the loo and was immediately sick, no doubt caused by lack of food, high temperature and the stress incurred by having to run the born again gauntlet. What happened, he wondered vaguely, to the Christian ethos of love thy neighbour and turn the other cheek? The virulence and violence of the born again Christians filled him with dismay – they obviously hated his guts with a passion bordering on paranoia – and no one likes to be on the receiving end of that kind of hatred.

'I've forgotten the flaming float!' Rob told him when he returned from the toilet. 'I'll have to nip back and get it…'

'Rather you than me!' Stephen exclaimed. 'Run as fast as you can and whatever you do don't get involved in any arguments or conversations…'

So Rob ran back to the car, grabbed the bag of float change and hurried back through the conflict – the heat of which, if anything, had intensified quite considerably.

But as is the case in many different kinds of conflict there are moments of levity, and Rob was treated to an amazing spectacle that he's chuckled about ever since.

The red faced man with the dog collar had given his hairdresser from hell banner to one of his mates and was now standing in the middle of the street, arms reaching skywards in supplication...

'Go inside that building and... YOU WILL ALL GO TO HELL!' he roared triumphantly.

An attractive and rather well built young lady in a pink mini skirt walked out into the street to face the ranting clergyman – Rob said afterwards that it looked a bit like a set up for the shoot out at the OK Coral – and wagged a warning finger under the protester's nose.

'So, we're all going to hell, are we?' she asked conversationally. 'Well, do you know what I think about that? Ummm, well *this* is what I think about that!'

She turned her back upon her adversary, hoiked up her skirt, flicked down her panties and gave the gasping churchman and his acolytes the most devasting moony that Chester had seen in many a year. As she walked back to the crowd there was a huge cheer and a thunderous round of applause.

'What was all the noise?' Stephen asked anxiously as Rob closed the door behind him.

'Some girl has just moony'd the vicar!' Rob reported gleefully.

'You're joking!'

'I'm not joking at all!'

Steve's pale face split into a grin. 'Well, when she comes in, tell her well done and give her a free ticket!'

All kinds of people come to Stephen's demos. There are working class families, aristocrats in disguise, TV celebs, other mediums, members of the police force and other professionals... Some of them come seeking contact with departed loved ones, others come just to assess the evidence without looking for personal messages. Increasingly more and more young people come just to find out what it's all about, and there are occasions when Stephen gets visits from members of the clergy, some of them wearing their dog collars with stern expressions, some of them minus their dog collars with open inquisitive minds. Predominently it is a female audience – on average a good 70% - but the percentage of men in the audience is steadily on the increase and, as I've said before, these are not just guys who have been dragged along by wives or girlfriends to provide company and transport – they are there of their own volition.

Occasionally, of course, you get some people who come along just for a laugh. There's nothing on the telly, there are no football fixtures, and maybe they've just been thrown out of the local pub for being drunk and disorderly...

Sad to say, four such people found their way into Stephen's demonstration on this particular night in Chester and unfortunately there were problems right from the beginning. They began innocuously enough with the quartet's unwillingness to be quiet, and Stephen had to be quite firm from the platform to get their attention. He started his presentation, but within ten minutes there were giggles and loud whispers coming from the side of the room where the four people were sitting. Stephen didn't have to do anything to sort this out for there were plenty of "hushes" and "shhhhhs" from the audience in the immediate vicinity, but about half way through the first half the male member of the quartet started heckling with ascerbic taunts such as "bollocks" and even "what a load of old shite!"

This is where Stephen stopped his demonstration and quietly asked the organisers to remove the disruptive element from the building with instructions that they should have their ticket money refunded and not be allowed to re-enter. This met with a huge roar of applause and approval from the rest of the audience, and Steve got on with the rest of the evening.

In the meantime, about fifteen minutes into the demonstration, Rob had slipped out of the building and had gone over to the nearest pub. The audience was in, the protesters had gone and for the first time in several hours he was able to relax. He ordered a gin and tonic, lit a cigarette and sat down to read the local newspaper. He did the crossword, smoked another cigarette, drank another gin and then got totally absorbed in an article about the controversy raging over the proposed extension to Manchester airport. Time passed...

And when suddenly he found himself wondering what time it was exactly and looked at his watch, he realised to his horror that he'd been gone for far too long and that Stephen would be finishing the demonstration in less than ten minutes' time. Grabbing the big heavy briefcase which contained, among other things, the float for the book sales (his next and last job for the evening), Rob marched out into the street, crossed the road to The Guild Hall and found that someone had taken it into their heads to lock the door.

He couldn't get in.

It was raining.

Hard.

And he didn't have a coat.

He banged on the door and nobody answered. He rang the bell and nobody answered. He tried ringing the bell again and this time, in a flash of inspiration, did three short rings, three long rings and another three short rings – SOS in morse code – and still nobody answered.

Beginning to panic slightly because he knew that he couldn't do the book sale if he wasn't at the book stall to do it and that Stephen couldn't do it either if he didn't have any change, he came up with the brilliant idea of sending a text message through to Steve, full well knowing that although in "silent" mode Stephen should still feel the vibration and would pick it up as soon as he left the stage. Tapping urgently on the keys he managed to spell out – *help I'm at the* – before the battery expired at the phone went dead.

It started raining even harder and his designer jeans were leaking through the expensive holes in the knees and his nice white starched shirt was now little more than a limp white rag.

Ten minutes later the doors burst open and the crowd emerged, chatting and laughing, and carrying Rob on a wave of humanity half way down the steps before he could fight his way back and force access to the building. He managed to get to the book stall in time to sell one book, and by then the hall was empty.

'I got locked out!' he told Stephen plaintively.

Fifteen minutes later they were leaving Chester heading back through the motorway system towards Leeds. Stephen was fast asleep and snoring while Rob did battle behind the wheel, fighting the tiredness and straining his eyes against the driving rain which had descended all across the northern half of England. Five miles short of Hartshead Moor service station and less than twenty minutes from home, the car suddenly coughed and spluttered, then the engine died and they coasted to a stop on the hard shoulder.

Rob groaned. 'Now what?' he said miserably.

'Wassamatta?' Stephen asked, struggling up from his sleep.

'You're never going to believe this,' Rob sighed. 'But, we've broken down.'

'Broken down? How?'

'I don't know how and I don't know why but we've broken down.'

'Can't you fix it?'

'Stephen, as you well know, the only thing I know about cars is how to drive them,' Rob found it hard to keep the exasperation out of his voice.

'You know more than me,' Stephen retorted grumpily. 'Oh well, who do we phone? The AA, The RAC or Green Flag?'

'Well you're in the AA, I'm in the RAC and the car is covered by Green Flag, so what I'm going to do is phone all of them and see who gets here first. Give me your phone. Mine's dead.'

'Are you sure this is a good idea?' Stephen wanted to know. 'I mean, what happens if they all arrive at once?'

'I'll deal with that problem if it happens,' Rob told him tartly.

The three companies in question did not all arrive at the same time but the truck from Green Flag and the van from the AA pulled on to the hard shoulder within five minutes of each other and there was then some protracted discussion between the two operatives as to who was going to do what, who had been called first and who had precedence. In the end the Green Flag man drove away, leaving it to the chap from the AA, who lifted the bonnet of the broken down car and started prodding around with spanners and screw drivers, shouting various instructions to Rob, who was anxiously sat behind the wheel waiting to hear the healthy welcoming broom broom of a mended engine.

In the end the AA technician came round to the driver's side window, scratching his head. 'D'you mind if I get in and have a try, sir... Ah, thank you very much.'

Rob got out and started getting wet again while the nice man from the AA sat behind the steering wheel tweaking the ignition key and peering intently at all the dials.

'Ah, so that's it!'

He got back out of the car, let Rob in and stuck a genial head through the window.

'Well, gentlemen, I think I've solved the problem,' he said reassuringly.

'Don't tell me the big end's gone or anything like that,' Stephen moaned. He knew nothing about cars but had heard a lot about "big ends" and knew they could be expensive things to have repaired.'

'Oh no sir, nothing as Draconian as that!' The AA man chuckled. 'I dunno how to break this to you lads, but, er, you seem to have run out of petrol.'

'Run out of petrol?' exclaimed Rob, looking at Stephen in disbelief.

'Run out of petrol?' Stephen shouted, staring at Rob accusingly.

'Run out of petrol!' the AA man confirmed. 'I've got a can in the back of the van so I can go and get you some from Hartshead Moor but, er, there is going to be an extra charge for this service because, er, you see you haven't technically broken down, you've just more sort of, er, just come to a stop.'

'I told you to fill her up this morning,' Stephen said tersely as the AA van disappeared into the mist.

'I told you that I didn't have my cards with me and you said not to worry because you'd do it later when you went out to the post office.' Rob retorted.

'But I didn't go to the post office because you said we could post all the stuff tomorrow,' Stephen shot back. 'So why didn't you put some petrol in the car before we left this afternoon?'

'Well, you were driving so I thought that if we needed it you'd automatically stop and fill her up.'

'But I told you I thought you'd already filled it up!'

'Well, didn't you look at the petrol guage?'

'No, but why should I? I thought you'd already put the petrol in.'

'Well, I thought you would.'

'I thought you had.'

etc. etc. etc.


Time back to Castleford, two a.m.

The perfect end to a perfect day?

In Rob Green's words – 'I *don't* think so!'

# Chapter Sixteen:    *Finding Archie May*

Most spiritualist mediums have a spirit guide, and indeed sometimes a number of guides, that work with them and help forge the links between the world of spirit and the world of man.  Whilst it is true that Stephen Holbrook has a number of guides, principle among these is a gentleman called Archie May.

Working on Stephen's psychic impressions, Archie would have been a sergeant in the first world war, either killed in action during the war or, if not killed, then certainly seriously maimed.  Whenever Archie puts in a spiritual appearance, Stephen's left arm becomes icy cold and goes into a form of paralysis, and Stephen feels that Sergeant May probably lost his left arm as a result of being caught in an explosion of some sort.  To all intents and purposes Archie is a somewhat dour and taciturn character, who nevertheless does stirling work in organising (with military precision?) the queues of spirit people who are seeking to make contact with their loved ones on the earthplane.

Many mediums seem to have acquired Indian braves or Chinese mandarins as their guides and there are no shortages of Atlantean priests and Egyptian goddesses – and the trouble with all this is that it's extremely difficult to verify the existence of such an entity in real life.  However, given that Stephen's guide Archie was a serving NCO less than 100 years ago and given the tenuous information that we have through Steve's psychic vision, we felt that it might be possible to identify Stephen's spirit guide as a real person from history.  Not a high priest or a goddess, not an Indian war chief or a Chinese nobleman, but a modest one armed sergeant from the trenches of the great war.

This was a project that I had in mind when writing both of Stephen's earlier books but, what with publishing deadlines and word counts, the project never got off the ground – and nor would it have done so in this book were it not for a casual conversation over a dinner party table a few months ago.

My wife and I had been invited to dinner by a couple of very good friends and over the coffee and the mints our hostess, an attractive blond lady called Jan Seddon, started telling us about her new found hobby and interest in geneology. I remarked quite casually that she could put her hobby to good use if she could come up with anything on Sergeant Archie May – she said she'd willingly have a crack at it and I promptly forgot all about it until about three weeks later when she sent me an email with some listings of first world war medal awards and, damn it all, at the bottom of the list there was an Archibald May. In truth there were about a dozen Archie Mays who had served in various regiments, but there was only one *Sergeant* Archie May, and all I could see from Jan's list was that he'd served with The Queen's Regiment and that his regimental number was G/1262.

There was one of those little icon windows you're supposed to access for further information, so I clicked on said icon and was informed that Sergeant Archie May had been awarded a couple of medals – but that was it. No further info. Not even anything to indicate why the two medals had been awarded or even what the medals were – they were simply "service" medals – and that to a military illiterate like myself could have meant any damn thing at all.

The work was piling up for our first tour of the year so I shoved Jan's list to one side while I dealt with the more pressing business of placing adverts and booking hotel rooms. But three weeks later I was sorting out my office desk and coming across the list acted on impulse and instinct and, first getting the number from dear old Maureen, I put a phone call through to the Royal British Legion in London and found myself talking to a charming chap called Tim West.

After listening while I told him what I was looking for, Mr West went off for a moment to rifle (sic) through some of his papers, and returned to tell me that what had once been The Queen's Regiment was now The Princess of Wales' Regiment, but that there was a Major Russell based in Cantebury who was the regiment's archivist who should be able to help.

I duly telephoned Major Russell to be told he was on leave for the next week, so I waited ten days and phoned again, this time to be told that Major Russell was overseas, and no I wasn't privy to be told as to when he might be returning to the UK. Was there, I asked, anyone else covering Major Russell's role as regimental archivist? No, unfortunately, there wasn't – so for the time being the trail had gone cold.

I saw Jan Seddon again a short while later when she and her husband Bill came over for wine and tapas at my place. She asked me how I was getting on with Archie and I brought her up to speed – not that there was any speed at all as we'd arrived at a full stop.

Jan said that she'd see what else she could find out and a few days later phoned me to say that as far as she could discover there were only three Archibald Mays who had made sergeant and who had served in the first world war... She had no more information than that but her news was encouraging because if Stephen was right in his perceptions, we had narrowed our list of possible candidates down to three. God knows what we'd have done if there'd been three hundred Sergeant Archie Mays, but there weren't three hundred, there were just three, and all I had to do next was find out who they were, whether they'd lost an arm and whether or not some surviving family member might have an old photograph. Sounds fairly straight forward, but I had no idea how to go about this task, or even how to begin.

Enter Allan Potts.

Allan and his wife Heidi live in Corwen and, apart from his family, Allan has two passionate interests, namely all things appertaining to body mind and spirit – and geneology! While Allan has always been interested in matters of a spiritual nature, his interest in geneology was sparked a number of years ago when his father presented him with an old box that had been handed down through the family for the better part of two hundred years. Allan describes it as a fascinating object; a small writing case with numerous secret compartments and a big brass plate on the front saying where the portmanteau was made and who it was made for – and deciding to trace its history opened the door to what was initially a new hobby and subsequently an absolute obsession. He has amassed an enormous CD Rom library and armed with no small degree of IT expertise he has become an effective and expert genealogical researcher. While he might take issue with this somewhat glowing description of his talents, I've been checking up on him (sorry mate!) and this is certainly what his family and friends think of him, not to mention a few secret admirers down at the Town Hall and the local library.

It was his other interest, however, that took Allan and Heidi over to Wrexham a few months ago. Allan had heard of Stephen Holbrook from a number of sources and had been told how accurate he was. A free evening coincided with Stephen's demonstration and a last minute impulsive decision saw Allan and Heidi going to see Stephen for the first time.

Allan told me he was extremely impressed by the evening and although he didn't get a message he still bought one of Steve's books – "Out Of This World".

Allan: 'It was really rather strange, because although I'd never met Stephen before, when I went up to get the book signed Stephen said he could see that I was very much involved in some kind of spiritual work and he felt compelled to give me his other book "Light In The Darkness" which he suggested I read first…'

So Allan set to and began reading the book Stephen and I had put together back in 1999 – and was particularly intrigued by the chapter in that book which dealt with Archie May. In "Light" I had said that identifying Archie would make a very interesting subject and to "watch this space".

Wondering if I had made any headway with this quest since writing the book in 1999, Allan sent an email to Stephen's manager Rob, asking if he could be of any assistance – and Rob immediately passed the email on to me. This came at a highly opportune moment and I wasted no time at all in getting in touch with Allan, bringing him up to date on the progress I had made thus far.

A couple of days later Allan got back to me, confirming the information I had already received from Jan Seddon, namely that there were three sergeants called Archie May who had served in the 14-18 war. One of them had been Scottish, while another had been Australian, and both Allan and I were inclined to ignore these two candidates because we felt that had Steve's Archie May been either Scots or Aussie, he would have picked up some intimation of that fact through his spiritual liaisons. Also, it has to be said that we both felt we were on to a winner with the third candidate insofar as according to the national census of 1901 *this* Archie had been born and bred in Liverpool and Stephen has a number of family links with this part of the world, going back two, three and four generations. Secondly, prior to volunteering in 1914 our Liverpudlian Archie May had been a hairdresser's assistant, which given Stephen's history as a hairdresser, was, we felt, either a very spooky coincidence or a clear indication that we were on the right track.

The only problem seemed to be that all three of these sergeants survived the war, so now we were looking for an NCO who was possibly maimed, but not necessarily killed and, indeed, if we extrapolate on this theme it seems highly probable that Archie *was* just maimed rather than killed!

Stephen gets the psychic impression of a military man with a crippled arm, and if Archie had died from his wounds on the battlefield, then following the "all wounds are healed in the passing" philosophy we are inclined to believe that Archie must have learned to live with the infliction of his disability to the extent that the disability (the dysfunctional left arm) became an intrinsic part of his earthplane identity.

Thus far, working from that 1901 census, Allan (at July 2006) has discovered the identities of Archie's parents and brothers and sisters... We have ascertained that he married in 1916 and that he died in 1926 but are no nearer to knowing for sure whether this is Stephen's Archie May.

Suffice to say the investigation continued, and because by mid-August of 2006 we were getting uncomfortably close to our copy deadline, I played a hunch and placed a small advert in the personal column of a Liverpool weekly newspaper asking if anyone had information appertaining to a Sargeant Archie or Archibald May who had served in the Great War and who had passed over in 1926. I thought of offering a reward for the information but that would have been crass and potentially would have opened the doors for a bag full of false claims.

Bingo!

I only had one response to my advert and this came from a lady called Florence Aptree of Formby who told me that her great uncle had been called Archibald May, and although she knew he had served in the first world war, she was unable to confirm his rank, didn't know whether or not he'd been wounded, and wasn't sure of the exact year of his death, although she did think that it would have been some time in the 1920's.

Did she, I asked, have a photograph or a picture of her uncle?

She said that she might have, because there was an old box up in the attick full of old family pictures. She promised to look and agreed to send me anything that she found.

And this is where it gets a little bit interesting!

Obviously Florence Aptree wanted to know why I was interested in someone called Archie May, and I ended up telling her all about Stephen and his work and how I was trying to establish the identity of his principle spirit guide. Florence was quite excited by this information because she and all her family, as far back as she could remember, were committed spiritualists and her Grandfather (Archie's brother, if we were on the right track) had been a practising medium! Coincidence or what?

Florence sent me a small dog eared image of her great uncle which I duly scanned in and copied on the computer before sending it back with a big box of chocolates and a profusion of thanks. In some ways it was rather an odd little picture, cut from a newspaper or magazine rather than a print from a negative, and instead of formally depicting a soldier in full uniform, it was a grabbed shot of two squaddies leaning out of a railways carriage window as the train took them off to the Great War that so very few returned from.

My next step was to show the copied photograph to Stephen – totally convinced that he would be able to identify Archie from the somewhat faded image that I eagerly thrust before his eyes.

'Archie May!' I exclaimed in triumph and then went on to tell him about my research and my contact with Archie's great neice.

'Ummm,' Stephen said thoughtfully. And then again another long 'Ummm.'

'Come on,' I pushed him. 'Tell me what you think. Is it him or not?'

'Ummm,' for the third time. 'I don't doubt that this is Archie May on the strength of all the evidence you've puilled together, but as to whether this is *my* Archie May I'm just not sure.'

'Well does it look like him?' I wanted to know.

'James, I don't know because I've never seen Archie's face clearly, I've only ever sensed his presence and received a psychic impression, and I'm ever so sorry but,' he studied the photograph intently, 'somehow this just doesn't ring a bell with me, it doesn't feel right.'

I felt crushed and disappointed. 'But we only had three Archie's to go on and this one seemed the most obvious cvandidate – I mean, there's the hairdressing factor and the Liverpool link and then there's the fact that all of Archie family seem to be spiritualists...'

'James, I'm not saying that this *isn't* Archie, only that I'm not sure about it and I need to think about it for a while...'

I have to tell you that this put me in a foul mood, but then two days later and quite unexpectedly, I had a phone call from Steve.

'Have you had a close look at that photograph you gave me?' he asked. 'Y'know, the one of Archie?'

'Not since I gave you your copy the other day, no. Why?'

'Have another look now and tell me if you see anything unusual...'

'Okay.' I rummaged around my desk 'till I found the picture. I studied it intently but I didn't know what I was looking for. 'What am I looking for?' I asked, hoping he'd give me some kind of clue.

'Well, look at the number on the carriage door... I think it's supposed to be number three but one of the one's has got rubbed out and so it looks more like an eleven, doesn't it?'

I had to concede that he had a point, which was very interesting because Steve's got this thing about numbers and for the last four years the number 11 has been like a spiritual beacon guide for him... In fact the times he has found himself staying in room number 11, or on the $11^{th}$ floor of this or that hotel, or coming down to breakfast and finding that he's sat on table 11 – frankly, it's quite amazing! But it doesn't stop there. Key dates in his life over this last four year period have always centred around the 11$^{th}$ of any given month... Important meetings that have led to major changes have occurred either at 11 at night or at 11 in the morning; it is a profound synchronicity, the potency of which cannot be ignored.

'Right now, and here's another thing, have a look at the railway carriage around the window where the two men are leaning out of... Can you see any faces in the paneling?'

I looked very closely. 'Er, no, to tell you the truth I can't.'

'Neither could I at first, but if you study it hard enough you start to see them... And there's something else that struck me last night. I mean, I'm looking at a photograph, and I'm wondering if this chap really could be my spirit guide and it suddenly dawns on me that the only things I can see about him are his face and his left arm – his *left* arm, James – and suddenly I got this little rush of confidence and conviction, and although I still wouldn't swear to it on a stack of bibles, I've come round to thinking that this just *might* be my Archie May after all!'

And that, dear reader, is about as far as we've come. Somewhere in the photographic section you'll find the picture that Florence sent me and if Steve has any more thoughts on this matter before we go to press, you'll be the first to know.

# Chapter Seventeen: *Jamie Beebo*

Although it has a most awful downside the internet is a very wonderful thing. As an educational tool and a source of information it has made volumes of encyclopedias obsolete almost overnight and has opened up channels of communication that only a few years ago would have been the stuff of science fiction. It is a window on the world that gives ordinary people the opportunity to tell the most extraordinary of stories. Some of those stories can be very funny, other tales can be sad; there can be reports of political cowardice and personal courage, and nowhere will you find a braver and more courageous report than the one you will encounter should you choose to visit www.beebo.info

Upon accessing this website you will be drawn into the world of Jamie "Beebo" Rendall and although I could tell you Jamie's story by quoting ad verbatim what it says on his website, it is probably more appropriate if I just publish the letter that Jamie's mum Kelly wrote to Stephen Holbrook a few weeks ago.

In Kelly Rendall's own words...

"Jamie was born in April 2000 – a millennium baby, the cutest little chap who always smiled and rarely cried. Everyone always told me how lucky I was to have such a good baby who flourished as a toddler and became such a beautiful well mannered child. He was never unwell, so it was unusual when he did fall ill after the birth of our second child Charlie in June 2003. For quite a few months Jamie had been waking up in the morning with leg pains, which our doctor thought were just 'growing' pains, but after Charlie's birth Jamie started getting a lot of tummy aches with lots of vomiting and chronic high temperature.

After about five weeks of this our doctor finally took us a bit more seriously and sent Jamie off for some tests at our local hospital. The doctors at the hospital did an ultrasound scan and discovered a large mass in Jamie's abdomen. We cried our eyes out when we were told that Jamie had cancer and that he would have to go to Bristol Children's Hospital for more tests!

The following day we drove nearly two hours with Jamie to Bristol where for the next four days he endured a whole barrage of different tests including exploratory surgery, a biopsy, CT scans, MRI scans, blood tests and bone marrow aspirates. Jamie was as good as gold and although we were worried sick, never once did he lose his sense of humour.

The worst part of the nightmare, or so we thought, was waiting for the results, but when the results finally did come through the nightmare began in earnest. Apparently Jamie had a rare and aggressive type of cancer of the sympathetic nervous system called Neuroblastoma. Jamie would need an intensive program of treatment, but he would never be cured and only stood a 20% chance of surviving the next five years.

Despite these slim odds Jamie was a tough little boy – a real fighter – and he pulled through a year of grueling treatment. Everyone commented on how well behaved Jamie was – he never complained about the cancer treatment and always took his medicines without arguing. He remained positive about the whole thing, was always smiling and happy, and in short he was an absolute pleasure to be with. He was finally allowed back home in May 2004 and the following year was absolutely fantastic. Jamie was declared in remission and even started school...

We were thrilled to bits, but we knew that Jamie could relapse at any time and sometimes it felt like we were walking on egg shells just waiting for our bubble of happiness to burst.

Despite this we still went into complete shock when Jamie did relapse at the end of May 2005 and we were told that Jamie only had a few weeks left to live.

We just couldn't accept it. He didn't actually look, or act, like a child with a few weeks to live and it was hard for us to believe.

Jamie started oral chemo, which was a slim chance, more of a grasp at straws, but in the three months that followed we made sure that every day was memorable for Jamie; we went to Legoland Denmark, he had a helicopter, Porsche, Ferrari, fire engine rides. We spoiled him rotten and made sure we took lots of home movies and photos, as it became obvious that despite efforts, his health was not improving. The oral chemo was stopped and Jamie required blood transfusions daily. He lost most of his hair and looked so skinny and pale; it was so painful to watch him waste away before our eyes.

The time came to tell Jamie that he was going to die and it was me that broke it to him one day in the car, driving to the hospital. He was telling me about how he looked forward to returning to school and being able to go swimming. Jamie was unable to go swimming because he had a central line for his blood tests, transfusions and medication. He'd assumed that because his treatment had stopped that he was better, so I gently explained to him that he wasn't better, because the medicine hadn't worked.

Jamie asked me the question, 'Am I going to die?' and I didn't know what to say, so I told him he might, as the doctors can't always make people better. He'd experienced his cancer buddy die just a few months before, but seemed determined that he wasn't going to die himself. We talked at length with Jamie about death and told him that his grandfather was in heaven to look after him. It terrified us to think of Jamie being alone on the other side, missing us, and we tried to make him not feel scared. One of the worst things, apart from seeing the physical deterioration of Jamie, was watching his personality also deteriorate and, as each day passed, we were losing the Jamie we knew and loved.

In the end I kept thinking how Jamie wasn't even there anymore; in our eyes his spirit had slowly ebbed away before his death. When Jamie finally gave up fighting on 31st August 2005, he was in hospital, with his father and me by his side. It was traumatic by all accounts, and I wouldn't wish the experience on my worst enemy.

The next few weeks blurred past, with a beautiful funeral, a horse drawn carriage and convoy of motorbikes. We buried Jamie with favourite toys and his granddad's ring which we hoped would be a link for him in the other world.

Since he died we've had a few signs/messages from Jamie…

First was in the hospital, just after he'd passed away. We were in the parent's bedroom, waiting for the nurses to wash and dress Jamie. I was laid on the bed, with my head on my husband David's lap, and I could feel David's breath on my face, as he was looking down at me. David's breath smelled of Jamie and made me feel calm and comforted. I smiled and after a few minutes told David that his breath smelled of Jamie. David may have changed his breathing, as it stopped then.

Second was David hearing Jamie call his name, one night in bed, before going to sleep.

Third was a message through my friend, mother to a boy called Davey, that Jamie was friends with while in Bristol Hospital. Davey had Osteosarcoma and had relapsed, then died in January. She has a friend whose sister is psychic and has had a message from Davey, through this psychic, shortly after Davey died. I had said to my friend that I was worried that Jamie was scared or upset and wished I knew he was ok. The same day, at the hospital, when I had signed the forms to release Jamie to the funeral directors, the nurse had asked if I wanted Jamie's central line to be removed. I had said yes, gladly, as Jamie had often said that he would like to go swimming when he had his line out and I'd had to tell him that he wasn't having his line out, because he wasn't getting better. My friend Mel phoned me one evening, a few days later, to say that her friend was talking to her sister on the phone and mentioned that one of Davey's friends had died. Just as she was telling her, the psychic said she could see a small boy before her. She said he was little, with blond, rebellious hair, sat cross legged, and smiling. He didn't speak to her, but she said he had nothing on but a pair of swimming trunks. When my friend told me, it didn't click and I said it must have been his pull-ups, as Jamie hated clothes and mostly just wore a pull-up. Later when I told Jamie's Nana Pat, she reminded me about his line being removed and so it must have been swimming trunks after all. Jamie was thanking me for having his line removed.

Fourth was a message through my husband's uncle, up country near Grimsby, from a man at his uncle's work that he doesn't actually know. His uncle had been approached by this man once before and given a message for David's Nan, from his deceased Granddad.

This time the man said he kept seeing a little boy, with gorgeous blue eyes. He had said that he is happy and can do all the things he couldn't when he was on the line. We have translated it to: he can do all the things he couldn't when he had his line in.

Then I went to see Steve Holbrook on Sunday, 18th September, two weeks after the funeral. We sat amongst the crowd, listening in amazement to the messages that people were getting, until Steve suddenly said, 'Somebody's lost their son to the spirit world'. I raised my hand and Steve asked for my voice. 'Was he only little, my love? How old was he?'

And then even before I could answer Stephen shouted out 'Number one' – which is our house number. 'House number one, god bless him. He's telling me he lived at house number one and that he was five years old! Was he five? He's here and, you know something my love, I bet you can feel a tingling across here...' Stephen indicated his chest and shoulders '...and down your sides – can you feel it? Well that's him.'

I was shaking and felt tingly all over!!! And already in tears, trying to hold it together.

'Now, he lived at number one and you live at number one and he comes back to be with you – and, you know something my love, you still question and you still think if only... why... if only I had done this or that or the other... Do you understand?'

I understood very well because I'd blamed myself for not pushing the doctors harder or trying different treatments.

'Stop it,' Stephen said. 'You're a fabulous mother and for goodness sake if you feel like crying you have a jolly good cry. Don't bother answering me, just nod your head! You know something, I can help you and I can take some of that pain away. All around here, now, can you feel it? That's good, that's the healing coming through. I can tell you something now, he is... fabulous! And he's just said 'I'm perfect, Mum, absolutely perfect – there's nothing wrong with me.''

The cancer had affected Jamie badly, causing tumours in his head and black/yellow eyes. He lost a lot of weight and ended up looking like a baby bird with huge eyes.

Stephen pointed a finger to the side of his head. 'And he's just said I'm fine in here.'

His tumours were causing him headaches, partial deafness, and he lost his sight the day he died.

'And he's brought me a beautiful blue love heart and he says Thanks, Mum, I've still got it.'

Jamie knew I liked hearts; he'd bought me a purple love heart cushion for a gift when he was well.

'He's just said he's well and you need to know he's ok.'

My only reason for going to see Steve was to know that Jamie was ok, not sad, scared or angry.

'After he'd gone to the spirit world you touched his eyes!'

Jamie's eyes were so large, compared to his bony face that his eyes wouldn't stay shut after he'd died, so I reached over to try and close them. And before Jamie had become ill, he'd always slept with his eyes partially

217

open; we had an ongoing family joke about him being nosey!

'I'm going to tell you something – five going on fifty five!'

Jamie had always been old for his years and very grown up; he was more like an old man at times!

'He had been here before!'

People had often said that of Jamie, he was always so laid back and calm, like he'd seen it all before, he took life in his stride.

'And he was so special!'

Every mother thinks her child is special but the truth is that everyone who met Jamie said this of him; he had a special sparkle, twinkle in his eyes and a cheeky grin. He touched many people, who met him only once.

'He's got a teddy with him and he's just said he's got the teddy, but it didn't go in his coffin with him.'

Jamie had a thing about cuddly monkeys after his Auntie had bought him one. Every time we visited the hospital, he wanted to buy another, and soon we had a collection. I liked one in the shop, but Jamie never chose it, so after he died, I bought it and swapped it for his favourite, so he had my choice in his coffin, and we kept his favourite!

'The monkey was just the right size!'

When the hospital staff washed and dressed Jamie, to send down to the funeral directors, they put his monkey under one arm and we commented how it was just the right size.

'I take it the monkey's got a nose? The nose is cock-eyed, have a look.'

We pondered for ages about this part… the monkey he had was fine, but I'd said that Jamie's nose had looked strange at the chapel of rest. Later we

218

discovered another monkey at home, that Jamie had recorded a voice message into at diagnosis… it had a cock-eyed nose!

'Seaside!'

We live on the coast and liked to spend a lot of time on the beach.

'Tell my Mum not to be scared.'

My grief had taken over me and at times felt like panic attacks, I'd feel shaky and breathless and scared. The thought of Jamie appearing to me in ghost form had terrified me. Later that evening at home, Jamie appeared to me, so he must have been pre-warning me.

'He's seen your granddad.'

His great granddad really, but we always referred to him as Granddad Jim, who would be in heaven waiting to look after him. Steve asked to speak to my mother-in-law, who'd come with me, as it was her father that was with Jamie…

'You never thought you'd be hearing from him in one of these spooky places!'

Jamie's great grandfather was a skeptic!

'He's just said 'I can't believe it – I've got the lad, he's with me!' And, do you know something, you always said he'd look after him and he *is* looking after him, because he's got a heart of gold.'

Then Steve came back to me. 'Your little boy is back. Did he have to have something done to his toes? He's wiggling them, why would he do that?'

At the time, we didn't really understand what this meant, but later on found out he was referring to his dad's toes.

Steve assured me that even though it's sad, I now know that Jamie is with me. It was spot on. He answered all my worries and questions, and made me

219

feel totally at peace, like a weight had been lifted from my shoulders.

The following week, we saw a load of balloons in a nightclub which were silver, but had a blue light shining on them. Then later on that evening, someone walked past us with one of those balloons and as they passed us it escaped them and floated off into the air!!! Jamie loved to release balloons, it was a ritual we'd started while he was in hospital. We'd sometimes tie a Polo mint to the string and it amused Jamie to see it float away. At Jamie's baptism, shortly after he relapsed, he started taking balloons outside and, much to the other children's displeasure, he was releasing them into the sky and laughing so much that the other children joined in too and they all laughed and released the baptism party balloons.

I counted the months until Steve Holbrook returned to my area and six months later I went to see him again, and this time I took my husband, his best friend and my auntie. All three were skeptics and sat and watched, not knowing whether to believe or not, until fifteen minutes before the end when Steve said, 'I've got a five year old boy.'

David said he came over all tingly and knew this was Jamie. We both put our hands up and Steve passed on the messages that he loves David/Daddy and acknowledged the new baby due soon... that he haunts Sam, the play lady whom he'd worshipped at the hospital. He'd seen my auntie writing a birthday card that day and had caught me snoring when I'd been taking a nap.

Jamie was such a huge character, he was wise beyond his years, and had a special quality that meant he touched the heart of everyone who he met. Everyone commented on how polite he was, as he always said, 'Excuse me' before he spoke. We will miss Jamie so much, and every day seems empty without being able to hug and cuddle with him.

I owe so much to Steve for making it possible for us to communicate with Jamie, to know that he is ok has eased the pain, and made grieving more bearable.

Thank you Steve – With love from Kelly Rendall.

Both Stephen and I agree that the pain of losing a young child is probably the worst kind of pain any human being can suffer. It causes a cut to the soul that never truly heals and with every passing month and each interminable year the parent forever wonders how the life of their dead child would have unfolded had it lived. This experience changes lives for ever and there are some parents, especially the mothers, who never recover from this blow, falling into the shadow existence of a half life, or if not a half life, then a life in which a huge chunk of their heart and soul is missing.

In light of this, is has to be acknowledged that Kelly and David Rendall have done something positive to ensure that the premature passing of their beautiful young son was not in vain. Their website www.beebo.info provides a network of support to other parents who have children afflicted by a terminal illness, has an information board about all medical advances as they come on line, and provides clear and concise information in understandable English about Neuroblastoma and Osteosarcoma. Kelly and David's work has created a common bond for other parents who have gone through or are going through the despair and agony that they themselves experienced, and in the process of putting their website together they have not created a maudlin sentimental shrine to Jamie's memory, but have lit a beacon of knowledge and hope that shines across the land. Kelly and David have a message for every other parent out there in the world, and it is simply this:

*"Let your children sleep in your bed.*
*Have more patience.*
*Let them make messes.*
*Don't take anything for granted.*
*Tell them you love them all the time."*

# Chapter Eighteen: *Robbie*

In some respects Robbie Holbrook, Steve's eldest son, is a very ordinary twelve year old boy. In other respects, however, he is an *extraordinary* twelve year old boy!

When you meet him for the first time you become immediately aware of the fact that here is a nice kid, who is *still* a boy, not yet fallen victim to the slings and arrows of modern day teenism. There are no hoodie jackets, no nasty words in his vocabulary, no angsty moods of non-communication, no embryonic traits of anti-social behaviour…

This doesn't mean that he's a saint or a little angel. Steve and Caroline would be the first people on this planet to explode that marticular myth, and in Robbie's own words:- *"You must be flaming joking!"* But nevertheless, he's a polite young man with a sunny, open disposition and although he's observant and doesn't miss much, there's none of the weary streetwise cynicism that seems to affect so many of our children these days.

I've known Robbie since he was five years old and even going back to the day that I first met him in 1999 he struck me as being special in some way. He was interesting and interested and carried with him an aura which belied his tender years. They say that 'it takes one to know one' and although I am not clairvoyant and I am not a medium, I do have some psychic ability and I recognised this ability in Robbie from day one.

When I mentioned this to Stephen all those years ago he seemed halfway between dubious and bemused, but as Robbie has grown Stephen also has become aware of the latent energy in his eldest son, and along with that energy there has been a keen and burgeoning interest in his father's work which has manifested itself in a host of questions which, for the better part, Stephen has not been fully able to answer.

It's quite possible that Stephen felt that Robbie's interest in spiritualism stemmed from the natural trait of any son wanting to follow in the footsteps of his father and that, as such, it was something that Robbie would grow out of once he got a bit older. In fact, the reverse was true and the older Robbie became the more curious he became and the more questions he started asking. In the end, as a means to satiate his son's curiosity, Stephen started taking him along to some of his local demonstrations and this was where the fun really started!

Robbie would sit close to Stephen, sometimes on the front row, sometimes in the wings of the theatre, sometimes, depending on the venue, even on the edge of the stage. Frequently, at the end of the demonstration, Robbie would remonstrate with his father, saying something like:- *"When you were talking to the lady in the red jumper about her little girl why didn't you tell her about the 7th of May?"* Stephen would ask Robbie why he should have mentioned the 7th of May and Robbie would calmly announce that it was the little girl's birthday.

This happened on too many occasions for it to be a fluke and Stephen slowly came to realise that if Robbie was picking up this extra information on the back of the messages that he, Stephen, was passing to the audience then it was a powerful indication that Robbie had some clairvoyant gifts of his own.

It wasn't a case of putting this theory to the test exactly, but Stephen started taking Robbie along to a few more of his demonstrations, now deliberately sitting him off to one side of the stage, and suggesting that Robbie pick up whatever he could pick up, whether it was connected to one of the messages or whether it was something quite independent.

The results were neither startling nor amazing but over many weeks Robbie brought through snippits of information, a name here, a date there, which were corroborated either by Stephen himself or by the person that Robbie was linking with and it was quite enough to give Stephen some serious pause for thought. It was obvious that Robbie's interest in spiritualism was not a passing fancy and it was also obvious that he had some natural aptitude – the question was, what to do with it and how to develop it?

In the early spring of 2006 spirit intervened and provided Stephen with the most perfect solution. Out of the blue he received a telephone call asking if he would conduct a spiritual development circle at a local college in Normanton, which is just around the corner from where he lives in Castleford. Looking at his diary for 2006 and 2007 he knew that he could not make such a commitment but he was more than happy to recommend an old friend and fellow medium, Val Atkins.

I think mainly because the introduction came through Stephen, Val agreed to take the course and as this course was, as I've said, very local, Stephen asked Robbie if he might like to take part in it. With Val in charge, Stephen knew that Robbie would be in safe hands; Val is a medium of many years' experience and is a lynch pin member of the spiritualist church. Over the years she has given Stephen a number of messages, all of which have proved to be highly accurate so far, and if he was going to entrust his son's spiritual development to anyone, Val was the obvious choice.

Robbie was highly enthusiastic and at the time of writing (July 2006) he has been sitting in Val's development circle for almost eight weeks. It has to be said that in the opinions of both Val and Stephen he has come on leaps and bounds, and on a personal note I find it most refreshing that a centre of learning such as The Freeston Business and Enterprise College has the wisdom and open mindedness to include clairvoyance and spiritual development on its curriculum. This certainly would not have happened only a few short years ago and it must be taken as an encouraging sign of enlightenment in these tense and troubled times.

Steve and I were kicking a few thoughts around the other week and Robbie cropped up in our conversation. I tentatively suggested that it might be a worthwhile exercise to conduct an interview with Robbie (a) to get a 12 year old boy's slant on the subject of spiritualism – bearing in mind that although there are many many development circles up and running at any given time in the UK not many of them will have a 12 year old sitting in circle – and (b) to try and get some idea of how a 12 year old handles the concepts of clairvoyance and life after death.

I actually thought that Stephen, who jealously guards his family life to a point of paranoia, would veto the idea, but instead he was all for it and, more importantly, so was Robbie. Thus, on the 7th of July I drove over to Ossett and while Stephen was demonstrating to a full house in the Town Hall, Robbie and I, accompanied by Val Atkins, sat in one of the small committee rooms and with my tape recorder running I started the interview by asking him what he wanted to do when he left school? Would he, for example, like to do what his father did for a living, or did he have other ambitions?

Robbie: "Well, actually, what I really fancy doing is being a fireman but if it got to the point where I thought spirit wanted me to concentrate on being a medium, then I'd give up being a fireman and I'd do what my Dad does full time. But I'm not in any great hurry and I know I've got lots to learn yet which is why, for now, I'm really happy to sit in Val's development circle."

I asked him if he thought he was special in any way and he answered – "No, not really James, I'm just me, and all I really want to do is to help people. If I can help them by being a fireman then I'd be happy with that or if I can help them by giving them a message from the spirit world, then that would make me very happy too."

I wondered if he might be phased out or be a bit worried by standing up in front of three hundred people?

Robbie:- "No not really, I mean maybe I'd be a bit nervous at first but I'd do what my Dad did and start by doing demonstrations for small groups, say twenty or thirty people, and work up from there and maybe I'll be doing a lot of stuff in the spiritualist churches – yes, I know I'll be doing that – but at the end of the day, whether there's thirty people or three hundred people, everyone is looking for some help and I'm looking to help them, so I'm pretty sure everything would be all right, wouldn't it?"

Stephen hates doing one-to-one readings and goes to the most extraordinary lengths to avoid doing them, and I wondered how Robbie felt about doing personal readings.

Robbie:- "I'd rather do groups, but if someone needed some help then I wouldn't turn them away. If someone was desperate to hear from someone that they'd lost, then I couldn't just turn them away, could I? Well, I wouldn't turn them away. I wouldn't be able to. Well, I suppose that I *could*, but I'd feel awful about it, so I wouldn't do that."

What about money? Would he charge for such a service? To give Robbie credit where credit was due, he was appalled by this thought. "Oh no, I couldn't charge for giving somebody a message!"

What if he was hungry and had no money to pay the bills or buy food? "Well in those circumstances I suppose I would have to charge something but I wouldn't like having to do it. I mean my Dad charges for his tickets at the demonstrations but then he's got to because it's his job, but having said that if there's someone who really needs a message but they haven't got any money to pay for a ticket, he always lets them in for free and I know I'd do the same as that."

I asked him if he was in any way frightened by being in contact with the spirit world, pointing out that to a lot of other people talking to the dead could be seen as more than just a little bit spooky and scary.

Robbie:- "No I'm not scared! How can you be scared about talking to people that love you? I mean, if I saw a ghost or something like that then I might be scared, but talking to the spirit people isn't at all scary because it's not the same."

There was a whole line of questioning here that I could have followed, but I chose not to go that route for this was a subject that Stephen and I had already discussed at some length and any opinion that Robbie might have expressed on the subject was very likely to have been influenced by what his father had said or written. Instead, I changed the subject slightly and drew

228

Robbie's attention to the fact that since he'd been sitting in development circle with Val and since he'd been going to more and more of his father's demonstrations, he had increasingly picked up more and more information, so much so that at the end of the evening Stephen had got into the habit of relaying Robbie's information to the audience to see if it connected with anyone. Quite recently Stephen had asked, on Robbie's behalf, if someone over to the left of the auditorium had lost their father in the month of March and if September was in any way significant.

A gentleman had put his hand up to confirm that yes, he had lost his father in the month of March and that yes, it was his father's birthday in September. Not bad for a 12 year old in training and I know lots of experienced mediums who'd feel quite pleased at being able to pull in this amount of information.

You could ask any audience 'has someone lost their father recently' and by the law of averages, you'd be pretty sure of getting an affirmative answer from somewhere in the crowd, but to specify a month (March) gives a layer of credence to the proceedings because it narrows the odds down quite dramatically, and then to follow it up with a September connection (that also proves to be relevant in the form of it being a birthday month) reduces the odds of being right down to a very tight margin indeed.

I asked Robbie how he felt when he was getting a message, and how did the message come through to him. Did he, like his father, hear voices or did he, like some other mediums, get his information through seeing pictures?

Robbie: "Mainly it's a voice that I hear in my ear, as though someone is standing next to me, but sometimes the voice can be very muffled and they have to say what they're saying over and over again until I can hear it clearly. Sometimes, maybe ten percent of the time, I get pictures and when that happens it's like watching a video, but not like *watching* it, exactly, more like being in it and part of it although I know that nobody can see me because I'm at the back of what's happening, like watching a TV but from inside the TV. It's a bit weird really..."

Not weird to me, I have to say, for Robbie's words clearly indicate the developing gifts of clair*voyance* and clair*audience*. A potent double whammy combination of potential that could, a few years from now, provide us with a medium even more powerful than Stephen!

*(When I shared this thought with Steve he was quite pleased and has already started planning for his early retirement!)*

A little while previously Stephen had told me that Robbie had picked up a very detailed message involving a car accident and a young girl called Amy, and that he had "seen" this in his video footage mode. When I asked Robbie to tell me about Amy and the car accident he looked at me blankly for a minute, and then the penny dropped and realization dawned.

Robbie: "It wasn't Amy, it was *Chloe!*" He tut tutted dismissively. "Flaming Heck, my Dad can't get anything right, can he? I kept telling him that the girl's name was Chloe and he will insist on calling her Amy... No, right, well anyway, yes, my Dad was giving out this message about someone who had been killed in a car crash and while he was doing it, it was like I was sitting in the back of the car watching everything that was going on and it was a silver car and I told my Dad this. Then we came to this crossroads and this *other* car came out of nowhere and crashed into the side of us at full speed, and I went with Chloe while they took her to the hospital but she fell asleep before she got there and never woke up… Honest James, I saw it all so clearly just like I was really there, and I *told* my Dad to tell the lady in the audience that Chloe had just fallen asleep without feeling anything but by the time we got to the end of the demonstration he must have forgotten about it because he never mentioned it. I mean he's my Dad and I love him but he does forget a lot of things…"

I put it to him that he seemed like a very confident young person… "Yes, I suppose you could say that, but only in some ways. I mean I'm confident about what I do at home and I'm confident about my work with spirits, er… I'm not always so confident at school though."

My next question was about how he felt after sitting in a development circle… Was it tiring, exciting, or what? "Actually James, it's all just very relaxing and I always come away from Val's classes feeling better than I felt when I went in."

I wondered if he thought his mediumistic abilities had got any stronger since he'd started attending Val's classes. "Yes James, definitely yes!"

Finally, I asked him, as best he could, to tell me what his long term ambitions were. "Well, I know I've got some time to go, but I want to finish school and become a fireman and while I'm doing that I want to develop my gift and work in the spiritualist churches and then maybe a bit later on, when I'm ready, I want to be able to do what my Dad does. But that's only if spirit wants me to do it, and I suppose the other big thing is that whatever I do, I want to make my Mum and Dad feel proud of me."

After I'd finished interviewing Robbie I went and sat on the steps outside the main entrance while Robbie sneaked up onto the balcony to watch his Dad do his stuff. Like most council buildings these days, Ossett Town Hall is a no smoking zone, and after nearly forty five minutes of conversation I was ready for a hit of the weed. I filled my pipe – a long Sherlock Holmes church warden – and took great delight in puffing out plumes of blue smoke into the balmy evening air. In my poor opinion the English atmosphere is already poisoned and polluted and I didn't think that my small contribution was going to make much difference one way or the other. I took out my pen and notepad and began writing up the notes from my conversation with Stephen's son, revelling in the warmth of the beautiful summer evening and the aromatic buzz I was getting from Holland's finest Amphora.

Frankly I was in no rush to drive home. I'd already checked the Radio Times and if you weren't into sports, soaps or so called reality TV there was absolutely nothing worth watching on the box, so I knew I'd either end up doing household chores or sitting in front of the computer. Worse, I might even end up arguing with my wife on the relevant worth of TV licences. Much better to sit on those nice warm steps, smoke a marvellous pipe and think a few positive thoughts about Robbie Holbrook.

In my opinion the boy was clearly psychic and a natural born medium and, as Stephen was later to remind me, there were too many occasions where Robbie had already given clear indications of his developing gifts and abilities....

When he was only four years old he had an imaginary friend. Let's face it, many kids do, but the unusual thing about Robbie's friend was that he only ever came out to play with him while he was in the pre-school kindergarten. The superviser, a lovely lady called Angela, brought this to Stephen's attention, but as I've said, many kids have these little friends and Stephen didn't pay it very much heed. However, over the weeks, Robbie's behaviour became increasingly odd. Rather than playing with the other children he only ever played with his imaginary friend and could frequently be heard in deep and animated conversation with his playmate, who was, he said, a nice little boy called Archie.

This was where Steve sat up and took a bit of notice. The coincidence concerning Robbie's invisible friend called Archie and Stephen's principle guide who also happened to be called Archie was not lost on him, and he questioned his son very carefully about his new found friend.

Remembering that Robbie was only just four years old, he answered his father's questions as best he could... There was this little boy, very thin and with fair hair, always wearing short grey trousers and a grey shirt, who came to play with him whenever he was with Angela's play group. Because Robbie's behaviour was unsettling some of the other children in the group Stephen suggested that if Archie did come to play, it might be a good idea to play quietly and not to let the other children know that Archie was around.

With some sort of equilibrium set in place Stephen was happy to let things ride for the time being, but then a few weeks later something occurred that put this business of an invisible friend in a whole new light.

With the lengthening days of the late spring, Angela took her young charges on a nature trail walk around the grounds of the old manor house in which the kindergarten was situated. They counted butterflies, identified wild flowers, and the children had a thoroughly marvellous time scampering up and down the long paths that led through the mature gardens and copses of old trees.

Angela had strolled through the gardens a few times on her own but she had never explored them thoroughly, and thus she was as surprised as the children when they turned into one shady corner of the garden to find three small gravestones set against an ivy strewn wall. Bending down to read the epitaphs she saw that they were the graves of three children, one called David, one called Hannah – and one called Archie! For a few seconds her blood ran cold because as far as she was concerned she had found the resting place of Robbie's invisible friend.

On another occasion a couple of years later when Robbie was six, the Holbrook family was driving to spend a week's holiday at a friend's caravan in Hunstanton. What with Steve and Caroline (who was nursing the new baby Ellie) and the two boys Robbie and Bradley in the back, it was quite a car full. The day was hot, the traffic was heavy, baby Ellie was crying and Stephen, who had been driving nonstop for two hours minus any air conditioning in the old Montego, was feeling quite frazzled. It was already nearly half past ten and there were at least another fifty miles to do before they would reach their destination. Another fifty miles meant at least another hour of doing battle with East Anglia's less than perfect road system.

All of a sudden, from the back seat, Robbie piped up. 'Dad, can I ask you something?'

'Yes love, what is it?'

'What would happen if a helicopter crashed into the sea and eleven people were killed?'

'Oh Robbie, what are you asking a question like that for?' Stephen was tired and distracted. 'I mean, why are you asking me that kind of question?'

'Well, what would happen?' Robbie insisted on knowing.

'Robbie, how should I know?'

'I just thought…'

'Can't you play with Bradley or do a game or something?' Stephen swerved to miss a tractor that had suddenly pulled out of a side road without so much as a by your leave or any kind of warning.

There was a moody silence from the back of the car but it only lasted for ten seconds. 'I mean, Dad, if a helicopter crashed into the sea and eleven people were on board, do you think that there'd be rescue boats and ambulances and maybe some fire engines and stuff like that?'

Forced by his son's insistence, Stephen had to think for a minute with that part of his brain that wasn't working overtime to keep the car on the road while his eyes were trying to fall shut. The previous evening had been a late night and he'd only had about three and a half hours' sleep. He was now paying the price for his workaholism.

'Er, yes Robbie, I suppose there'd be rescue boats and ambulances. There might be fire engines too and there might even be other helicopters up in the air looking for survivors…'

'Right. Thanks, Dad.' Robbie fell silent and no more was said about helicopters crashing into the sea. The subject seemed closed.

But some three hours later as they were settling into their caravan and Caroline was in the process of preparing some lunch while Stephen was playing outside on the grass with the children, a news flash on the radio caught her attention, and she immediately yelled out to her husband...

'Steve, be *quick*, come and listen to this *now!*'

Stephen responded immediately to Caroline's note of urgency and together they listened in silence as the newsreader reported that a Chinook helicopter had just crashed in the North Sea a few miles off Cromer and that eleven people were believed to have lost their lives. The Cromer lifeboat had been dispatched to the scene, along with Coast Guard and air sea rescue units. Ambulances were standing by at Cromer harbour, but there were not expected to be any survivors.

Steve and Caroline stood and looked at each other blankly. This was the two o'clock news bulletin. The Chinook was reported to have gone down a few minutes after one... And yet Robbie had been asking his questions from the back of the car two and a half hours earlier, at half past ten.

As Stephen said then and still says to this day, explanations please on a post card, c/o the publishers!

# Chapter Nineteen:       *Alvis Ormady*

I relit my pipe and was just thinking it was about time I made a move, when someone came and sat down on the step next to me.

'Ah, a fellow pipe smoker! D'you happen to have a light, my friend? Bloody English matches! Bloody useless these days!'

It was a very soft Irish brogue – not the guttural Northern whine of Belfast but the gentler lilt of Galway or County Cork. He was about my size (short fat and round) and maybe a little older, say early mid sixties. He reminded me of myself insofar as he had a beard and moustache (and although mine was grey his was Santa Claus white) and he wore a bright green shirt hanging loose over blue denim jeans that were tucked into calf length boots made of soft tan leather. Like me, he also wore glasses, but while my frames were Specsavers silver, his were bright red polycarbonate, straight out of Dame Edna Everidge's dressing room

Without thinking I handed over my Zippo.

'Thank you, m'dear!' he spun the wheel and got his bowl glowing. 'And...' puff puff... 'Bloody Zippos aren't what...' puff puff... 'they used to be. Once upon a time they'd...' puff puff ... 'light every time, but...' puff puff ... 'not so these days!'

'They've still got a lifetime guarantee,' I said lamely, doing my best to defend the smoker's prime and iconic artefect.

'Yes they have at that, and I've bought m'self a bell, you know! I light my pipe and see the disapproving faces of my friends then I ring the effing bell as loud as I can and start shouting *'Unclean! Unclean!'* at the top of my voice. It pisses m'wife off something rotten,' he smiled mischievously and I could see he was missing a couple of teeth, 'but it makes me feel one helluva sight better.'

He zapped the Zippo again making sure he had a free and even second burn (yes, these are pipe smoker's terms and you're not supposed to know what they mean) and then passed the lighter back to me.

'You're Jim Christie, aren't you? Never met you before, but sort of recognise you from your man Holbrook's demonstrations and I recognise you from your picture in one of the books.'

Part of me winced. I hate being called Jim or Jimmy and anyone who knows my history will recall that there's a damn good reason for it. On the other hand I've got an ego that enjoys being stroked now and again.

'Yes,' I admitted. 'Guilty as charged. I'm James Christie.'

'Ah well now, I'm Alvis Ormady and for what it's worth, I'm very pleased to meet you, Mr James Christie.'

He shoved out his hand – gnarled and with old scab wounds from eczema – and for the sake of good form I had little choice other than to take it in my own hand and respond to the cursory shake with a shake of my own. There was none of this hand gripping macho pumping routine, but (sorry Alvis!) I have to say I didn't particularly like this physical contact; my psychic hackles were in defensive mode and (old habits dying hard) I found myself thinking of flaming pentagrams and six rayed stars. There was something slightly odd about this Mr Ormady and I remembered that first shot in the Forest Gump movie where Tom Hanks is sitting by the bus stop. He's wearing a shirt buttoned right up to the top but he isn't wearing a tie and you immediately

238

twig that there's something that isn't quite right with this character.

'Er, aren't you going in for the demonstration?' I asked, jerking my thumb in the general direction of the entrance behind us. 'Stephen's only just started so you won't have missed much.'

'Nah,' he shook his head. 'Tonight I've brought someone along who needs a message much more than I do so I'm quite happy to sit out here and let your man get on with it. He's pretty damn good, y'know.'

'Yes, I know he is,' I retorted rather smugly, preening myself (not nice) and bathing in Stephen's reflected glory. God, I can be overbearingly pompous at times... 'I gather you're familiar with Stephen's work?'

He laughed. 'Ah for Heaven's sake you're talking about the man as though he's an actor or an artist or something and to use his own words, he's only a bloody medium, but yes, I'm "familiar with his work" as you put it. I've seen him demonstrate four times and I've had a message on every occasion – now I bet that's a bit of a record? – so tonight I'm quite content to stay out of the way and have a chat with you while my lady in there gets her message!'

'There's no guarantee...' I began.

'No, of course there's no guarantee but I'm betting you a bottle of Jamiesons or whatever you drink that my lady *will* get a message from your man tonight and, for God's sake, on the subject of drink, is there anywhere in this damn town where we can get a drink, preferably a room temperature Guinness but at a pinch I'll settle for a pint of something sensible that comes out of a wooden cask rather than a tin barrel?'

Now, I have to admit that there was part of me that wanted to bring this conversation to a close. At that

239

time I didn't know Alvis quite as well as I do now, and I freely admit that I did not feel too comfortable in his company. He had neither said nor done anything to offend but his manner was excessively familiar and he had that Irish cockiness which some folk find endearing but which I find quite irritating.

On the other hand my own limited psychic faculties suggested that this meeting might not be quite so accidental as it appeared and my journalist's nose was twitching with the possibility of a story. I was mindful of what he had said – four messages from four different demonstrations – and I know people who follow Stephen around the country who never get a message from one year to the next. So maybe this Mr Alvis Ormady was worth half an hour of my time after all.

As for finding a drink, I knew Ossett no better than he did, so we ended up going down the steps into the small cellar bar that is attached to the Town Hall. It's one of those modern disco bars with dischordant music and flashing lights, with a clientele of girls in nightdresses and boys with holes in their jeans; both sexes wear their tattoos with pride and each sex looks at the other with vapid expressions of predatory disdain. This early in the evening we more or less had the place to ourselves, and compared to what would be blasting out of those disco speakers an hour or so later, Robbie Williams and Madonna were relatively easy listening.

There was no draft ale and the Guinness was ice cold out of the pump so he had a large whisky and I had a gin and tonic. We took our drinks over to a (relatively) quiet corner and watched the half naked girls wind the bovine boys around their little fingers.

'My Christ,' Alvis commented, the Christ coming out as Chroyst, 'back in Ireland those girlies would be locked up by the Garda on charges of indecent exposure. What in God's name are the parents doing, letting their children out onto the streets lookin' like that?'

I shrugged. 'It's summer and as far as they're concerned, they're probably the height of fashion, and as for the parents, well probably...'

I let it hang... I know bugger all about parenting and I know even less about high fashion in the North of England circa 2006. What I did know, however, was that I hadn't come into this bar to talk conversational pleasantries.

'Anyway...' I toked at the churchwarden, now filled with Alvis Ormady's Mick McQuade while his was filled with my Amphora – which is another pipe smoker's ritual, you smoke mine and I'll smoke yours – 'have you got a story for me?'

'A story?'

'You've had four messages at four of Stephen's demos and there's got to be a story there somewhere?'

'Oh yes, I see what you mean! Well, yes, I suppose when you put it like that I do have a story for you, though I'll bet you a crate of Ireland's finest you'll never be able to publish it.'

He sipped at the whisky, lit his pipe and he started talking. An hour later, I was still listening and he was right – half of his story is completely unpublishable, another thirty percent is irrelevant, but the other twenty percent, the bits about the messages he's had from Stephen, are very relevant indeed. In truth, Alvis Ormady's tale is worthy of a book in its own right, as it is I have to compress the essence of it into just a few pages.

Alvis Ormady was born in a small village on the banks of The River Shannon in Western Ireland in 1936. The seventh son of a seventh son, he was gifted with a feyness and a degree of second sight that soon separated him from the crowd and gave him an extremely lonely and isolated childhood. Much against his own will and inclination he was ordained into the Catholic priesthood but within only a few short years was willingly tempted by sex and alcohol, and quit the priesthood in favour of more libertine and artistic pursuits in Dublin.

In 1966 he met and married Mary Caitlin O'Hara, three years his senior who already had some small fame as a minor poet and folk musician. She did much to promote Alvis's painting, but by 1968 he was earning more as a folk musician following his wife around some of the traditional Irish folk circuits that were ubiquitous in their day. They did not earn a fortune, but they did earn enough to live on, and for a time they were extremely happy.

In 1971 Mary became pregnant and gave birth to a daughter whom they called Florence after Mary's mother. Unfortunately fatherhood did not sit naturally on Alvis's shoulders, and in 1973 Mary divorced him on grounds of adultery.

Three weeks after the divorce both Mary and Florence were killed in the infamous air crash on the island of Tenerife when a whole plane load of tourists crashed into the side of Mount Teide killing all on board. In Alvis's own words, this was the beginning of a monumental guilt trip that still gives him problems to this very day.

At the time, however, rather than sobering him up, it opened the door to greater depths of hedonism and under the banner of Irish folk poet and philosopher he travelled the world throughout the better part of the 1970's drinking and whoring wherever he went. He was in San Francisco in the summer of 1979 when three things occurred in the space of a month that brought him up against a brick wall with a life changing jolt. One, back in Ireland his mother died quietly in her sleep. Two, he was diagnosed with testicular cancer. Three, he fell in love, and the way he tells it – *"My God, here I was, forty three years old with hundreds of notches on my gun and for the very first time ever, I'd actually fallen in love. My God, man, I didn't know what to do with myself. I was in emotional agony and I just wanted to die..."*

His wish may well have been answered insofar as the testicular cancer was quite advanced – and was complicated by a mutated strain of venereal disease. And while Alvis arguably should have been burying his mother and could have been courting his new love interest, he was flat on his back in a hospital ward having one testical removed and being pumped so full of drugs he didn't know whether it was Monday or Tuesday or June or July.

Alvis beat the cancer and walked away in remission on his 44th birthday. It is not right to say he walked away a new man, but he did walk away a different man, determined to clean up his life and tidy up his act.

He quietly began to court his new lady and within six months Sandra Kassman had become Sandra Ormady. They went to Ireland for their honeymoon and although Alvis was able to pay his last respects at his mother's grave, the greeting he and his bride received from the rest of his family was cool bordering on hostile and, indeed, his father Joe Ormady, ninety year old patriarch of the family, flatly refused to see him or make him welcome in the family home.

With a heavy heart – and a curious wife – Alvis left Shannon and they spent a desultory fortnight driving around Ireland... In the rain. Seeing the sights. And Alvis got depressed and started drinking and the honeymoon descended into one very sorry affair indeed.

It transpired that Alvis had been less than honest with his new bride and when, through the whisky fumes and Irish angst, some of the truth about his earlier lifestyle came out, Sandra Ormady nee Kassman began to realise she'd made one bloody great mistake and within three weeks of being back in the United States she'd walked out on Alvis, hellbent on getting her own name back.

Which she did quite successfully along with more that sixty percent of Alvis's worldly goods – and by then, he did have quite a few worldly goods. The only problem was that from Alvis's point of view, while Sandra was welcome to her own name she was *not* entitled to sixty percent of his worldly goods. In fact, when he thought about it over several bottles of something strong and malty, she wasn't entitled to any damn thing at all, least of all the twelve new paintings that were drying in his studio – and by then, Alvis's paintings were selling for well in the region of three or four thousand dollars a throw.

Cutting a long story short, Alvis was caught by his recently decreed ex-wife and her new boyfriend, whilst in the act of breaking into his own home, to nick his own artwork. There was a fight, and in the process of the fight Alvis managed to (accidentally) break Sandra's nose and (very intentionally) crack the new boyfriend's skull with the heavy gilt frame that surrounded one of his favourite portraits. Which put him in a coma for two months. And then the boyfriend died. And Alvis went to prison for six years for manslaughter.

Alvis was released three and a half years later. It was 1984 and he was 49 years old. He had an American passport and an Irish passport, around $140 in loose change and an awful lot more knowledge than he'd had three and a half years earlier. *"Not much to do in prison, Mr Christie, other than read books and to be ever mindful of your arse. I minded my arse and I read an awful lot of books."* Feeling that he had outlived his welcome in the USA and remembering his last experience in Ireland, he made his way to Spain (and how he got there, ladies and gentlemen, would take up another forty pages). Applying some of his literary knowledge gleaned in Orange County's Facility of Detentions, he managed to take the Casino in Marbella for the equivalent of £28K in two long and carefully prepared nights at the roulette wheel. Then, a week later, another night in Gibraltar's Casino gained him a staggering £42K. *"Nothing illegal, I promise you, but once you know how the system works, then you can work out a way of beating the system."*

In 1984 the property market was already booming in Spain, but there were still many bargains to be had, especially if the careful investor looked a few kilometres inland away from the much more expensive costas. With his Casino winnings Alvis bought two houses, one for £6000 and one for £15000. He sold them both in 1994, the six grand house going for £60K and the fifteen thousand pound house going for £210K. He had lived well for ten years, had got a sun tan, a third

245

wife, a beautiful Spanish girl half his age called Juanita, and he'd read a lot more books!

On the strength of his reading he moved to the UK in 1995 and bought a small cottage just outside Glastonbury with a picture postcard view of The Tor and St Michael's Tower. Immersing himself in the Glastonbury scene of New Age contradiction and confusion and searching for that inner something that might bring a modicum of peace and calm to his troubled spirit (not to mention his somewhat turbulent and troubled life), he found very few answers but the answers he *did* find edged him further away from the commercialism of New Age philosophy and pushed him along a more meaningful spiritual pathway of self examination and personal awareness. It would be wrong to say he had rediscovered religion after half a lifetime of absenteeism – but he certainly had made contact with spirit, even if, at this time, it was only his own inner spirit.

Unable to cope with the awful English weather, Juanita went back to Andalucia in 1998 and, once again, Alvis was on his own. *"Didn't phase me too much by then, because once you get to a certain age after living a certain kind of life, you learn how to be on your own. Thank God we're still great friends and we talk on the phone every week and she sells a lot of my stuff from her gallery in Marbella and although I knew from the beginning I could have gone back with her, my gut was saying that I should let her go – set her free – and that my place was here in Glastonbury beneath that magnificent old Tor. And besides, what does a modern young woman with beauty and brains want with a battered old fart like me? As long as I've got my booze, my brushes, my poetry and my freedom, then that's all I*

246

*need. But for a lot of other people, Juanita among 'em, that's no longer enough in this crazy day and age."*

It was around this time that Alvis first attended a spiritualist church.

He went for the social contact as much as anything else, but, as he admitted slyly, he was rather taken by a certain lady who had turned down his dinner invitation because it was one of her church evenings. Once he had been reassured that this was the spiritualist church and not the Catholic or C of E variety, he was happy to keep her company.

I do not know which service he went to or which medium he saw, but the evening impressed him sufficiently to start him on a new quest of reading and research, and for the following year he travelled all over the Southwest taking part in church services and attending demonstrations of clairvoyance wherever he could find them.

In the spring of 2001 he and his new girlfriend went to Paignton in Devon for "a dirty week among the rock pools" and there Alvis came across Stephen Holbrook for the first time and also received his first message via a medium from the world of spirit.

Alvis: 'We were about half way through the evening and this guy was blowing my mind away, I mean his messages were so damn fast and so bloody accurate, and I'd simply never seen anyone work like him before. After some of the doddering old dears I'd seen around the churches, yer man Holbrook was like a breath of fresh air and then, damn me, he was asking if there was anyone over on my side of the hall who had Irish links and who could connect with a big letter A. Well now I'm telling you, as quick as a flash I put my hand up, and then he was telling me that I'd lost my mother a few years ago, that her name was Bridget, that she'd died of pneumonia, that she'd been buried beneath a cherry tree, and that I'd been miles away at the time and hadn't been able to attend the funeral, for which I'd always felt eternally guilty, and that it had not gone down too well at all with the rest of the family. He told me not to worry, because it wasn't much of a funeral and I didn't miss anything special, but she'd been watching me when I'd visited the grave later on with the pretty American lady. Said that it was a shame about the American lady's nose and, of course, although yer man couldn't have had a clue what he was talking about, I knew all right, because that was the nose I'd broken less than six months after having visited my mother's grave. Totally amazing…

And then, if that wasn't enough, he told me he had a message for me from someone called Harry, and that Harry had drowned in a river when he was still a young boy. He told me that Harry was fine but he was sorry he hadn't be able to pay me for the bet…

And again, yer man Mr Holbrook couldn't have known what the hell he was talking about, but the truth of the matter is that when I was about six or seven years old I used to play with one of the village lads, my best mate actually, and he was called Harry. One day we were larking around down on the banks of The Shannon and he bet me sixpence that he could swim out to yonder rock and back under water. I thought he was bloody mad so I bet him a shilling – and all right, it was a shilling that I didn't have – that he damn well couldn't! The river isn't too good on that stretch and I really didn't want him to do it. My old sixth sense was working over time and what I should have done was hit him with a brick or tie his hands to a tree or something, but he was bigger than me and a lot braver and the silly sod did it anyway. In he went and down he went, and the poor silly bugger never came up again and they found his body two days later half a mile down the estuary... Now that was something that happened sixty three years ago, and I'm ashamed to admit it but I'd almost forgotten about it myself until yer man brought it up...

Anyway, I was impressed, so six months later I went to see him in Bristol and damn me if I didn't get another message. To be sure, it was short, but there was no harm in it for that and it did me a lot of good...

Holbrook was looking over at my side of the room and wanting to know if anyone could make anything of the 4$^{th}$ of August... Nobody could, and then it struck me that it was my birthday, so up went my hand and I told him that 4$^{th}$ of August was my birthday and he said 'Happy Birthday' and everyone laughed. Then he said the date was special for some other reason and then I realised that I'd started my prison sentence in The States on the 4$^{th}$ of August, but I wasn't going to admit that to a room full of strangers, so I just said that yes, it was significant. He then asked who Joe was and I told him that was my father's name. Stephen told me that Joe had passed over near to Christmas with cancer and he was saying sorry for not being as understanding as he could have been, but there were a lot of things he hadn't known about which if he had known about would certainly have made a difference. He said that Joe knew I'd been worrying about some sort of cancerous condition but that everything was absolutely okay and although I needed some medication, whatever was worrying me wasn't cancer.

Well, once you've had cancer you *always* worry about it coming back and around about then I'd been getting some nasty aches in my groin and I'd been putting two and two together and getting five. So, on the strength of what my father said through Stephen, I went and saw my doctor and within half a dozen weeks I was as right as rain.

Third time I saw Stephen was in Liverpool, somewhere around 2003. In between times I'd seen all the other mediums who were doing the rounds, had never had a message from any of them and, without wanting to do anybody down, Stephen's the best of the lot and I'm not just saying that because I have had messages from him. It's his overall style and the speed of the messages and the rightness of the connections that makes it so bloody good.

Anyway, as I was saying, I went up to Liverpool and this time Stephen was trying to make a link with a big letter O and someone who could connect with the date of February 14th that was nothing at all to do with St Valentines day. Also, that 2pm in the afternoon was significant in some way. Well up went my hand again because O is for Ormady, and I walked out of prison a free man at 2pm on February the 14th, so you could certainly say that was a significant date all right. Anyway, Stephen said he was sending love and best wishes from someone called Frank and did I know anybody called Frank? Well I certainly did know Frank, he's my brother for God's sake, but as far as I was concerned, I couldn't very well be getting a message from that Frank because he was still alive and well back in Galway. I sure as hell couldn't think of anyone else called Frank... But then Stephen gave me the willies because he told me that Frank was with Black Bob, and did Black Bob mean anything?

Well, I suppose you could say that it meant everything because Black Bob was an old sheepdog, a family pet, and Frank and I would argue like hell when we were kids as to who was going to take him for the evening walk… It was a short message and because I couldn't take it fully, Stephen went on to some one else fairly quickly, but when I got home that night I made a few phone calls back to Ireland and learned that my brother Frank had been killed in a head on collision the previous week and that the funeral had taken place only that very same morning.'

He shook his head from side to side, finished the whisky and looked a little bewildered. 'For Christ's sake, my brother's dead, only freshly put in his grave, and because I'm the black sheep of the family no one's even bothered to let me know, and God knows when I *would* have found out, if ever, without the bloody message from yer man in Liverpool.'

'What about the fourth message?' I asked quietly.

'Now that would have been earlier this year in Leicester… Y'want to know about that, do you?'

'Yes, please.'

'Right, well I was on my own, doing some work for the de Montfort University and I suddenly opened the bloody newspaper and there was yer man's face smiling up at me out of the "what's on" column. So down I trot, talk to your lovely lady on the door, get my ticket and go and sit very quietly at the back. There's no way, or so I think, that I'm going to get another message, but that's not why I went. This time I just wanted to watch the crowd, get their reactions to what was going on and see if there was anything I could pick up myself about how Stephen does what he does.

'Then, damn me, would you believe it, I get the first message of the night. Stephen says he wants to talk to a gentleman somewhere towards the back of the room who's badly fallen out with his family and that an August birthday should be relevant. So up goes my hand yet again, and then he's telling me that although things have never been right between me and my family and that they never will be right, something is going to change soon that's going to bring us all a lot closer. He tells me that although my father and mother are in the spirit world, I've still got brothers and sisters and nieces and nephews who in some way are going to need my help. He wants to know who Brenda is and I tell him I've got a sister called Brenda and he emphasises that she's still down here on the earthplane and I tell him yes, that's true. Then he tells me that Brenda has recently lost her husband – which was something that I didn't know – and that his name is Keith and that he wants me to get in touch with Brenda to tell her that he's okay and to thank her for putting the rose and the photograph in his coffin before they closed the lid.

Then he wants to know who Lynne or Linda is and I tell him that I don't know and he tells me that I'm going to meet someone by this name who is going to have a really big influence on me.

Then he wants to know if I've just bought a new car and I tell him yes, and he asks me if it's a blue car, and again I tell him yes and then he wants to know if it's only got two seats, and again I tell him yes. Then he wants to know if I've parked it somewhere safe, and I tell him I bloody well hope so, which gets a laugh from the audience but gets me worrying...

Then he really gets me by telling me he's got a lady with him who got killed in a plane crash and that she's got a little girl with her... Now, I tell you, I've learned a fair old bit about this spiritualism business, and I've been priviliged to already have had three messages from Stephen Holbrook, but when he went into this message it was somehow so unexpected and I had a small attack of the emotional wobbles for a minute... Anyway Stephen said this air accident would have happened quite a long time ago and that it would have happened a long way out of England and that a lot of people would have lost their lives at the same time... He said he had someone called Mary with him and could I understand that name? I told him that I could – and that everything else was right as well. He told me that Mary was saying that her daughter had grown up into being a beautiful young woman in the spirit world and although she had never known me properly when she was alive, she had been watching me through my life trying to help a bit here and there whenever she could and especially when it came to "the books" – if I knew what that meant, which obviously I did because although I'd never been a reader when I was a kid, I've read avidly as an adult...

Finally he said that Mary knew things had been a bit rough lately and that I'd been rather lonely ever since someone had moved out of my life a couple of years before, but she promised me that things would start getting better now and that it wasn't my fault she got on the damn plane. She said that I should carry on with my painting but she was sorry that I'd given up playing the guitar and the banjo... And then that was it, he was off somewhere else with a message for somebody else in the room and, to tell you the truth, I couldn't sit through the rest of the evening and I slipped out of the side door,

253

sat on the kerb by my car (that someone had keyscored from nose to tail) and for the first time in twenty odd years I had a really good cry.

And that, Jimbo, is the end of my story.'

The clientele had increased five fold and they were noisy with it. Also the music had moved into raucous heavy metal mode and I figured that it was time to leave. We moved out into the fresh evening air and sat ourselves down on the steps where this conversation had started an hour and a lifetime ago.

The summer sun was low in the sky casting a golden glow across the uncompromisingly northern townscape and although we could still hear the distant thump thump of mind fracturing music from the disco with the occasional reassuring bursts of laughter coming from Stephen's demonstration in the hall behind us, it was relatively peaceful.

'Got to be an epilogue,' I said thoughtfully.

'An epilogue?' he echoed.

'Yes – like, what happened with your sister Brenda?'

'Oh I wrote her a nice letter telling her what Stephen had passed on to me, and although she was grateful and amazed, because damn it she *had* put a rose and a photograph in the coffin before they closed the lid, she didn't really want to take the correspondence any further. It's the Irish Catholic thing...' he looked mournful. 'All my family think I've gone over to the other side and that I'm batting for The Devil's team... Although having said that, I did get a very nice letter from Brenda's grandaughter, if you like my great neice, saying that she was starting university in Bristol come the autumn and it would be nice if we could meet up for a cup of tea and forge some kind of family connection, so I suppose that's a start.'

'That'd be the Lynne or the Linda that Steve spoke about?'

'Good God no, that would be Charlotte! Lynne's in the hall getting her message.'

'You're pretty sure about that?'

'Ah, seventh son of a seventh son, and all that,' he teased. And then, much more seriously. 'Of course, I can't *guarantee* Lynne is going to get a message tonight. I mean, if I could, I'd be in there doing Holbrook's work for him instead of painting chocolate box covers for little old ladies and bloody great murals for northern town council offices, but let's just say I'll be very surprised if she doesn't get one.'

'Er, do you mind if I hang around, er, just to sort of find out?'

'My dear chap it's a free country – or so they say but I'm really not so sure any more – and you've been excellent company. It's been quite cathartic telling my story all at once, all in one go, so to speak and if you decide to use any of it in your next book do for God's sake spell my name right, will you? You'd be amazed at how many people get it wrong...' He spelt it out for me and I studiously wrote it down in my note book.

Five minutes later there was a big burst of applause from inside the hall, and a few seconds after that the entrance doors swung open and the crowds started to make their exit. Alvis and I stood to one side and after two or three minutes a quite startling young woman walked over towards us.

She must have been in her mid twenties. Had legs up to her arm pits, wore a very short mini skirt with very long black suede boots and had Gossard breasts which strained against a black bra that was barely concealed by a black lace blouse. She wore Goth make-up on a most beautifully chiselled face and she had bright shiny green hair slicked to her skull in a close cropped bob cut.

She spared me a passing glance, then reached over and kissed Alvis full on the mouth. 'You okay, hon?' she asked. 'Hope you've not been bored waiting for me?'

'Hell no,' he beamed at her genially, pride of possession writ large across his Father Christmas visage. 'I've been talking to yer man Jimmy Christie here, who's written the books you've been reading and by the sound of it, he's going to put me in his next one!'

'That's cool.' She turned her gaze on me. Big green eyes that matched the colour of her hair, quizzical, amused and filled with quiet challenge... Okay, said those eyes, he's old enough to be my grandfather, but we're together, we're an item. If you think that's odd or wrong in any way, it's your problem, so deal with it and don't even raise an eyebrow in my direction or I'll claw your heart out and eat you for breakfast.

'I hope you write nice things about my husband,' she said in a polite and neutral tone, but behind the civility there was another challenge that said if you can't write nice things about him then don't write anything at all, otherwise I'll see you in court and I'll sue your arse off.

'I'll try very hard to write nice things about Alvis' I promised her, which is why this chapter is a bit like The Bible insofar as there's a helluva sight more been left out of it than ever went into it.

'I was, er, just wondering what you thought of the evening and whether you happened to get a message or not?'

'Yes, it was really cool and of course I got a message...' she leaned over and kissed Alvis on the end of his Irish nose. Then she flashed me a dazzling smile. 'Alvis said that I would and he's always right about things like that.'

## Chapter Twenty:  *Stephen on Stage*

Stephen is standing in the middle of the stage in front of four hundred people.  To those four hundred people, he is standing solitary and alone, but from Stephen's point of view the stage is a very busy little corner of the world.  He can't see very much – there are blue and silver spotlights bathing the stage in a molten glow and two of the lights are badly angled denying him a clear view of the crowd of people out there in the auditorium – which is bad because he needs to see the audience to deliver the messages.

And he knows that there will be messages, because all around him there is a hive of spirit activity.  He sees nothing with his human eye, but he senses Archie May's presence behind him and in his psychic imagination conjures up a picture of the army sergeant marching up and down shepherding the waiting spirits into some kind of order.

He is also aware of little Christopher sitting over somewhere to his right and knows that one of the early messages, perhaps even the first message of the evening, will involve a child.  As if to confirm this theory, his nose starts itching, which is always a clear indication of spirit children waiting to come through.

Over to his left there is the dark shadowy energy of his other key guide, a large black guy called Warren, and Warren's presence indicates that there will probably be suicides trying to make the link between life and death and, if not suicides, then certainly someone who has passed over as the result of aggression and violence.

This is always a time of tension and on this occasion the atmosphere is particularly tense and electrifying.  There is a lot of disturbance in the ether and Stephen senses that Archie is having his work cut out keeping everything in order.

He is coming to the end of his five minute introductory speech, his left arm is now freezing cold and is locked in paralysis. He smells damp canvas and mud and feels Archie May moving closer. He hears no words in his ear but in his head he senses Archie's voice saying *"All right, Stephen..."*

And then there is an impression, vague and ill-defined, of a gentleman sitting in a wheelchair and pointing with a crooked finger to his heart. A voice, this time a voice that he can hear in his ear and not just in his head, but as though coming from a very long way away, and so far away that Stephen has to strain to hear what is being said – and the voice is saying *"April – died April – heartacker..."*

'I want to come to someone who lost someone to the spirit world in April, and this would have been a gentleman who spent some time in a wheelchair and passed over from some sort of heart condition or heart attack...'

Stephen is looking into the audience, wishing he could see the people out there a little more clearly, and he's almost certain that he wants to be talking to a lady somewhere over to the left of the theatre. It comes as no surprise to hear a female voice call out from the left of the aisles. 'Yes, over here. I lost my Dad in April...' Stephen detects a note of trepidation in the lady's voice and knows he needs to proceed carefully.

*"Freddy! Reddy! Eddy! Eff-Red Effred..."* This is the voice calling down a long corridor of space and time from the gentleman in the wheelchair.

'Who's Fred or Freddy?' Stephen asks the lady in the audience.

'That's my Dad's name!' The lady is astounded.

'Don't be surprised, love,' Stephen says gently. 'I'm supposed to get it right!'

Stephen's mental image of a man in a wheelchair gets stronger and now, although still not 100% coherent, the gentleman's voice is now louder – as though he's shouting at Stephen from across the stage.

*"Friday at twoshclock – Shhriday twopee-emtwo…"*

'He's telling me something about Friday and something that happened at two o'clock in the afternoon, now don't be nice to me, my love, but do you know what he's going on about…?'

There is a gasp from the lady. 'Oh God, he died at two o'clock on the Friday afternoon!'

*"Shtrook! Iyaddashtroke Shtroke andthen artacker."*

'He's telling me, my love, that although he passed over from a heart attack, before he had the heart attack, he also had a stroke….'

*"Wheelshare wheelshare!"*

'…and that it was the stroke that put him in the wheelchair and was responsible for his speech going all odd – he couldn't get his words out properly…'

'Yes, that's absolutely right! Oh my God!'

'No love, it's just Stephen Holbrook…' Stephen becomes aware of an intensifying energy lifted on the laughter of the audience. Now the wheelchair is much closer, but the gentleman is no longer sitting in it, but standing next to it. In his mind's eye, Stephen sees the gentleman called Freddy smiling into the audience in the direction of his daughter.

*"Fine now, no problems."* The words are clear and distinct without impediment or distortion.

'He's telling me that he's fine now and that he's out of the wheelchair and he's got his voice back…'

*"Love to Jamie and Diana…"*

'He's sending his love to James and Diana?'

'That my husband and daughter!'

*"Seen Sally – Sally still laughing!"*

'He's telling me that he's seen Sally and he wants you to know that she's still laughing…'

*"Love to Nora thanks for all the care and attention. Thanks for looking after me."*

'Who's Nora?'

'I'm Nora!'

'Well, your Dad is sending you all of his love and he wants to say a big thank you for all the care and attention you gave him and for looking after him the way do did! Do you understand?'

'Yes, yes I do….'

'And who is Sally? This would have been a lady with a great sense of humour who laughed a lot.'

'My best friend was called Sally and she died a year ago and you're right, she had a fabulous sense of humour. We were all always in stitches whenever she was around.'

Stephen senses that Christopher has moved positon from over on the right hand corner of the stage and from somewhere distant he can hear a girl crying and demanding to be able to talk to her Mummy…. It's all very distant but in a heartbeat the energies shift and as the gentleman called Freddy walks his wheelchair into the wings, Christopher's energy strengthens and Stephen imagines he hears a muffled *"Sorry"* from the world of spirit. Then something hard kicks him in the side of his leg and when he looks down he sees a pretty pair of blue shoes filled with white stockinged feet. Even as he looks, one of the shoes pivots round and kicks him in the leg again, and while he is only seeing

261

this as a psychic projection of thought, the impact of the sharp little foot is very real indeed.

*"I want to talk to my Mummy,"* a tearful and angry little voice is coming from the level of Stephen's belt buckle and is wailing up at him plaintively. *"Oh please, why won't you let me talk to my Mummy."*

'Of course we can talk to your Mummy,' Stephen thinkspeaks. 'But there are a lot of people here sweetheart, so can you tell me what she's called?'

*"She's called my MUMMY!"* the little girl sobs. *"I'm only six and I want to talk to my Mummy."*

'I've got a little girl here,' Stephen speaks to the audience, 'who would have passed over when she only six years old... and she's wearing a pair of bright blue shoes... Can anyone...'

'Me! Me! Over here! Over here!'

A lady five rows back on the right is waving her hand frantically in the air.

*"That's my Mummy,"* the little girl exclaims in delight as her sobbing suddenly begins to recede. *"Oh Mummy I love you, I love you..."*

'She's telling you that she loves you very much...'

*"Love Biffo too... Tell Mummy I've still got Biffo..."*

'She's telling me that she's still got Biffo and that she loves Biffo too...' Stephen hasn't got a clue what the hell he's talking about but he hopes that the little girl's mother might.. 'Do you know what she's going on about, my love?'

'Oh yes,' says the mother with tears streaming down her face. 'Biffo was her favourite cuddly toy, a big brown woolly bear, and we put him in the coffin with her before they closed the lid...'

*"Grampy Tom is looking after me now..."*

'Who's Tom?' Stephen asks.

'Oh God, that's my Father, Suzie's granddad...'

'Well she just wants you to know that she's with Granddad Tom and that he's looking after her...'

*"Tell Mummy I've got my goldilocks again..."*

Stephen gets a mental flash of Shirly Temple curly blond hair but behind the flash image of all the hair there is another darker image of a small child on a hospital bed with tubes and drips fitted to its arms and stomach. This child has no hair at all... Stephen's olfactory senses are suddenly overwhelmed by the smell of iodine and disinfectant.

'My love, she's showing me a hospital bed and there would have been lots of tubes and all the stuff you'd associate with a life support system...'

*"I'd got the lookeema."* Says the little girl called Suzie pontifically as though it was something to be very proud of. *"And Mummy said I had to be a brave little girl because not every little girl gets to have the lookeema!"*

'She's telling me.' Stephen says carefully, 'that she had leukaemia and that she lost all her hair, but that you're not to worry, because do you know what? She's got it all back and she's your little Goldilocks again. And she's telling me that you said she was a very brave little girl because not everyone gets leukaemia...'

'I always called her my Little Goldilocks...'

'And did she pass over with leukaemia?'

'Yes...'

Stephen senses a subtle change in the atmosphere. He looks down and can no longer see the white socks and little blue shoes. When she speaks, the little girl's voice is just a shade more distant than it was before, as though she's moved back, somewhere behind Stephen in the direction of the curtains.

*"Mummy must stop crying. I don't like it when Mummy cries because it makes me upset and she doesn't need to cry because I'm in my nice new home with Granddad Tom and Auntie Ellen...'*

'Who's Ellen or Helen?' Stephen needs to know.

'That's my sister Ellen. She died three years ago...'

'Well, Suzie says she's with Granddad Tom and Auntie Ellen and that they're looking after her in her nice new home and she's telling me that you've been doing a lot of crying, my love, but that you've got to stop crying now because she's absolutely fine...'

*"Chips!"* The little girl calls out from somewhere beyond the stage, *"Chips and red sauce was my favourite but Mummy's got to stop eating chips now... Chips, chips chips, oh and I did like beans... Beans and chips were my favourite..."*

'She's telling me about the beans and chips,' Stephen smiles kindly at the mother in the audience. 'She really liked her chips, especially with lots of red sauce, but she's telling me that this is more or less what you've been living on yourself lately, and that you've got to stop eating the chips now...'

*"Or I'll have a very fat Mummy!"* the little girl giggles.

'Or you'll soon get fat...' there is laughter from the audience but Stephen doesn't hear it as he's straining to catch what Suzie is telling him...

*"As fat as Uncle Danny Dan and he's very very fat... A very fat man."* The child's voice is now very distant – it's clear but as though coming from a very long way away – Stephen is aware of some major psychic disturbance coming from the opposite side of the stage and in his mind's eye he pictures Warren having an

264

argument with someone that Stephen can't see and whoever this person is, he's very angry and unhappy…

'Who's Dan or Danny?'

'That's my brother – Suzie's Uncle.'

'And is he, er, quite a large gentleman?'

'Totally enormous, like 20 stones!'

'Well Suzie's saying that if you keep trying to live on chips and red sauce you'll end up being just like her Uncle Dan…' There is more laughter, but again Stephen doesn't hear it. Someone – or something – has just hit him on the back of his head with something very hard and heavy.

For a moment he is dazed and the stage spins. Psychic, imaginary or otherwise, from Stephen's point of view the blow has been a hard physical blow. He's felt it. It has made him feel sick and dizzy. The lights spin and he has to sit down.

The audience? They see Stephen take a sip of water and lean on the edge of the table that is set in the middle of the stage.

In his nostrils there is the acrid smell of smoke… Smoke and something worse, the smell of burning flesh. In his psychic mind the whole of the left hand side of the stage is on fire, his spirit guide Warren is waving his arms – Stephen doesn't know whether it is some kind of warning or whether the guide is trying to fend something off from the other side. There is a sense of chaos and carnage, there are a number of different voices shouting all at once, and then Stephen hears a ringing bell and has a flash mental image of a fire engine. He opens his mouth to speak but…

*"Not yet, Stephen."* This is Archie May's quietly controlling voice. *"Not quite ready… Warren?"*

265

Stephen isn't sure whether Warren is talking to him or to Archie when he says – or seems to say – *"No, not yet... Ah yes, all right Andrew Firehead Andrew Firehead Andrew Firehead for Father Father Father..."*

Stephen now becomes aware of a tall young man in a shredded fireman's uniform. He is minus his helmet. He has fair hair which is matted with blood. This young man is extremely agitated and angry. Stephen senses that Warren has one arm around him – holding him back? – and that there are many other figures rushing around behind both Warren and his ward. The smell of smoke and the sound of roaring flames assails his senses, and although he is not aware that it is happening, his left arm is twisting into the most impossible of orthopaedic angles and he is holding on to the table with his right hand with such force that he is breaking three of his finger nails. He is choking on the smoke and can hardly breath. In another part of his body, something disengages and he has to clench the muscles of his sphincter to avoid the most extreme kind of public embarrassment.

He feels utterly dreadful and unaware that he is speaking out loud he says firmly and forcefully: 'Take this off me now!' And two breaths later – 'Take this off me NOW or I'm not doing it.'

Most of the audience are bemused, having no idea what he is talking about. Perhaps a small percentage want to accuse him of theatrics and showmanship. But there is no showmanship here. It's a genuine ultimatum and another two or three breaths later some of the symptoms Stephen is experiencing begin to subside.

'I want,' Stephen addresses the audience abruptly, 'to talk to a gentleman, I think somewhere near the back

266

of the room, who has lost a son in some kind of explosion or accident involving a fire, and I think...'

'Here,' a loud clear dignified male voice from the back of the room.

'Andrew?' Stephen asks quizzically. 'Do you know who Andy or Andrew is?'

'Andrew is my son,' comes the voice in response. 'Most of his young friends called him Andy.'

*"Tell him it was Halloween!"*

Stephen is unsure whether this is Andrew's voice or Warren's voice. Nevertheless, he asks 'Why is the 31st of October significant?'

'My son died on the night of October 31st,' comes the terse reply.

*"Fire man eighty three... Tell him fire man eighty three..."*

Stephen is now sure that this is Andrew speaking and not just Warren acting as intermediary.

'Sir, please don't be nice to me, just give me a yes or no – but can I ask – was your son a fireman?'

'Yes, he was.'

'And he died in a fire?'

'Yes, he did.'

'And why is the number eighty three significant? He's telling me eight and three. Eighty three?'

'His station number was eighty three.'

*"Say sorry but it wasn't my fault... Please tell him I didn't want to die."*

'He's telling you that he's sorry but it wasn't his fault and that he really didn't want to die and...'

And again something slams into the back of Stephen's head, taking his breath away and causing explosions of stars and sparks behind his eyes. The pain is excruciating, and his ethereal body is sent flying flat on its face…

The audience, however, simply see Stephen bow his head for a second and take a deep breath before saying in an intensely angry voice to some unseen person behind him and off to one side – 'I told you before, take it OFF me…'

And then, readdressing the elderly gentleman at the back of the room – 'Sir, he's telling me that he died instantly from a massive blow to the back of the head.'

'Yes, that's quite right.' The gentleman coughed. 'Bloody roof came down on top of him.'

A tremendous and overwhelming feeling of sadness descends upon Stephen's shoulders. There is a mental impression of universities and quiet quadrangles and students in gowns and mortar boards…

*"He wanted me to go to Oxford and study law but I failed all the exams and ended up in the fire service which was great because that was exactly the right place for me to be until…"*

'He's telling me that you wanted him to go to university and become a lawyer but that he wasn't happy there…'

*"Real disappointment to him, I suppose… Sorry about that…"*

'He's telling me that he's sorry he was such a disappointment to you…'

'It wasn't that he was a disappointment, but…'

Stephen is aware that Warren has released his grip on Andrew and that the spirit of the fireman has now moved much closer to the front of the stage and is looking directly over the heads of the crowd towards his father a hundred feet distant on the back row. Again, Stephen is not seeing this in human visionary terms but only in the form of a psychic projection. However, when Andrew speaks again it is from three feet short of Stephen's left ear.

*"Total bloody disappointment!"* Andrew laughs quietly and sadly. *"There were lots of arguments. Wouldn't have been so bad if it wasn't for Henry."*

'He's telling me that there were lots of arguments,' Stephen said, and then: 'Who's Henry?'

'Henry is my other son. Andrew's brother.' The bitterness in the elderly gentleman's voice is so profound that it immediately makes Stephen wonder what ever happened with Henry? As though picking up on the thought wave, Andrew provides an immediate answer.

*"Wanted to be an actor. Dad made him go into the army. Hung himself at the training barracks after the first month..."*

For good measure Stephen experiences the sudden and most unwelcome sensation of something rough wrapped around his throat trapping his windpipe and cutting off his air supply.... He turns and snarls into what the audience perceives to be empty space...

'Take if off me or I'm closing this down right now!'

The sensation immediately subsides but there is a trickle of moisture at the end of his left nostril and when Stephen brings a casual hand to his face he realises that the moisture is blood and he has started a nose bleed.

'Sir, about Henry, did he want to be an actor or something like that?'

'Damn fool,' the gentleman mutters inaudibly.

'Did he go into the army?' Stephen pushes gently, not wanting to cause any distress to the gentleman but still looking for confirmation.

'Yes, he did.'

269

'And was there some kind of accident…?'

'Accident?'  The elderly gentleman is sounding dazed.  'No, not really.  He was… he was unwell and he became very depressed and unhappy, and he ended up taking his own life.'

*"Oh for goodness sake, tell him not to feel so bad about it.  Henry's okay and I'm okay and we do as best we can to look after Gillian…"*

'He's telling me that he and Henry are looking after Gillian.  Who's Gillian, please?'

'My late wife – the boys' mother.'

Stephen sees bonfires and fireworks, rockets and sparklers.  It's obviously Bonfire Night.

'Sir, I'm getting Bonfire Night.  November the 5$^{th}$.  Now please don't be nice to me, but does this mean anything to you?'

'My wife died on November 5$^{th}$.'

A voice – female – wafting out of nowhere is calling for Malcolm.

'Who's Malcolm?'  Stephen asks.

'I'm Malcolm.  That's my name.'

*"Might as well mention Uncle Pete,"* Andew's discarnate voice suggests.

'Who's Pete?'  Stephen asks.

'That's my late brother,' the gentleman called Malcolm acknowledges.

'Carry on like this and we'll have a coach party coming through!'  Stephen tries to lighten the leaden atmosphere but is only partially successful.  There is such a deep wellspring of anguish emanating from the back of the room the the audience at large has been drawn into the fugue.

Lord, he thinks, give me something – anything – to lighten things up a bit.

*"You might want to mention Martha,"* Andrew says meaningfully. *"She's his sort of part-time lady friend of these last few years and if he doesn't do something about her soon she's going to bugger off with someone else. And you might want to mention Lucy... that's our sister and she's got a wonderful family but he hardly ever pays them any attention which is a bit of a shame really because there's plenty of love for him there if he wants it, and oh bollocks I think I've got to go now be-"*

The link is suddenly broken and Stephen is left on an empty stage, spiritless and guideless. There's a vacuum and a worrying void. Where'd everyone go?

'Andrew is telling me that there's a lot of love around you, sir, but that you've got to do something to go and find it. He's been mentioning Lucy and Martha and he's telling me that you need to do some work in those areas... Do you understand?'

'Yes, er, I think so...'

'Thank you very much sir...'


Stephen walks up and down the stage. Glances at his watch. It is only five minutes past eight. He has been on stage for only twenty minutes. It feels like twenty hours. He doesn't know where he's going next or what he's going to be saying next. He's on his own until a soft feminine voice whispers gently in his ear...

*"Well if you're free can I just say hello to my husband and my little boy? They're sitting here on the front row..."*

Stephen looks down at the front row, and sure enough off to one side there is a gentleman in his mid thirties sitting with a little boy, perhaps about eight or nine, and wearing a red school cap.

271

Stephen has a mental impression of a tall lady, very attractive with long dark hair. She is rubbing her breasts but there is absolutely nothing sexual about this gesture.

*"Breast cancer,"* she says simply. *"My goodness, but these two lumps hurt like hell when I was alive but we're all sorted out now and everything's back to normal..."*

'I need,' Stephen speaks meaningfully, looking in the general direction of the gentleman and the schoolboy, 'to talk to a gentleman who has lost his wife to breast cancer...'

*"June..."* says the lady with the long dark hair.

'And the month of June should be significant,' Stephen adds hopefully.

Stephen is relieved and rewarded when the gentleman with the schoolboy puts his hand up cautiously. The little boy is looking at his father with an expression of wonderment and curiosity on his young face.

'Yes sir, what do you understand?' Stephen asks encouragingly.

'My wife died of breast cancer earlier this year,' it is a soft masculine voice with a burr of a west country accent. 'But it was in February... Er... but my wife's name, well, er, she was called June, so I think this might be a message for me...'

There is a note of absolute desperation in this man's voice... but there is also an element of fear and apprehension.

*"Sorry,"* says the lady spirit called June, and she is speaking both inside and outside of Stephen's head. *"He's just a bit nervous. He never used to believe in any of this before I went."*

272

Stephen needs to put this gentleman at his ease. 'Your wife's a bit surprised to see you here tonight,' he jokes, 'because you never used to believe in anything like this, did you?'

'Er, no.'

'Well she's really glad you've changed your mind and she's really pleased to see you here tonight.'

This is what Stephen is saying but he's actually thinking something along the lines of 'Come on, June, there's nobody else on this stage except you and me so make the most of it and tell me what you want me to say. The June spirit does not let him down.

*"Tell him he's doing a fantastic job, an absolutely fantastic job with Robin and I'm extraordinarily proud of them both!"*

'Who's Robin?' Stephen asks innocently, full well knowing who Robin is.

'This is my son, Robin...' The father leans across and wraps his arm protectively around the little boy.

'Well, June is damned proud of the pair of you,' Stephen exclaims triumphantly.

The June spirit moves closer and Stephen picks up the distinctive scent of Dune perfume. Stephen is an expert on perfumes.

'Did your wife wear Dune perfume a lot?' he asks.

'Yes, it was her favourite scent.'

'Well, she's wearing it tonight, just for you!'

*"He sprays it on the pillow every night..."*

There is a lump of emotion rising in Stephen's throat and there is the salt tang of tears welling up behind his eyes. 'She says she watches you when you spray the pillow with her perfume every night before you go to bed.'

*"Six months six years..."*

Stephen risks being wrong and interprets the message the way he feels June wants it interpreted. 'She's telling me she's only been gone for six months but for you it must seem like six years…'

He can't see her, but Stephen knows that June is crying. He can see her husband crying on the front row. Stephen is also crying and rubs his eyes with the back of his hand.

Stephen is aware of the fact that June is somewhere on his right – she is between him and her family on the front row. He "sees" her looking at them longingly, so full of yearning, so full of regret, and in this second he know that no words are needed. Theirs is, for these few seconds, a silent communication of soul and spirit. He feels a steadying hand on his left shoulder and picks up the smell of leather and damp canvas. This is Archie May, suddenly moving in close to bring physical as well as spiritual support.

*"She has the baby safe,"* Archie says quietly, and superimposed over the top of Archie's words, Stephen hears June say the same thing…

*"I've got the baby safe!"*

Stephen passes on the message, sees its impact upon the bereaved husband and feels the waves of pain wash up over the edge of the stage. Privately he thinks: 'What baby?'

*"Holiday in Gran Canaria… Fell because I wasn't well…"*

Stephen is given a flash vision of a long flight of steps. He is aware of a moment's giddiness, then he is tumbling and falling and there is the most dreadful pain in his abdomen.

'She's telling me about the accident on the steps, where she lost the baby…'

'Yes, we lost the baby on holiday…'

*"We'd decided if it was a girl we would call her Tammy or Tamsin, Tamsin, Tammy for short. We really wanted a girl. Tell Barry we've got a beautiful little girl called Tammy…"*

'Who's Barry or Harry?' Stephen asks.

'I'm Barry,' says the front row father.

'June's telling me she's looking after Tammy… that if you had a little girl you were going to call her Tammy…'

'That's right.' The words are short and blurted out with an energy of their own volition.

*"Good idea, the new school for Matthew…"*

'Who's Matthew?'

The small boy with the red school cap tentatively puts his hand up in the air but his father answers for him. 'This is my son, Matthew.'

'Have you been talking about sorting out a new school?' Stephen asks.

'Yes, we have.'

'Well, June thinks it's a great idea.'

In the eye of his mind Stephen sees a poster for the new Pirates of The Caribbean movie. He's also given a flash vision of a big carton of popcorn being spilled over the cinema floor.

'Have you recently been to the cinema?' he asks.

'Er, yes, we went the other night.'

'And was it to see this new pirate film they've brought out?'

'Yes, we went to see Pirates of The Caribbean!'

'And did one of you spill a big bucket of popcorn all over the place?'

'God, yes, I did…'

'Well she was watching and she thought it was a great laugh.'

*"Loved going to the movies. Vivienne Leigh, Gone With The Wind..."* June has now moved back much closer to Stephen and he feels her presence very close to him. Again there is the unsusual phenomena of his being able to hear her voice in two dimensions, outside his head through his right ear and actually inside his head impinging itself on the synapsis of his brain. *"Gone With The Wind was my favourite movie of all time. I watched it at least once a month. Used to drive Barry mad so that was when he'd go out and do his...."* Stephen misses the next couple of words because from somewhere on a very base level there is a mobile phone ringing in the audience. *"...but Barry knew how much I loved it and he put the video in my coffin with me so that, as he put it, I could watch my favourite film up in heaven."*

Stephen goes and sits down on the edge of the stage only a few feet away from the father and son. 'June's saying that she used to love to go to the movies and how Vivien Leigh was her favourite film star and how Gone with The Wind was her favourite film... She's saying thank you for... Oh, did you put the film *in* her coffin with her so she could watch it when she got over to the other side?'

Barry the father nods mutely. He is lost for words.

*"Tibs and Wrinkles,"*

'What?' Stephen asks, looking in the direction of the empty space which is, in fact, filled by the life force of the visiting spirit.

*"Tibs and Wrinkles..."* This is Archie May's voice speaking into Stephen's other ear. *"Matthews's pets, over here with us...'*

Stephen is given a clairvoyant vision of a large tabby cat and a small nondescript rodent belting the blazes out of a wheel... Hamster?

He leans forwards, nearly falls off the edge of the stage and makes eye contact with the little boy called Matthew. This is unusual. Matthew is very young. But Stephen is suffused with such incredible feelings of love and protection that he simply follows his gut instincts and goes where June leads him and Archie allows him to go.

He opens his mouth to speak and although the voice is his, the words are most certainly not. They come directly from a mother to her son.

'Matthew, your Mummy wants you to know that you are a very special little boy, that she loves you very very much and that she's relying on you to look after your Daddy... And although she's not here to look after you herself, she's with you every hour of every day and is going to do everything she can to help your Daddy look after you, Okay? What's more, she's telling me that she's looking after a big grey pussy cat called Tibs or Tibby and that Wrinkles is still having a great time on his wheel, but most of all she wants to say that she is ever so proud of you and that she loves you very very much...'

We are *all* in tears so it is just as well that out of the corner of his eye Stephen sees a friendly and familiar face waving at him from the rear entrance and he breathes a sigh of eternal relief. It is the interval. He can take a twenty minute break. He's been on stage for forty five minutes. It feels like a week.

## Chapter Twenty One:  *Stratford-upon-Avon*

Our mid-summer tour of 2006 was not one of the easiest tours we've ever put on the road.  The weather was incredibly hot and sticky and we were in the middle of world cup fever followed by Wimbledon fortnight. Nationally the sales of BBQ grills and air conditioning units had broken all records and the last place that a lot of people wanted to be was in a small theatre or hotel suite taking part in an evening of clairvoyance.  As you can imagine our attendance numbers were well down, and although as a promoter I worried, Steve took it philosophically in his stride – *"James, to tell you the truth I wouldn't mind sitting in a nice garden having a lovely barbie and a few bottles of wine with my family and friends, but if only three people turn up to a demonstration and one of them gets the message that could change their lives, then I know I'm doing the right thing and I'm in the right place..."* – which was very noble of him, but even he sweated when we turned up in hotel rooms that had no fans or air con and with security windows that wouldn't open more than half an inch. We both joked that we'd be better off sleeping in the car which, old though it was, did have air conditioning that worked very well.  In all seriousness, the car was sometimes the most comfortable place to be.

Our tour dates took us to Hereford, Stratford-upon-Avon, Portsmouth, Southampton, Corby and Stamford in Lincolnshire before we trecked back up to Yorkshire and the north of England.  Some bright spark recently commented that whoever booked Stephen's dates should first of all take a look at a map of England and rationalise the zig zag pathway we plot across the country, but when you have limited dates to work with in the first place and you're booking venues twelve and sometimes eighteen months in advance, it isn't always easy to get them nicely dove tailed in harmony with an AA road map.

Scatty though Stephen's tour dates might seem they're a helluva lot more rational than some of the tour dates I got lumbered with back in the bad old band days of the 1960's when we'd be in Frankfurt on Friday, Berlin on Saturday, Hambourg on Sunday, Munich on Monday and back to Hambourg on Tuesday – and all in the back of a smelly old Bedford van with four other unwashed musicians drinking copious amounts of 1664 and smoking something slightly more far out than Benson & Hedges!

Although we had pretty good nights in Portsmouth and Southampton, the highlight of our tour was The Falcon Hotel in Stratford. Both Steve and I love this venue – it's a small and intimate hotel that always makes us more than welcome – and we are both very fond of the lovely old Shakespearean town in which, over the years we have been going there, we have made a number of very good friends. I have another reason for being fond of Stratford insofar as over the years Stephen has brought through some truly phenomenal evidence. One such piece of evidence found its way into our first book and this was the story of a beautiful little baby boy called Callum who passed over when he was only a ferw months old – but another piece of evidence came through on the night of $23^{rd}$ July 2006 which is certainly worthy of some mention in these pages.

It doesn't all of the demonstrations but at Stratford I have got into the habit of loitering in the reception area of the hotel just to say hello to old friends and familiar faces as they arrive for the evening. On this occasion, as the audience was filtering through the entrance, I noticed a particularly pretty girl with short blond hair and a gorgeous smile. She had clear eyes and flawless skin and she moved with such graceful confidence that one immediately thought of very svelte pussy cats and slinky models on high fashion catwalks.

Rob, who was standing next to me, noticed that my attention had become locked upon this young lady. 'Now now James,' he said with a mischievous tease to his voice. 'You're old enough to be her father!'

'I'm old enough to be her bloody grandfather!' I retorted lightly, matching his bantering tone, and not letting on that I was just a little distressed by his assumptive remark... Why is it, I wonder, that one cannot be interested in or even "attracted" to a member of the opposite sex without everyone assuming that there is a sexual agenda somewhere? In this young woman's case, she was certainly quite stunning and had I been thirty years younger I may well have gone over and introduced myself, but the thing about her that had caught my attention in the first place was not her physical presence but rather the very strong psychic aura that she carried with her. It seemed to me that this girl was not just out to attend an evening of clairvoyance, but that she had come to The Falcon Hotel on a mission.

'I bet you,' I said to Rob as the girl disappeared into the auditorium, 'I bet you a drink of your choice that she gets a message tonight!'

He cast me a shrewd glance. 'You picking something up?'

'Maybe. I don't know. Want to take the bet?'

Rob declined, which was just as well, because as it turned out, he would have lost. The young lady in question *did* get her message, and Steve was so cock-a-hoop about it, that he talked to her for a little while at the end of the demonstration and finally brought her over to meet me. She and I had a few words, and she willingly agreed to send in her story for this book. For my part I was very pleased that she had got what she had come for, and I couldn't fail to notice that she left The Falcon on a very different vibration to the one she had brought with her when she had arrived. A lot of the tension had gone from her, and now an inner beauty radiated from behind her eyes.

Anyway, here is Alice's letter, unedited.

'Hi James

My name is Alice, and we met last night 23/07/06 in Stratford upon Avon. You asked me to write to you and tell you a bit about my dad who had passed over and the things that Stephen had said to me.

18 months ago my dad found out he had a brain tumour. He fought and fought and three operations and eighteen months later the grade 4 brain tumour finally got the better of him and on the 28th Dec 2005 my dad passed away peacefully. I am a true believer of the spirit world and that there is somewhere you go to after you pass over. I talk to my dad's picture and feel him with me sometimes, so when I saw Stephen's advert in the paper I thought why not… I would love to go and even as it has been so soon after his passing if dad can't come through it will still be amazing to see what happens for the other people that do have messages.

Once I booked tickets to come and see Stephen I couldn't stop thinking about it and how much I would love it if dad came through but I had to keep telling myself it doesn't matter if he doesn't because it just might not the right time.

On Sunday 23/07/06 at around 11.00 my husband said he was going to go to the shops and would I like to go with him? I said no as I just wasn't in the mood. I had butterflies all morning and afternoon just not knowing what to expect. In my living room I have a big picture of my dad which was taken at my wedding reception. He always had such a cheeky smile and I loved the photo so I had it made a lot bigger and it sits right where I can see him while I'm sat on the sofa. I chat away to him all the time and cry and yell but it just makes him feel closer to me when I see his cheeky smile. At around 11.30am I looked over to dad and I said dad PLEASE PLEASE try and come through tonight just so I know you are OK. I miss you so much and just knowing that you're all right would really help me so very much.

Sunday evening finally arrived and God, was my tummy doing rollie pollies..! I had to just keep saying "chill out Alice he may not be able to make it!"

Anyway 7:30 came and Stephen started the show. He spent about 10 minutes just explaining everything to us which was very interesting and I made sure I took it all in. During his introduction Stephen kept looking at me and I was not scared but almost nervous so I would look away. Once he finished his introduction he began and straight away asked who had lost their dad recently?

Two of us put our hands up, another lady and myself, and I thought oh dad please let this be you but Stephen went over to the other lady and asked her to let him hear her voice, and when she answered, he said no the message wasn't for her and then he came over to me and asked me why the month of March was important.

My whole body just had a freezing cold feeling all the way from my head to my toes.

He'd done it! He'd come through!

I told Stephen that March was my dad's birthday. Then Steve asked me if I'd noticed that he'd kept looking at me during the introduction... He said "I bet you thought I fancied you" and we all laughed but then he said "your dad's here and he kept interrupting me during my introduction, and that's why I kept looking in your direction!"

I couldn't believe it. I'd waited six months for this and I know a lot of people that have waited for years and years to get a message so six months is nothing - but to me it was an absolute ages. My dad meant absolutely everything to me. Anyway Stephen went on to say how my dad had known a lot more than what he'd let on which now, when I look back on it, I can see that he did. Steve also told us how, when dad was dying, we were all so worried that he was in pain but then he put my mind at rest by saying he was not in any pain any more and that he was really enjoying it over there in the spirit world and that he was especially enjoying having some space.... which made me laugh because dad did enjoy his space but with mum and I always there he didn't get much especially when it came to watching TV as we would always want to watch the soaps. So when Stephen was going on about space I just giggled to myself. But out of it all what really got me was when Stephen turned around and said "at 11.30 this morning you chatted to your dad didn't you?"

My heart must have stopped for a quick second before I said yes. "And you asked him please please dad try and come through... Well guess what! Your dad has had today booked for the last 10 days and there was no way he was going to miss it."

It still gives me Goosebumps and makes me cry now. My dad never let me down as a child or a teenager and even now he's on the other side he still hasn't let me down. He would have known how heartbroken his little girl would have been if he didn't come through so I know he would have tried so hard to contact Stephen and I just cant say thank you enough to Stephen because he really has helped me so much. I am very new to all of this and just to know that my dad is ok and that he loves me and the family has made me look at it all in a totally different way. I think Stephen is a very special, kind man. And I just still cant believe out of 100-200 people that my dad came through to Stephen and not only did he come through but he came through first and was trying to interrupt Stephen during his introduction! Well dad I got your message loud and clear and I love you too!! Everything that Stephen said to me I knew was from my dad and there were things that no one else would know and Stephen got everything down to a T with what he told me. The only thing that has worried me is, he asked if I had a little girl and I said no.

Then he asked what was happening in April and I said my Anniversary he said no its not that… Then he said "Good luck because that's when your little girl will be with you"… Well I'll be coming to see Stephen in September and we'll just have to wait and see if I am two months gone. But for the time being I want to say thank you once again to everyone that I met on 23/07/06 and for making it such an amazing experience.'

I think that Alice's story illustrates an extremely important aspect not just of Stephen's work but indeed the whole concept of post mortem communication. Alice Egerton is an extremely beautiful young woman full of intelegence and the vibrancy of life. She has a good job, great friends and a family who love her dearly – and yet, until she received the message from Stephen to prove that her father's spirit lived on, all of these wonderful gifts were overshadowed by the feeling of bereftness caused by the loss of a deeply loved parent. One could say that we should not dwell on the past but seek to move forwards into whatever our futures hold for us, but sometimes this is very difficult to do, especially if we do not have closure on a situation that has caused us such profound distress and loss. How do you tell someone to forget their right arm if they have lost that right arm in some dreadful accident? How do you tell the mother to forget her dead child, or the daughter to forget her dead father? The truth is that you can't and to do so would be insulting! There are some losses that we simply never adjust to, and perhaps that is part of what living is all about. But it is not always easy and nor should we ever assume that it becomes any easier with the passing of time. All that happens is that we learn to live with our loss and our heart ache – that's all any of us can hope for really – but at least with Stephen Holbrook's intervention perhaps we are given a modicum of extra strength to get on with the business of living, knowing that at the end of the day death finally reunites us with those whom we have lost and those who have gone on before.

As a lovely footnote to Alice Egerton's evidence I was talking to her Mum the other day and she was all too eager to tell me that Alice is now expecting her first baby, which is due in April 2007 so yet again Steve got it dead right.

As I said earlier, we have made many friends in Stratford-upon-Avon and two such friends are Steve Devey and his vivacious artist wife Kay Whittaker; you may recall from an earlier chapter in this book that they dwell in The Shrieves House on Sheep Street where Stephen came across the angry little spirit that kept telling him to get out of her bed.

On the evening of 23$^{rd}$ July, Devey and Kay were our guests at The Falcon and after the demonstration we all trouped around to The Shrieves House for a few drinks and a bite of supper.

Devey, who is a spiritually enlightened soul, is immensely proud of his guardianship of The Shrieves House, and quite rightly so, for the original building was built in the 12$^{th}$ century, was renovated in 1406 and renovated again just after the English civil war. Since then it's been added to, improved, restructed and supported, but in essence it's pretty well the same house that stood there, half way up Sheep Street, way back in 1690 something or other.

Long before Devey and Kay took over the lease a dozen or so years ago, it had the reputation of being a *very* haunted house and with the amount of history that has taken place beneath its roof, I suppose that's hardly surprising.

Properties of this age need a lot of money constantly ploughed into them for ongoing maintenance and Devy has tried a number of business projects, some of which have worked, others which haven't. His latest fundraising scheme has been to turn the old barn at the back of the building into a living history museum, and although there is a lot of history packed into this museum, Devey is a businessman and he's well aware of the fact that he has to entertain the millions of tourists who flock to Stratford each year. As such, pinching a leaf out of Madam Tussaud's, he has built a number of tableaux depicting Stratford's back streets in the time of the great plague, an old ale house complete with real straw and ale on tap, and the coven corner of the three Stratford witches that Shakespeare took as his inspiration for the three famous witches in Macbeth. To take the guided tour is quite a spooky and unnerving experience, and since the museum has been open (about six years) there have been a number of ghostly appearances and supernatural occurrences.

Obviously, and I'm sure Devey won't mind me saying this, this is great business publicity, but to put it in some kind of context, this isn't just a proprietor spouting off in an attempt to get punters through his door. The Shrieves House has been investigated half a dozen times or more by serious psychic researchers, has been featured in the prestigious Vision Magazine and has even been the star of one of Derek Acorah's most haunted programs – and indeed on this particular show Mr Acorah was seemingly possessed by a malevolent energy and at the end of the broadcast he couldn't get out of the place fast enough.

In short, partially through media hype but more as the result of serious paranormal investigation by some very serious people who are acknowledged experts in their field, The Shrieves House has acquired the reputation of being one of the most haunted buildings in Britain.

For myself, I have to say that The Shrieves House has always embraced me with a warm and most gentle welcome, a protective energy that seems to offer security and sanctuary. I have on many occasions felt spiritual energies moving around me and they have always seemed to be soft and serene entities that have been interested and even sometimes delighted at my presence among them.

But this is the house I'm talking about here, and not the museum in the barn in the other part of the building. Here the atmosphere seems darker and sadder – but we must remember the nature of this part of the premises and allow for factors such as man made atmospherics and the all too powerful influences of autosuggestion.

So much for the background, but now let me tell you what happened on the night of July 26th and for a couple of reasons, I'm going to tell this from Rob Green's point of view as he was probably the most objective person present. And incidentally, you can expel some of that bated breath. This story isn't going to pan out the way you think.


Rob was in a very good mood as he strolled down Sheep Street from the Falcon with the rest of the party. His hotel room was spacious and cool and after the last couple of nights spent in stainless steel saunas in big bustling cities, the old world charm of Stratford and The Falcon Hotel was a blessed relief. Knowing that he didn't have a long night drive ahead of him he was well up for the idea of having a few drinks and relaxing with friends; also he was curious to see The Shrieves House. He'd heard Stephen talk about the building on a number of occasions and had heard the story of the little girl in the bedroom, and now he was looking forward to seeing the house for himself.

From the street the old mediaeval edifice looked quite splendid – exactly, he mused to himself, the way that a haunted house was *supposed* to look; all beams and plaster with mullioned bay windows. It reeked and creaked with age and history.

Devey opened the door with a big key and led the way into the building... and here was a most curious thing! As soon as Rob crossed the threshold he felt a rushing sensation of pressure around his temples and within less than a minute he was suffering from an uncomfortable headache.

Following Stephen through a labyrinth of dark passageways they finally arrived at the kitchen – a huge room with exposed beams and low ceilings and stable style doors that led out into a long thin courtyard that ran the whole depth of the house from the street to the end of the barn, about a hundred feet distant across an uneven patchwork of cobbles.

Thick clumps of ivy and damask rose climbed up the courtyard wall of the house and the whole area was littered with statues of nymphs and shepherds, gargoyles and goddesses, a couple of huge stone dogs, half a dozen overturned barrels, a set of stocks and a couple of long pews.

Taking a seat next to Stephen on one of the pews, he gratefully accepted an extremely generous glass of ice cold white wine from his host, and nursing his headache (which had not improved with being outside in the open air) he sipped at the wine sparingly and joined in with the general buzz and ambience of the conversation. On more than one occasion, however, he found himself looking up at the dark windows above him with a feeling of discomfort. He knew it was his imagination, but he couldn't get over the feeling that there was someone up there behind one of those windows watching what was going on in the courtyard below, perhaps with a degree of envy and wishing that they – it? – could join in.

Inevitably, the conversation came around to the subject of the new book (this one, the one you're reading now) and I happened to comment that one of the things that I would really like to have done with Stephen was put him in a haunted house for a few hours just to see what, if anything, he picked up. Borely Rectory had been mentioned, as had Stanstead Hall, plus a castle up in the north-east and a couple of hotels in York. The trouble was, of course, that there wasn't time to do everything and so sadly this idea of an all night vigil had gone out of the window.

Devey immediately suggested that he take us all on a tour around the museum. It was, he told us, a *very* hot spot for hauntings and strange goings on, attested to by quite a number of celebrities, including Derek Acorah, and also by half a dozen paranormalist groups who had spent the night there as part of their investigations.

I could see that neither Steve nor Rob were all that keen, but in the end they were persuaded to go for it (Devey can be *very* persuasive when he needs to be) and as Rob pointed out, it did fall within the remit of research work for the book. He said if they spent twenty minutes in a haunted museum it would shut me up and put me in my place if I started going on about spending a whole night in sleeping bags in some musty castle dungeon or some damp and dark wine cellar beneath one of York's famous watering holes.

Devey went and got lanterns. Yes, he could just have turned the flaming lights on, but that would have been against the ethos of the adventure and we all followed him into the old museum. Devey first, then Stephen, then me and lastly Rob.

Rob: 'Well, of course, it was all very dark and spooky and extremely atmospheric and while one part of me kept saying stop being so ridiculous another part of me did have a slight case of the jitters, so much so that I was very soon wishing that I'd just said no and had stayed outside in the fresh air with that nice glass of white wine I'd been drinking. For one thing, it was so dark I could hardly see where I was walking – Devey had the lantern but he was up in the front and all I had was this piddling little torch with a nearly flat battery.

Anyway, we were going down this long thin passageway and then we came to a long flight of open wooden stairs that led up onto the first floor, and as I was walking up the stairs I had this horrible feeling that someone was walking up behind me – which of course there wasn't, and it was just my imagination reacting to the mood and the environment. But having said that, and despite the fact that everyone was still basically in front of me, I really didn't like the feeling that I got at the top of those stairs – it was very different to the rest of the place and I don't think it had anything at all to do with the wax dummies of witches and plague victims. This was something a lot more subtle and I nearly said something, but then we were moving off into another part of the building which, according to Devey, was where the majority of happenings happened, and it was also where some visiting clairvoyant had been possessed by whatever was passing through at the time.

Well, anyway, this was where Devey turned his lantern off and told us just to be very quiet and concentrate on our breathing in the pitch black and tune into the atmosphere around us and see what we could pick up. I thought, there's no way I'm going to pick up anything here and then something lightly tapped me on the back of my head and I nearly jumped out of my skin!

I nearly shouted out loud, but then I got a grip on myself and thought no way am I going to make a fool of myself – I mean, it could have been a spider or a flake of wood dropping from the ceiling and, for all I know, bearing in mind I wasn't quite sure where everyone else was standing, it might have been James or Steve having a lark. In any case, no one else felt anything and despite what James says, I was the least psychic of the lot and I wasn't going to let my imagination get the better of me.

So then we went back to the top of the stairs – the bit of the building that I disliked the most – and Devey turned the lantern out again and we did the breathing tuning in thing again and just for a moment, and it was only for a second or so, I got the impression that there was someone else with us breathing much more heavily than the rest of us... Devey said he felt it and James admitted that he felt *something* but nothing else came of it and nothing else happened and I suppose that was it... We all trouped out of the museum and I went back to my glass of wine.'

The party broke up around half past midnight and we left The Shrieves House initially intending to walk back to the hotel, but it was an incredibly hot and muggy night and we needed to clear our heads, so we strolled back to The Falcon the long way around, via the river and the RSC Theatre. There was that lovely childhood smell of mud on the night air and a suggestion of moving shadows enhanced by suppressed giggles – young couples doing what young couples do in the long grass out of sight of the public eye.

Stephen was unusually quiet but Rob was quite eager to know what we had both thought of our recent experience.

We sat on a bench near some moored rowing boats and, being the boy scout I always wanted to be, I produced the small flask of brandy that I had in my camera bag. While I will frequently carry a camera bag, I do not always carry flasks of brandy, but I'd recently bought the flask at one of the Spanish Paradores and the novelty hadn't yet worn off.

We sipped from the flask.

'Well, come on, what do you think?' Rob wanted to know.

'It was a bit anti climactic,' I ventured.

Stephen sighed tiredly. 'I think that our host was totally desperate for something to happen,' he suggested. 'He was almost willing a haunting on us, but it's always the way, when you push for something in the spirit world, nothing much ever happens. I don't doubt for a minute that the building is haunted but I've got to tell you, I didn't pick up a thing. Not a single solitary thing. So...' He looked at me shrewdly, 'I don't know what kind of a clairvoyant that makes me, because if I've got it right, there *have* been all kinds of psychic goings on at The Shrieves House, haven't there?'

'Yes, there have,' I confirmed, thinking of all the reports I'd heard about, not least of which had been the occasion when the Vision team had held their all night session in the museum. 'Lots of poltergeist activity, quite a number of materialisations and even that case of possession when the TV crew were on hand.'

'So why didn't I get anything?' he wanted to know.

I shrugged. 'Dunno. But like you say, with all things paranormal you don't just throw the light switch and expect something to happen.'

Stephen said something that sounded vaguely like "harrumph" but I suppose he could just have been clearing his throat.

And then, quite out of the blue, he said – 'You know, there are times when I get really cross, no, not just cross, but downright flaming angry with spirit!'

This was a totally untypical comment and I guess Rob and I both looked at him with slightly slack jaws.

'That's a helluva thing to say,' I said, 'coming from you, of all people.'

'Yes, but it's true, though,' Stephen said adamantly. 'Look, I haven't told you this, in fact I haven't told anybody anything about this, but d'you remember a good few weeks ago, just before we went on our holiday to Tenerife? Well, about a week before we went I woke up in the middle of the night with this awful dream – and it was one of those spirit dreams that are more than just a dream – and in this dream I was being told that Robbie had a brain tumour!

'I tell you, what with all the health problems we've had in the family over the last couple of years it scared the living daylights out of me. But as I say, we were all set to go off on this big family holiday and I knew I just had to keep my mouth shut because I didn't want to worry anybody – but what I really wanted to do was haul Robbie down to the hospital and demand that he be given a brain scan.

'I didn't because can you, for one moment, just imagine how it might have sounded. "Hello, I'm Steve Holbrook and I'm a clairvoyant and I've had this nasty dream about my eldest son having a brain tumour so I'd like you to give him a brain scan right here and now just to put my mind at rest." For heaven's sake,' he laughed shortly and without humour, 'they'd have thrown me out on my ear with a good old telling off for wasting NHS time.

'So anyway, we all trailed off to Tenerife and everything was okay for the first seven or eight days, although for me the holiday was spoiled because I couldn't get the dream out of my head. Then, damn me, at the beginning of the second week Robbie was taken ill in the night... He was thrashing and sweating in bed and when I checked on him his eyes were rolled right up into his head and there was this little trickle of blood coming out from the side of his mouth. I threw a complete wobbler... Ended up yelling at Caroline to call an ambulance and we all dashed down to the hospital in the middle of the night, got Robbie checked in... And d'you know he looked so poorly and he was in and out of consciousness all the time, and there was this one occasion when he looked up at me and asked me if he had a brain tumour...

'Well, that just hauled the dream into point blank focus and I couldn't just ignore it. So I had to tell him that he *might* have a brain tumour, but that the doctors in Tenerife were some of the best doctors in the world and whatever was wrong with him, they were certain to be able to put it right.

'And it was quite amazing really, because without me even having to ask or make any kind of fuss, they automatically did a brain scan on Robbie and when the results came back he was absolutely clear. They said he'd had a minor epileptic fit and that he would have to undergo some tests when he got back to the UK, but there were no tumours or any other lurking nasties.

'So, if there *wasn't* any brain tumour, why did spirit send me that flaming dream that caused me all that anguish and unnecessary worry? …And, if you're wondering what this has got to do with Devey and his haunted museum, then it's the same question, isn't it? If the place is as haunted as we all think it is, where were my spirit friends when I needed them to make the link?'

'Whoah, hang on! Hang on a minute!' Rob exclaimed. 'Stephen, these are two completely different situations and there aren't any similarities at all between hoping to prove that The Shrieves House is haunted and coming up with an answer as to why you had that horrible dream. James, for God's sake, you tell him!'

'Steve, Rob's quite right and you said it yourself, when you go *looking* for a ghost, you never damn well find one. Not for real anyway.'

'All right,' Stephen snapped, 'so why-' he took another gulp of the brandy from the flask while Rob and I exchanged anxious glances, 'why did spirit send me that dreadful dream?'

'Come on, Steve, you're the expert,' Rob said very gently. 'Maybe spirit just sent you the dream so that you'd be alert to Robbie's problem when it did crop up. Or,' he thought for a moment, 'maybe it's more subtle and more complicated than that. Maybe because they know of Robbie's own talents and they know how important you are to each other, and maybe because they know how important you're *going* to be to each other in the years to come, they psyched you up with this brain tumour thing so that when Robbie asked you if that's what he had, you had the strength to give him a straight and honest answer without waffling on and trying to obfuscate everything… You know, a father and son trust thing… And, of course, there's a third factor, isn't there?

'You had the dream, you wanted Robbie to have a brain scan to make sure he was okay but you knew you couldn't just walk down to the hospital and demand that kind of attention without something more than a dream to back up your demand. So, while you're on holiday Robbie comes down with a health problem that automatically makes sure he *gets* a brain scan, and now you know he's in the clear and you can put your mind at rest…'

Rob trailed off lamely, but I thought he'd done a fabulous job of reasoning and my respect for this guy, which was already very high, went up another couple of notches.

We finished the brandy (hey, look, it was only a very small flask, right?) and headed back towards our hotel. Stephen was tired and drained, but I have to say his psychic vibration was much brighter than it had been earlier in the evening and I vaguely wondered what the results might be were we to go back to The Shrieves House and camp out on our own for a few hours. It was not, however, an idea that I had any intention of putting to the test.

'Robbie's okay now, isn't he?' I asked tentatively.

'He's fine,' Stephen smiled wanly. 'Which is more that I am right now. I'm knackered. It's been a long night and I'm ready for my bed.'

# Chapter Twenty Two:    *Heat*

Stamford, in Lincolnshire, is one of the most attractive small towns in England and if I was staying in the UK I'd probably buy a place there, or maybe somewhere in Suffolk. But I'm not staying in the UK and by the end of 2006 I expect to be resident in Southern France with my wife, eight cats, and a load of unfulfilled dreams and ambitions which the way I see it, are mountains just waiting to be climbed.

But I love Stamford – its streets and it people, its rather odd shops, its golden stone and its welcoming ambience. In particular, I love The George Hotel with which I've had an ongoing association since 1972, and I have tried deliberately to schedule Stephen's tours so that I can enjoy an overnight stay in this most wonderful of watering holes.

Shock horror when we tried to book The George for the evening of 28th July to coincide with Stephen's demonstration at The Stamford Arts Centre. The George was full! No room at the inn! So we had to find an alternative, and we ended up at a place called The Lawns Hotel, about a quarter of a mile out of town.

It has to be said that The Lawns was quite lovely – an old Jacobean house, with well appointed rooms, a terrace and a truly delightful cloistered garden filled with carefully cultivated rhododendron, ivy and jasmine, a profusion of roses and a plethora of palms and ferns. Okay, it *wasn't* The George, but we were all well pleased with the alternative.

Stephen did a stunning demonstration at The Arts Centre and then we went and pigged out at The Thai Orchid, which is one of our favourite Stamford restaurants. I guess we rolled back to The Lawns at around 11.15pm at which point in time we met the owner of the hotel, an extremely genial ex-RAF officer called Tom.

Was there anything we wanted?

Well, it was stiflingly hot and none of us was ready for bed. We'd all got very full tummies and had drunk just enough wine to make us want some more – so we asked for a bottle of Rioja and a bottle of Pinot Grigio and wondered if it would be okay to go and drink it out in the garden?

Absolutely no problem, and within a few moments we were sat outside on the terrace at a big round table beneath an enormous square canvas umbrella with two nice bottles of vine and four glasses – the fourth glass being for mine host Tom whom we had invited to join us for a night cap after he'd finished his closing down chores for the night.

This was without doubt the hottest night of the summer and the humidity reminded me of Florida on a bad day in August. There were a few odd flurries of rain – not even enough water falling to be described as a shower, just a spit here and a splatter over there – while in the distance an electrical storm cast jagged forks of lightening into the parched earth, counterpointed with ongoing and somewhat ominous rumbles of thunder.

Along with the heady scent of the flowers and the garden foliage, you could smell, and indeed almost taste the rain on the air, but it was rain that teased and tantalised like a mischievous lover, hinting at the joys of a great deluge and yet persistently refusing to fall.

We were sitting in companionable silence and then Stephen started laughing. Rob and I both raised questioning eyebrows.

'Are you going to share the joke, then?' Rob asked in his usual ascerbic way.

'No joke really,' Stephen chortled. 'It's just that we walked around that bloody museum the other night looking for ghosts or wayward spirits and I didn't see a damn thing. Yet here we are in Stamford less than two days later, and I've got to tell you guys, that I have a very sad little ghost in my bedroom and I've just seen her behind your heads, looking at us out of the dining room window.'

Rob and I both spun around in our seats and although we saw the dining room window (we couldn't very well *not* see it as it was barely ten feet away), we certainly were not aware of anyone watching us. Being all too well aware of Stephen's history with ghosts, including little old men and angry children, I pressed him for more information.

'Oh, not much to tell,' he said off-handedly. 'But when we checked in this afternoon, there was this lady in an old fashioned sort of dress, sat in the corner of my bedroom crying her heart out. I mean, we didn't have a conversation or anything like that, but I got a kind of picture image of her story and I guess that because her husband was chasing and catching everything else in the house that wore a skirt, she got thoroughly depressed and ended up killing herself by taking poison. I just sent out a few peaceful thoughts, telling her that it was 2006 and it was time for her to move on to somewhere else where she could find a bit more happiness... and I think that what's happened is that she's just given me a mental wave from the dining room window to say that she's on her way.'

'And is this a ghost you've seen – or a spirit?' I asked quickly, extremely keen to hear his answer.

Stephen smiled sadly but there was a definite twinkle in his eye. 'Ah James, I know where you're coming from, but I really don't know. This wasn't a spirit like I'll have contact with during one of my demonstrations but it wasn't a cold ghost like the two I've come across before... So I don't really know, I'm afraid. This was something different. Something new.'

'Your atunement must be changing,' I said pontifically, and then blushed in the darkness at the pomposity of my remark.

'Ummm, well it's 2006 and if you remember I always said a lot of things would change in 2006, and when you think about it, the changes that have happened this year have been quite incredible. I mean, for instance, I've taken Rob on as my manager and he takes care of all the business aspects that used to snarl up my day. He does ninety percent of the driving for me so I don't get nearly as tired as I used to do. I'm taking some proper holidays for the first time in my life, and I'm really getting to spend some quality time with my kids.

'From Rob's point of view, he's now an itinerant self employed manager and a year ago he was flogging cossies and arm bands for Speedo. It might not have been the most fantastic job in the world but it was a job he did well and at least there was a regular salary coming in. Also, he's had to relocate from Nottingham to Castleford – so you could say there have been a few changes in his life, couldn't you?

'And for heaven's sake, just look at you and Jo. You're selling up here and you're moving off to France in November and as well as the books you've written about me, you've got a big novel out there which is selling reasonably well and you're got your other book about those séances down in Spain – and I bet you never thought you'd be in this position when you were looking at your own future a couple of years ago.

'And bringing it back to me, well, good Lord, we're all going on this clairvoyant cruise in October and I never thought I'd ever do anything like that, and then there's this business of going to Jordan in 2008 and maybe opening a healing centre somewhere near you in France. And, for God's sake, I always swore I'd *never* do any television work until the kids were grown up and here I am discussing a TV contract with ITV and Jane McDonald. And that, as much as anything, is truly amazing!'

He wasn't far wrong in that because God knows how many times he'd turned a whole host of TV companies down when they'd come knocking on his door. But then, as he said, things change and circumstances change, and when one of his oldest friends, the cruise ship diva Jane McDonald, had come to him with a novel and very new idea for a TV show, he'd been sufficiently interested to meet with the producer and programme controller. Very probably prompted by Jane, they had broached the subject in such a way that he'd felt he could give a conditional yes to what was being offered. At the time of writing, late summer 2006, negotiations are still in a tentative and preliminary stage, but the fact that for the very first time Stephen has given his blessing to a TV production that will feature his work as a medium is a very major step for him. Although I doubt that anything is likely to happen for many months, yet, if and when it *does* happen, there'll be a new kind of pressure and a different kind of heat coming into Stephen's life. I've got this wager with

Stephen. Basically I've bet him five hundred quid that if the show gets as far as a pilot programme being broadcast, he'll be on prime time terrestrial telly within a year. Watch this space, or if you don't like that idea, keep watching the box.

There was a triple fork of lightening that lit up the whole of the sky over to the west and within a few seconds the detonation of thunder rumbled across Stamford like a broadside from a world war two battleship, rattling the rooftops and causing us to glance up at the dark and starless heavens.

'Storm's getting closer,' Rob commented casually, which was probably the most obvious understatement of the evening. The way I saw it the storm was getting closer and more ominous with every passing minute. And yet it was quite weird. There wasn't a breath of a breeze and our clothes clung to us like damp rags. Just ever so slightly unnerved by the power of the elements, we poured more wine into our anxious glasses.

'How are you doing with the book?' Stephen asked, taking me slightly by surprise. My mind had been flitting all over the place and at first I wasn't sure which book he was talking about. Did he mean this one, or was he referring to book sales of my great occult novel which, to date, had sold about all of thirty one copies? I assumed he was talking about "Survival" and answered accordingly.

'Pretty well okay... Got a couple more chapters to do and I'm still waiting for some stuff about Archie May. We're still on schedule for an October launch if that's what you're worried about.'

'I was just wondering if we're going have to do the haunted house thing,' he mused, 'especially in light of what happened in Stratford and what I found up in my bedroom earlier today.'

'Don't think so,' I reassured him. 'Apart from anything else, I just don't think we've got the time, or the space for that matter. Which is a bit of a shame because there were loads more things I wanted to see going down in this book. I mean, the whole business about séances and ectoplasm and physical mediumship, for example. I really wanted us to be able to get our teeth into that because in my opinion it's this aspect of spiritualism that puts so many people off.'

'Save it for book four,' he said lightly – and I gave him a sideways look. We hadn't even finished book three and here he was talking about book four!

'Hang on Stephen,' Rob butted in. 'James has got a point about all this darkened room stuff. It does put a lot of people off and certainly, if my own experience is anything to go by, there are some questions here that do need to be asked. I mean, that transfiguration evening I went to with Jill Prior down in the west country earlier this year was an absolute disgrace!'

I remembered the incident Rob was referring to very well and it was this, as much as anything else, that had prompted me into wanting to do something on the subject of physical mediumship. People find it hard enough to accept what Stephen does on the public platform, and in light of spiritualism's somewhat chequered history, a lot of folk find the idea of rolling clouds of ectoplasm and the materialisation of spirit people from beyond the grave just a little bit hard to swallow. The fact that an awful lot of fraudulent faking went on in the early half of the 20$^{th}$ century hasn't done the cause much good, and this whole idea of doing things in darkened rooms is anathema to me. If it is to be done at all, do it with the lights on and remove all doubts and suspicions from the proceedings. I know that Rob shares my views on this and therefore when the opportunity presented itself for him to go and take part in a transfigurational séance, it seemed like too good an opportunity to miss.

I'll let him tell you what happened in his own words and you can come to your own conclusions.

Rob: 'I realised that being in this line of work, I did have to have some degree of knowledge about the various types of mediumship that there are. It wasn't just being on the door, selling tickets and books etc, there was a whole host of things that I needed to know about the actual nitty gritty of the concept of spiritualism. Each and every night, someone would come up and ask me a question, either thinking I was Steve (as some still do, even though Steve is sat next to me!), or just asking me because Steve was signing books. Questions regarding loved ones who had passed over, or how they could develop the psychic ability they had, or this or that. For the first few months, I did, to some all intents and purposes, wing it a little bit. That's not to say I hadn't got a clue what I was saying, because being around Steve all day gives you some sort of understanding, but I felt I needed more of a concrete background to base my answers on.

With this is mind, after much badgering and cajoling by Jill Prior (who had seen an event advertised in the local press), I went along to see a demonstration of transfiguration, which happened to be in the same town on the same night that Steve was demonstrating in the South West. I didn't really have a leg to stand on, I simply had to go! I did not want to suffer the famous, or should I say, infamous, look from Jill all night!

305

Before I begin, please forgive me for my basic layman's terms in this chapter, because I'm still very naïve and backward on the subject. Even though James still professes I have a deeply latent psychic ability, I'm still the cautious virgin I always was!

Transfiguration is where a medium goes into a form of trance in, apart from the hypnotic glow of an underlit red lamp, complete darkness. His spirit guide(s) will bring through the spirit of a person, and he/she will transform, facially, into that person. Depending how good they are, they can also take on the voice and personality of them. So far, sounds good, I'm sure you'll agree. For those who want more than just a message verbally, this sounds like the ideal avenue to get that little bit more.

Still, with my heart all a flutter, and my mind working overtime on how it could all be set up, I meandered in with Jill. We were ushered into a small room, and after exchanging small talk with the hosts, we took our seats. To be fair to Jill, she was also as nervous and guarded as me, so just as the lights went out, we gave each other's hand a reassuring squeeze. I thought, "Well, there's only ten people here, if I'm lucky he won't pick on me!" We were each assigned a number, as the guy didn't know our names, so that if a spirit came through, the guy just had to say, "Number Five, are you there?" to which we replied "Yes" obviously, and then the connection was made. I guess it's the same scenario when Steve asks for the voice, as that's where the energy is connected.

The room was pitch black, and it seemed to take forever for my eyes to adjust to the red glow of that lamp at the front of the room. I kept going in and out of focus,

306

trying too hard I guess, to zoom in on the guy's face. My first thought was that all I could see were two huge bushy eyebrows and a little thin moustache, the kind that a dashing cad would have worn in the 1940's. His helper explained to us what would happen, and that we could ask questions at any time.

He eventually spoke to the group in what I can only describe as a comedy style Englishman talking Chinese voice. This was his guide, an ancient Chinese warrior who brought the spirits through. Apparently, he also had a Red Indian chief, if the warrior was busy. One by one, he went to all the numbers in the group, relaying "messages" from beyond. This, for me, is where it all sort of goes down hill. I had been looking forward to some amazing detail, some fantastic face changing, but all I could see, no matter who he was meant to be, were those huge eyebrows and that 'tache. The information being given was at best very vague and most of it was totally meaningless.

It seemed as if the person receiving the message was the one who was driving it. He'd say "Number Two, I have an old man here, do you understand?" to which the reply was "Are you my father?" and he said "Yes". Rather than asking open ended questions where he really had to give a correct response, and something else other than a yes or no. Everyone seemed to be asking the questions they wanted to ask and, by doing so, showing the person they wanted to make a connection with. The guy simply used the information given to him to concoct a reply. Another example was where he was connected to Number Eight's father, apparently spot on to the recipient in its content, but Number Eight kept asking leading questions: are you with mum (yes), have you seen my brother (yes). What I'm trying to convey (albeit badly!) is that I would have said "Is there anyone else there with you?" which he would have had to think about it.

It just seemed a little contrived, too staged for me and for all I knew, these people in the group (who were all regulars) knew what to say and what to ask. So it looked good for Jill and I, who were obvious newcomers. This could be as far from the truth as can be, but it felt like that.

Well, anyway, this carried on for all the numbers in the room and, to a degree, I did secretly hope he wouldn't come to me, because I wouldn't know what to ask. Naturally, he came to me next, my stomach lurched, my eyes rolled, my face went deep red (thank goodness for the pitch black - I would have looked a candidate for The Ugly Show) and yes, you guessed it, I was speechless. There are those now who will be thinking Rob Green Speechless? Must have the wrong person, he's always jabbering on about something... but speechless I was. Jill had to nudge me before I responded. Actually this makes me see how Steve feels when he's asking a question on a demo and no-one answers, even though someone out there knows what he's talking about. Then they come up at the end and say that it was them he was talking to. Steve always gets annoyed, because it makes him look as if he hasn't got it right, and 99.9% of the time he has, it's just that some people are too scared to shout out "yes!"

The man who came to me (and I was secretly hoping it was my dad that would come through), looked like any other face that he'd morphed into that night - that's right, the huge eyebrows and the moustache. It didn't resemble anybody I know whatsoever. I asked non-leading questions and got non-specific answers (which was my own fault I guess).  Nothing I asked, and nothing he responded with, pointed to the fact that it was my dad, or anyone else I knew for that matter.  It was someone who was "looking over me" and "making sure I made the right decisions."  For goodness sake, I could have gone up there and said that!

All the other messages that night were along the same lines, very vague and just feeding off the questions he was given.  His face never changed form; the eyebrow/moustache combo.  Then, all of a sudden, with a sharp intake of breath and a tilt of the head, he came out of his trance, and the lights went on.  That was it.  In one way, I was disappointed because I wanted to see something different to what Steve does, something enlightening and revealing, that would change my guarded mind.  On the other hand, it turned out exactly as I thought it would, no proof, a big show, a waste of time and money.  I know there are those out there who will be screaming at me now, saying it was my own cynicism that made me closed off and not receptive, but believe me, I went in with eyes and ears open.  Whether the others in the group felt like that too, I really couldn't say.  It hasn't put me off trying again with someone else, but if that had been my one and only shot at it, I would have left feeling severely short changed.  I am still open to all forms of spiritualism, and I do learn things each and every day, so please, do still ask me questions, I'm not that bad!"

I've got to say that I know exactly where Rob is coming from – I've had enough similar experiences myself, and in my opinion there are some very misguided people out there whose ambitions and desires blind them to the

309

damage they do to those people who are foolish enough to believe in their delusions of spirituality.

In this area Rob and I have a common bond and as we tippled away at the wine, we were both riding our hobby horses, demanding that séances and so called transfigurations should be held in clear light. As for the business of mediums disappearing within the sanctuary of curtained cubicles to re-appear as some ghostly manifestation from the other world, we were quite adamant that the curtained cubicles should be thrown out of the window and whatever the medium was capable of doing should be done in full view of a scrutinising audience...

Stephen started laughing. 'It's just as well,' he chuckled with mirth, 'that there *isn't* any room in the book for this subject because the way you're both going on about it, well I can only say it would rub a lot of people up the wrong way, and it's *my* scalp they'll come looking for, not yours. My Lord, if I let you two loose on a word processor I'd soon be feeling the heat, so if I were you I'd shut up about it and let the subject drop for now.'

'But it's important!' I protested.

'It's not so important as hurting other peoples' feelings and whatever you and Rob say, it's me who'd end up wearing the big black hat of the baddie.'

'So what do *you* think about this physical mediumship bit and transfiguring faces that remain the same all night and people putting on funny Chinese voices to make people think that they've been taken over by some mad mandarin from beyond the great wall?' Rob can get quite tart when he's pushed into a corner and right now he was fighting for his right to have an opinion of his own.

310

'Hang on Rob, just a minute! It's not what I think that matters here, although I do concede that you do have a few valid points. What I'm more concerned about is not rubbishing the beliefs of other people. We get cross and hurt when some of those evangelical Christian groups start shouting us down and I'm not about to join their ranks by shouting other people down just because their way of doing things is different to mine.'

'Okay, that's fair enough,' I put in, 'but Stephen, come on, you can't deny that there are some very dubious practices going on there and there are some very dubious people involved in the process.'

'I don't deny it at all James, but I know that while I'm okay in all that I do, it doesn't give me the right to be critical and point the finger at anyboldy else. That's not my job. It's not what I'm here for. And if there are people out there doing things they really shouldn't be doing, ostensibly in the name of spirit or the concept of spirituality, then sooner or later spirit will catch up with them and catch them out. I don't need to do anything or say anything and if you and Rob are telling me that I *should* do or say something, then my response is no thank you – at least not yet and not now.'

There was now a tension around the table that had nothing to do with the impending storm born of nature's turbulent skies. Steve was issuing a policy statement that brooked no argument and if Rob and I didn't like it, then we were being told we would just have to lump it. There is, as I've mentioned before, a certain tone of voice that Stephen uses which clearly indicates that a subject is closed – not necessarily for the rest of all time, but certainly for the time being. It doesn't do any good to argue, plead, cajole, because then he just starts

311

getting angry and although he tries hard not to let it show, you know his fuse is fizzing and you also know you'd better back off because when the Holbrook rocket does go off, it goes off with a very big bang.

Even so, I would have still argued the toss were it not for the most incredible detonation of thunder that exploded directly over our heads, taking us completely by surprise and causing me to send my wine glass flying half way across the herbaceous border.

And then the rain started. At first a few plopping squelchy drops and then an absolute torrential downpour that fell vertically out of the night like a Burmese monsoon. Palm fronds and fern stems bent before the onslaught and the summer flowers were stripped of their petals. We could see the raindrops literally bouncing and dancing on the wide expanse of the lawn and the roar of the rain against the canvas canopy of our big square umbrella made normal conversation impossible. Part of me, maybe only a small part, had been ready to have an argument with Stephen on the subject we had been discussing, but now I reckoned I'd been saved by the storm.

The three of us sat there grinning stupidly at each other. This rain was long overdue and now its sudden arrival brought a sense of freshness and revitalisation, drenching away the dust and making the air redolent with the scent of ozone and earth. I'm not exactly sure how Rob and Steve were feeling but I was just about to kick off my shoes and tear off my shirt and go dancing around the garden in the storm, but at that moment a figure moved towards us from the bar, behind us and to the left, and we were joined by the hotelier Tom, who had a large bottle of brandy in one hand and four good sized brandy balloons in the other. The distance from

312

the bar to our table was less than five yards, but even in those five yards Tom had got absolutely drenched.

It didn't seem to bother him and as he pulled up a chair and passed around the cognac, he was smiling broadly. 'We're ready for this,' he called out above the sound of the rain. 'This'll help the gardeners and farmers – here, gentlemen, have a drink on the house. I just popped out to say I'm closing the bar now, but you're welcome to sit here as long as you like, and if you want me to leave you the bottle that's fine, I'll put it on your bill in the morning.'

Stephen was looking beyond the back of Tom's head, back towards the window of the dining room. 'Oh,' he said absently. 'Our ghostly lady's back watching us from the window. She must have forgotten something from earlier on.'

'Ghostly lady?' Tom echoed in alarm. 'No, there are no ghosts here, Mr Holbrook. It'll just be another guest coming in late from the town…'

'Not unless they can walk through walls, it won't,' Stephen said quietly and although I heard this comment, mine host Tom did not. And then – 'Hang on, I've just got to go and check something out and I need to spend a penny.'

Stephen got up from the table and ran through the teaming rain into the bar, and I saw him a second later walking across the dining room looking to his left and right before he disappeared from view. He returned less than three minutes later with a big self satisfied smirk wrapped around his face. He plonked himself back in his seat and grinned effusively across the table at Tom.

'Sorry mate, but you've definitely got a ghost in there. Just had to go and make sure while I went to the loo.  She's a lovely lady but she's very sad because when she was alive…'

'No, Mr Holbrook,' Tom said tersely, not allowing Stephen to finish his sentence.  Mine host was smiling brightly, but only with his teeth, and not with his eyes.  'When I say there are no ghosts here, I really do mean *there are no ghosts here!*  Now, if you'll excuse me, I'm off to my bed and I'll leave you gentlemen to enjoy the storm.'

Tom made an abrupt departure with a long rumble of thunder escorting him on his way and the rain began to fall even harder.

'Well what was that all about?' Rob asked.

'Like the man said,' I grinned, 'there are no ghosts here – because if there were, he'd be off like a shot.  I don't think it's the sort of thing that he could deal with easily…' I shot a glance at Steve. 'Is it?'

'Er no, probably not…'

We got well into the brandy and started telling silly jokes.  Rob told the one about the clairvoyant's palmistry parlour in Scarborough that had a big sign across the door that said "closed through unforeseen circumstances" and I told the one about the guy who went to the fortune teller at York races who told him five was his lucky number, so he put five quid on the fifth horse in the fifth race and the damn thing came in fifth.  Steve told the one about the mouse and the elephant – the mouse looks up at the elephant and says "ooh aren't you big" and the elephant looks down at the mouse and says "ummm, yes, but aren't you small" and the mouse looks back up at the elephant and says "yeah, well, I've been ill," – and when we found ourselves laughing our socks off at the mouse and the elephant joke, maybe we knew it was time to go to bed. Besides which, by then it was gone two in the morning, the rain was easing off and the thunder was moving off way to the east. Before we got up to go, however, there was one of those quite odd little moments of grace where three friends sat in companionable silence – three very different people, each with his own wishes wants and desires, each with his own agenda of priorities, but each in turn bound one to the other in the common bond of spiritualism and the deep abiding belief in life after death, not just because we wanted it to be so but because each of us in his own way *knew* it to be so.

Each of us, also, believing that whether we liked it or not, spirit was guiding and influencing our lives, pushing us and putting us in place for what ever new challenge or adventure – or lesson – was destined to come our way.

Rob trusted that spirit had brought him into contact with Stephen so he might find a true sense of purpose and direction in his life... I trusted that spirit was pushing me to the south of France where I would write wonderful poetry and provide a safe haven for friends and family when civil war and revolution came to the British Isles within the next dozen years or so.

And as for Stephen, well I knew what he felt. He trusted that spirit would keep him doing his work with honesty and integrity, and the only reward he hoped to receive from this commitment was to enjoy that sense of inner peace that came from knowing that he was doing the right thing.

Stephen's earthly world revolves around his family and his few close friends, and the absolute adoration of his three gorgeous children – but the fact of the matter is that Stephen is not like most other men. He has this

315

mandate from the world of spirit to be their ambassador, to be their go-between, to act as their telephone exchange, and as such there have been times when the demands of the spirit world have not coincided with the needs of the father, the friend and the man.

As such, Stephen's life has always been in a state of compromise, and this is a juggling act he has had to perform on a daily basis for the last twenty four years. He always believed that 2006 was going to be a special year, and thus far it has certainly been all of that. As I said way back in chapter one, my friend has changed a lot in the last six months or so and I suppose, on reflection, one of the biggest changes has been his determination to take more time off, to spend more time with his children, to take more holidays and take better care of his health. It seems that his spiritual allies have given him leave to do this...

But in those stormy rain lashed hours as we sat beneath our canvas umbrella in the garden of The Lawns Hotel in Stamford, I cast him a shrewd glance and I remember thinking that I hoped he was making the most of the brief respite because 2006 was not going to last for ever and I had this sneaky feeling that once the year turned the heat would be back on.

With a vengeance.

We checked out of the hotel the following morning after a late breakfast. The storm had passed and we were left with the leaden skies and dismal drizzle of a typical British summer. There was no sign of mine host, but a charming lady, who turned out to be Tom's wife handled the formalities of the credit cards and accounts, and as in the way of all good hoteliers, she said that she hoped we'd enjoyed our stay. Stephen told her that it had been a perfectly marvelous visit, thank you very much, and then – and I've no idea what made him do this – he apologised in case he'd upset Tom in any way.

Mrs Tom cocked her head to one side and asked how he thought he might have upset her husband.

'Well,' Stephen grinned sheepishly, 'I was going on about the hotel being a bit haunted, but Tom was quite certain that there were no ghosts here, and I just thought I might have upset him a bit, that's all.'

'Aha!' Mrs Tom exclaimed with a curiously sharp edge in her voice. 'Well Mr Holbrook, if there are no ghosts here you tell me why my husband simply will not go up onto the third floor on his own after dark. No ghosts here indeed. That's the biggest joke I've heard all week!'

Grinning like idiots we hauled our luggage out into the damp grey morning and stashed it away in the car. Steve got in the back and Rob climbed in the front with me. I gunned the engine and we did a dubious three point turn in the middle of the road.

In one of those delicious moments of synchronicity we all cast a parting glance at the hotel and we all said 'No, there are no ghosts here!' before cracking up into silly giggles.

We cruised out of Stamford heading north towards Yorkshire. We were just passing the petrol station on the outskirts of the town when Rob turned in his seat to talk to Steve.

'There's just one thing I don't understand,' he said.

'Ummm, what's that?' Stephen asked absently.

'What's the mouse's size got to do with the fact that it had been ill... I didn't get that part of the joke at all...'

317

## Chapter Twenty Three:    *The Opera*

She stood mysterious and monolithic in the early morning mist, a towering edifice of white with flashes of royal blue.  Standing on the quayside in Genoa and gazing up at this great ship, she seemed absolutely enormous – which indeed she was.

Twelve decks and fifty seven thousand tonnes of opulence and luxury, beckoning with the promise of excitement and adventure, this was the MSC Opera, just two years old and one of the finest cruise liners in the world.  She was to be my home for the next week, and was to prove to be one of Steve Holbrook's greatest challenges.

The idea of doing a "Clairvoyant Cruise" had been mooted early in 2006 when Steve had been contacted by a lady called Jean Merry who worked with a company called Cruise 365.  Jean had a lot of experience putting themed cruises together and some of her greatest successes had been in the genre of body mind and spirit.  Having heard of Stephen's reputation and subsequently seeing him demonstrate, she had approached him with the idea of doing a week's cruise in the Mediterranean.

At first Stephen hadn't been enthusiastic about the idea, but as I'd pointed out at the time, the least he could do was go and talk to Jean and see what it was all about.  This he duly did, and at their initial meeting, something clicked between them, and much to his own surprise, Steve agreed to give it a try... Not so much because he was over enamoured by the idea of a working holiday on board a cruise ship but because he really warmed to Jean and felt that there was some sort of psychic connection that made it a matter of spiritual intervention.  As he said to Rob on the way home – 'I'm

318

really not bothered about going on a cruise, but I liked that lady a lot and spirit is telling me that this is the right thing to do.'

For my part, I wasn't backwards in coming forwards. I loved the idea of spending a luxurious week in the Med and virtually invited myself along with the dangling carrot of doing private readings for people between helping Steve with the three or four shipboard demonstrations that were mooted at the time.

When asked by Cruise 365 to assess the degree of potential interest in the project, I was confident that providing the advertising and pre-cruise publicity was right, we should have a major success on our hands. However as spring rolled into summer it became obvious that something was wrong because the bookings for the cruise were abysmally low. When I asked a few leading questions, I discovered that all the adverts were being placed in Northern newspapers, and sad to say that there are not many people in Sunderland and Sheffield who are natural cruise clientele. Maybe I'd misunderstood something, but I was under the impression that the advertising campaign was to be a national campaign that would, of course, have encompassed Steve's stronghold territories on the south coast.

Either way, I ended up in the dog house and right the way through June, July and August it was a moot point as to whether we would be going or not. In August, Jean Merry pulled a rabbit out of the hat and by opening up Steve's demonstrations to the rest of the ship rather than keeping it closed to just our own small group, we got the green light and the trip was definitely on – which oddly enough was suddenly a bit inconvenient for me because I was in the process of moving a wife, seven cats and two businesses from North Yorkshire to the South of France. However, I wasn't going to miss this cruise for all the tea in China, so while Jean and Steve and Rob and forty other souls flew out from Manchester to Milan, I made my own way and flew out from Stanstead to Genoa and got to The Opera a good five hours before everybody else.

By the time that the main group arrived I'd conducted a bit of a reconnaissance trying to get an angle on the lay-out of the ship, and my first impression was one of labyrinthine four dimensional confusion and although I was to learn how to find my way around eventually, the first few days were more than a little confusing, and not just for me – which is something I'll ask you to bare in mind when we come to the next part of this chapter! I suppose, with two theatres, four cabaret lounges, six bars, three swimming pools, one discotheque, half a dozen shops and six hundred cabins all spread over eight passenger decks, things would *have* to be a bit confusing, wouldn't they?

Anyway our group got itself together on the first night for an introductory cocktail party – and to tell the truth everyone was half way between being jaded and downright weary so there wasn't a great deal of energy at this gathering and the proceedings were a little muted. What was extremely gratifying, however, was to see so many familiar faces from Stephen's UK venues, so in part it was a little like a family reunion. There was also a pleasant mood of camaraderie insofar as there were forty people on board this ship, all drawn from disparate walks of life from different parts of the United Kingdom, but all with one common bond – namely to share time space and experience with Stephen Holbrook!

320

By shipboard standards we all went to bed quite early, the Opera slipped anchor and promptly sailed into a force nine gale.

Now for a fifty seven thousand tonne ship a force nine gale is no great problem, but it has to be said that the ship does *move* when confronted by strong winds and eighteen foot waves. For some people this can be a lovely experience – the gentle rolling of the ship rocks you into sleep like a baby in a cradle – but for others, even the mildest sensation of movement is enough to bring on the symptoms of mal de mer, especially if you've had some rich food and have imbibed just a little too much of the old vino.

Er... How do I put this politely? Let's try it this way. Rob had had a wonderful dinner and because this was the first night he'd been able to relax properly for weeks, he'd had a few bevies, and he went to bed around midnight, prepared to sleep like that proverbial baby I was talking about a few seconds ago.

However, a rolling ship, a dry mouth and a rather full bladder brought him to wakefulness around three o'clock in the morning and he staggered, barely half conscious, to the odd little en-suite which is a feature of all the Opera's cleverly designed cabins.

So, Rob goes to the loo (only half awake, remember) then comes out of the loo, and *then* realizes that he needs a tissue because (bless him) he needs to blow his nose. So, he opens the loo door, steps inside to get a tissue, but then to his half asleep horror realizes that he's not in the loo, he's in the flaming corridor – silly bugger has mistaken his cabin door for the loo door – and what's worse, the cabin door is an automatic locker and his key card is on the inside. What is even worse than that is that the hero of this tale, is stark bollock naked.

Ah, dear reader, indeed the stuff oif nightmares!

All right, think about this for a minute. What would *you* do in such circumstances? No point in banging on the door, because there's nobody on the inside. The cabin's only occupant (you) is on the outside. You're naked, you're tired, you're not feeling very well and you don't know where the hell you are.

Okay, you know you're on a ship but it's a BIG ship and you've only just got on it, and you don't quite know where you are on this BIG ship. Yes, you could go and bang on Stephen's door, which would be easy if only you could remember what cabin Stephen was in. You could bang on James Christie's door, but you don't know what cabin he's in either. You could go and bang on Jean Merry's door, but you don't even know what *deck* her cabin is on.

Rob Green, ladies and gentlemen, is now very wide awake and he realises, to his horror, that he is going to have to go and find the reception and get a pass key for his cabin. So with one hand over his front and another hand over his bum he marches down the corridor until he comes to the mezzanine: here there is a plan of the ship and as far as he can see, he's on deck ten and the reception desk is on deck five. Thank God there is a lift. He gets into the lift, presses the button, and down he goes...

Adding insult to injury the lifts are decorated by mirrors. Big mirrors covering three walls and the whole of the ceiling. Everywhere Rob looks, Rob sees Rob reflected a hundred times in the kaleidoscopic effect of the mirrors' projection of multiple reflections.

Deck five. The lift door opens. Ahead of him is the reception desk. Is it manned by some dignified male night porter? Oh dear me no, it is not! For lo, behind the desk are two very young and beautiful Italian ladies whose jaws drop and whose hearts start fluttering a little faster as this naked man marches purposefully towards them.

Later on the cruise I was to make the acquaintance of one of these girls – a long leggy brunette called Alexandra who found her way to me for a Tarot reading. After the reading she narrated the events from the receptionists' point of view.

Alexandra: 'I had been talking with Maria about how expensive things had become just lately when all of a sudden the lift doors opened and this naked man came walking towards us. He did not seem to be embarrassed but he did seem to be very angry. Maria and me got the giggles because although he had his hand in front of himself to protect his modesty either his hand was very small or his modesty was very large. We tried to keep our faces very straight, and of course we found him a pass key as soon as possible, but, of course he had nowhere to put it, so he put it between his teeth and marched away towards the lifts with it in his mouth, while he tried to hide himself with his hands. But, as I say, he had very small hands. After he had gone, I realised that I could have lent him a jacket or a towel from the office, but I just didn't think of it at the time. Besides, he was such a nice looking man and it would have been such a shame to cover him up.'

Rob made it back to his cabin in one piece but he was not in the best of moods when he came down for breakfast the following morning. I heard his version of the story and I have to say that Alexandra's version was a lot more entertaining.

Our first port of call was Monte Carlo. Sounds really exciting and romantic, but the truth of the matter is that fron the deck of the Opera it looked about as exciting as Ferrybridge minus the cooling towers. It was a grey flat drizzling day and this most famous of Mediterranean cities was shrouded in mist. While a lot of people went ashore, the Holbrook party elected to remain on board; the previous weeks had seen us battling through a punishing work schedule and we all needed to chill out and catch up with some of life's basis commodities, such as sleep.

Day two of our cruise took us to Valencia, and as this was one of Spain's cities that I hadn't visited, I made the most of the opportunity and did grab a cab into the town to have a look around. A far cry from El Cid's final battle with the Moors, Valencia had much to offer even though I didn't have a great deal of time to appreciate it.

On this day the sun shone in brilliant Mediterannean brightness and Stephen and Rob remained chained to their sun loungers by the ship's main pool. Both Steve and Rob are a pair of real sun bunnies and at the first sight of a single fluffy white cloud they'll go leafing through the Yellow Pages or Vision Magazine in search of some cloud counselling. I used to feel that way myself – a cloud in a clear blue sky is an offence against nature and a pending threat of doom and disaster, but these days I don't have much time for sitting in the sun, either because I become too easily bored or because I realise I no longer have time for sitting in the sun, twiddling my thumbs and waiting for the sun tan to set in before it inevitably fades with the first flush of English winter. Too many things to do and too little time left to do them in.

Stephen's first demonstration was scheduled for that evening, and knowing that he was tense and nervous about it, I reckoned that anything he could do to get some R&R before the event had to be to everyone's advantage.

Although Steve has been demonstrating for more than twenty years, and over that period has demonstrated in some very strange venues, he was feeling justifiably tense and apprehensive about the Opera demonstrations: this was the first time he would be demonstrating at sea and more importantly, to the very small audiences we were expecting. With an audience of two to three hundred Steve comes into his own, lifted by the group energy that carries him along his psychic wave that enables him to enjoy contact with the world of spirit. With an audience of only forty or so the group energy, in theory at least, would be significantly diminished and Stephen was nervous about the outcome. More than being concerned for his own record and reputation, Stephen's prime consideration was for Jean Merry who had put this package together and, of course, for all the people who had paid a lot of money and had travelled more than a thousand miles to be part of this experience. Steve is quite pathological about not wanting to let people down and he puts himself through a load of grief and heartache whenever this spectre raises its ugly head.

The shipboard venue for the demonstrations was The Caruso Lounge which would comfortably seat about a hundred and fifty people. Because we were only expecting forty, Rob and I judiciously arranged the

325

chairs so that from Steve's point of view forty might look like eighty. Roger Prior who runs Steve's website and handles a lot of his West Country venues, was also on board and while Rob and I sorted the chairs, Roger sorted the microphone and the sound system. By six thirty we were up and ready. By six fifty five we had an audience of only twenty three people and by seven o'clock we had a panicky Stephen wondering where the blazes everyone else had got to. An audience of forty would have been difficult enough but an audience of only twenty three was downright near impossible.

This was the first and only occasion in all the years I'd known Stephen that I had seen him nervous and trembling with stage fright. I've watched him walk out to an audience of a thousand plus, calm and unruffled. I've seen him take the stage full well knowing that there are born again Christian hecklers in the audience just waiting to have a go, and it hasn't phased him in the slightest. But facing this small audience of twenty three people was a different matter entirely. True to say, each member of that audience would have seen Steve demonstrate many times before, so in one way it could have been argued that he was demonstrating to an audience of sympathetic allies. I think, however, the way Steve saw it was that he would be demonstrating to a group of well educated peers who might possibly be expecting far more than he could deliver.

Rob gave him a pep talk.

Roger gave him a pep talk.

I gave him a pep talk.

…And then between the three of us, we pushed him out onto the small cabaret floor just five minutes later than scheduled. Beneath his sun tan Stephen looked very pale and if he could have done a bolt out of the nearest porthole, I think he would have bolted. Trouble was, we were at sea and there was nowhere at all to bolt to.

It's easy to say after the event, but really, he needn't have worried. Once he got over his initial unease at the unfamiliarity of the situation, the messages came through thick and fast and by the end of the demonstration he was not only relaxed but elated by what he felt he had achieved. There had been eight or nine strong links, and because he'd had time to play with, he had taken his time with these messages and had brought out a greater degree of detail than might have been possible if he'd been trying to get around a couple of hundred people in the same amount of time. Certainly the members of the audience I spoke to had been significantly impressed with comments such as "better than ever before" or "it's the best show I've ever seen him do" coming thick and fast from all over the place.

It was at this time that a small seed of psychic thought found some fertile soil in my mind. Rough around the edges, it was ill defined and without cohesion – but I knew it had something to do with Steve having to tackle this small and intense audience situation. In the "pep" talk I'd told him to treat this night as a new experience, or to think of it as being a big séance, or to use it as an opportunity to practice and play with some fresh techniques – to experiment with his gift and to see if there were any new lessons to be learned... And at the time I'd been using whatever words came readily to hand to give Steve the lift he needed. After the event, however, those words still lingered in my head, searching for a deeper degree of meaning and purpose that I could not quite bring into focus at that point in time.

One of the most surprising and rewarding trends I have noticed over the last year or so is the growing number of young people who find their way into Stephen's audiences and on board the Opera two very special people seemed to be typical of this situation. If you met them in the street or in some trendy disco you would not think that 19 year old Stephen Smallwood and 17 year old Emma Elliott would be the kind of people who'd get much out of a demonstration of clairvoyance. Yet, on holiday with their respective families, they sat entranced throughout Stephen's three evenings on board ship and talking to them afterwards it was abundantly clear that they were very much in tune with Steve Holbrook's work and what he was trying to achieve. Neither were what you'd call committed spiritualists, but both were open minded and actually very excited about the idea of post mortem survival. These were not scatty brained teenagers but seriously minded young adults with that wonderful clarity of intelligence and intellect that can sometimes become so clouded when you get to your middle years and wake up one morning and wonder where the hell half your life has gone to in a blink of an eye... And for me, and Steve Holbrook also, people like Stephen and Emma are vitally important because they are the spiritual pioneers of this new generation... The questioners, the door openers, the answer-finders.

This doesn't make them boring anoracky geeks... Lord, nothing could be further from the truth. Emma is one of those lovely young girls who has a gorgeously attractive personality that makes you smile and feel good whenever you are in her company, and while

Stephen Smallwood may be the epitome of sartorial elegance when it comes to modern male fashion who probably wouldn't be seen dead in an anorack, believe me, he can boogie and bevie with the best of them as he proved on more than one occasion in Opera's sumptuous Byblos disco. There is nothing chavvy or aggressive or angsty about these two teenagers, and although they come from different backgrounds they are similar insofar as they seem to have inherited an unusual degree of sensitivity from their families, and as I say, for me, these people are so *important* because they are the spiritual ambassadors of tomorrow. On a personal note, it is the Stephen Smallwoods and the Emma Elliotts who shall inherit *my* world when I depart this mortal coil for that great cruise ship up in the sky.

In their different ways both Stephen and Emma were influential in helping me define a line of philosophical thought that in the first couple of days of the cruise was just a blurred psychic image at the wrong end of a coca cola bottle.

During Steve's first and second demonstration (the second demonstration was better attended with about forty five people present and was also a lot more energetic with one particularly amazing message being delivered) he forged many impressive links and brought through some truly amazing evidence.

One lady who had been following Stephen around North Yorkshire for the better part of a decade, finally got a message from her late husband, which was just as well, for as she told me afterwards – 'I'd have killed the old bugger if he hadn't come through!' And, by the way, she wasn't talking about Steve, but of her departed husband!

Another highly emotive message went to Angela Smallwood (Stephen Smallwood's Mum) who instead of getting her message all at once, got it in dribs and trickles over the better part of an hour. Steve would bring something through, then would move on to someone else, then would come back to Angela with some more information, then move on again to someone else, before yet again returning to Angela. He forged links with her departed brother and brought through a plethora of evidence with names, dates, anniversaries, and even mention of The Angel that Angela constantly carried with her. At first Angela didn't get the bit about the Angel until her son tactfully pointed out that she did have an Angel tattood high up on her shoulder that she'd had done to commemorate her brother's premature passing.

Talking to Angela afterwards she said something that put the experience very much into perspective. This, she said, was the first time she'd ever been out of England. It was the first time she'd ever flown. It was the first time she'd ever been on board a ship. And it was the first time she'd ever had a message from heaven. The holiday was fantastic, the flying had been exciting, the cruise ship was incredible, but the most *important* thing of all was the message from her brother!

Including Steve's third demonstration which came later in the cruise and in which he felt a marked absence of energy, it transpired that just about *everyone* in the Cruise 365 group had received a message – and the four or five people who hadn't have been given free seats for one of Stephen's evenings when he is next in their area. Without shadow of a doubt, however, the most spectacular link that Stephen forged on the cruise was a message that came through during the second shipboard demonstration, and for the impact of this message to be fully appreciated, you need to have some background information.

In February 1991 Jill and Roger Prior lost their lovely daughter Lisa in an accident that was all too common at that point in time. Lisa was a ballet dancer and dance teacher, living in London in rented student accommodation. Landlords being what landlords were back in those days, ungoverned by the health and safety regulations which are now thankfully and belatedly in place, were frequently inclined to cut a few corners to make an extra buck, and one particular corner that frequently got cut was in the servicing of boilers!

Lisa's boiler had developed a fault and hindered by a heavy overnight fall of snow the air vent had become blocked. Thus, when Lisa took a bath, her bathroom was pumped full of carbon monoxide fumes – these are fumes that you neither see nor smell – and Lisa literally fell asleep and died in her bath.

Jill and Roger's world disintegrated and they went through the very worst time in their lives. I shall not dwell upon their grief – in any case, it takes little imagination to understand what they must have gone through. Here was a beautiful young woman, just twenty three years old, full of talent, enthusiasm and sheer vibrancy of life, destroyed in her prime by some wanton act of landlordly neglect. The hurt, the anger, the sense of unfairness and outrage that the Priors felt was only marginally overshadowed by their deep and profound sense of loss. It hit them very hard and it took them a long time even just to begin to come to terms

331

with what had happened. To this day they still do not understand why it had to happen.

In search of this understanding Jill and Roger found themselves exploring the concepts of spiritualism and they started attending a number of spiritualist church services: they talked to people, they observed, they listened and they assessed. They did *not* go racing in embracing everything they saw and heard at its face value, but rather they moved with great caution and objectivity.

Their breakthrough came when they met Stephen Holbrook for the first time. Both Jill and Roger were impressed by his freshness and enthusiasm, his very down to earth attitude and the accuracy of his messages. At their very first meeting some sort of psychic connection was made, and Stephen went out on a limb and actually prophesied that sooner or later both Roger and Jill would be actively working in the field of spiritualism.

Neither of the Priors thought this was remotely possible, but over the years, and especially after they had moved down to Somerset, their interest in spiritualism steadily grew and they found themselves attending more and more spiritualist churches in search of the contact and the evidence that they craved.

Frankly, the quality of mediumship in Somerset at that time was not very good and they both missed their friendship with Stephen; Roger happened to comment quite casually that if only Steve could come down to Somerset he would blow a few minds and show them how it should be done. When Jill said something along the lines of "well why don't you try and arrange something?" Roger took her at her word, and after getting the okay from Stephen, he arranged some demonstrations in the area which were a huge success and led to a regular twice yearly tour down in the West Country for our lad up North. This was also the embryonic beginnings of Roger and Jill's small promotions company called Prior Engagements.

At the time of writing, Roger and Jill have been promoting Stephen for the last fifteen years. They have attended hundreds of his demonstrations and have witnessed some of the most compelling evidence. And yet never once in all that time have they received a message from their beloved Lisa, although this is something they have both often prayed for. Curiously Stephen reports that he has occasionally felt Lisa's presence next to him on the stage but that she has never come forward to make contact – which is typical of her character in life. She was dedicated but never pushy.

A couple of nights before departing for the cruise Roger found some quiet space and offered up a silent message… He asked Lisa to please please please make a big effort to come through and he pointed out that their other daughter Frances would be on board, and that it would mean so much to all of them if they could have a message even if it was only a short sentence of encouragement.

Twenty minutes into the second demonstration in The Caruso Lounge, Stephen did come through with a message for Jill Prior, but it wasn't from Lisa, it was from her grumpy old Father who had caused Jill no end of problems while he was alive and with whom Jill had quite a number of unresolved issues. To be fair, Jill was impressed and amazed that her Father had chosen to make contact at this time, but also I suspect that she was secretly resentful. This was *not* the person she either wanted or needed to hear from. Like Roger and Frances, she wanted to hear from Lisa!

Nothing is absolutely perfect and although MSC Opera was almost perfect in every way, one thing that did get on my nerves was the tannoy system that was prone to burst into life two or three times a day with some over-enthusiastic young man exclaiming that it was "Shooooow Time" in this or that location – he did it in five languages, and the fact that he felt compelled to preceed and end his announcements with his verbal impression of a trumpet fanfare – "Paaappapadaaa!" made it even more annoying.

Half way through Steve's message to Jill from her dad his microphone cut out as the tannoy exclaimed "Paaappapadaa – it's shooooow time!" There wasn't much Steve could do other than perch on the edge of his table making idle conversation with his audience until the announcement had run its five language course. At the end of the interruption, he got up and opened his mouth to carry on with the message he had been giving Jill from her late father, but then a glazed expression came over his face. He looked directly at Jill and Roger and said quite simply – 'I've got Lisa here with me.' His eyes were filled with tears and needless to say, after fifteen long years of waiting for a message from their daughter, and in Frances' case from a most precious and beloved little sister, the Priors were in tears as well.

Lisa's message was gentle and simple. She had felt no pain in her passing. She had fallen asleep and had awoken, as if from a dream, on the other side. She was most deeply saddened that she'd had no time to say goodbye but that she had maintained a constant watch over the family and that she sent her deepest and most heartfelt love to everyone... To back this up she provided dates and details and more than sufficient evidence to prove beyond all shadow of doubt that this was definitely Lisa making contact with Roger and Jill and Frances.

When I met up with the Priors after the demonstration they were still bubbling over with elation and exultation – and I do not use that word exultation lightly for it exactly and precisely describes their emotional state. Some hours later when we were in a more seriously analytical discussion of the events that had occurred, a couple of *very* interesting points came to light.

(1) The week before Lisa had passed away she had been approached by a company who wanted her to choreograph a modern ballet called "Showtime".

(2) The tannoy announcement that had preceeded Steve's message from Lisa had been for a modern ballet presentation in the Opera's main auditorium.

(3) The message for the Priors came through when their daughter Frances had been present – and this was the first time that all *three* members of the family had attended one of Steve's demonstrations together.

And this business of there being *three* family members together has given evidence to a private theory of mine that suggests a three-way vibration, perhaps reflecting the holy trinity of love, is a very powerful beacon for any visiting spirit to lock on to. Not knocking Roger or Jill in any way, I think it is entirely possible that Frances was the catalyst for the message from her baby sister and that Roger and Jill reaped the benefit of Frances's presence.

Certainly the "Shooooow Time" vibration would have been a most powerful magnet for above all else,

Lisa was a dancer and a choreographer and she would have responded to anything that hinted at the theatre, lights, music and the stage.

Now, although possibly a wee bit circumstantial, this is where it gets just a little bit weird and spooky.

Stephen does not let either me or Rob into the demonstrations. He says it puts him off. So once he's on, we're locked out. On the night of this important demonstration, once Stephen had started the evening, Rob disappeared back to his cabin to find some cigarettes, and I wandered off down the ship to have a quiet drink in my favourite watering hole called The Cabala Bar. There was no one there, just me, the Balinese bar manager and the piano player. The piano player didn't have an audience to play for and so he played for himself, and gently tinkled away on a rather bluesy version of Clare de Lune by Claude Debussy. I've always liked this piece of music and I very much liked what this musician was doing with it. I was happy to chill out with my brandy and coke and let Debussy's haunting music flow over me.

This would have been more or less the time that the Priors were getting their message and I can narrow the timing to a very narrow margin by virtue of that blasted tannoy announcement.

I subsequently learned from Roger that Clare de Lune was one of Lisa's favourite pieces of music and that the last time Roger and Jill had seen her dance, she had danced to that particular tune.

As a footnote to this section may I draw your attention to a truly wonderful little book called "One Moment In Time" by Jill Prior (Apex Publishing Ltd. ISBN: 1-904444-74-1). In this book Jill writes with great elegance and compassion about Lisa and how her

336

passing affected everyone in the Prior family. It is an absolute must for anyone interested in spiritualism and I would suggest that it is vital reading for any parent who has ever lost a child.

In summation, the cruise on board the Opera was a qualified success. We all made some new friends, we all drank too much and we all ate too much. As far as Steve and I were concerned, cruising was a totally new experience, and contrary to our expectation we never once felt trapped or claustrophobic. The weather was reasonably kind to us, and after the incredibly busy year we'd had, we did find just a little time to chill out and get a bit of a rest.

It has to be said that there were a few incidents of highly wry humour that are worth mentioning. I'm not sure if it was half way through Steve's first or second demonstration but at one point his attention was distracted by the arrival of two smartly dressed ship's officers who stood pontifically at the back of the Caruso lounge, giving Steve a cursory once over. Steve hates people standing at the back, so he politely but firmly asked the two officers to be seated and, if they elected to remain, they would be expected to put their hands up if they thought that there might be a message coming through for them.

Jean Merry hissed in a huge stage whisper that this was *The Captain* doing his rounds to which Stephen replied he didn't care if it was the Captain of the Star Ship Enterprise, it was *his* demonstration and if they were staying, they'd sit down and take part – or they could jolly well leave right now. The Captain and the first officer duly sat down!

Another incident that gives me a smile every time I think of it involved one of the tours that went around Rome while we were docked in Civitavecchia. One party got lumbered with a particularly inept guide who managed to lose various members of her grpoup on numerous occasions during the day. At one point, a lovely guy called Terry Nutman, rescued two lost damsels in distress and virtually had to spend the whole of the afternoon acting as Tail End Charlie rounding up the guide's increasing numbers of lost sheep. By the end of the day Terry was furious and when the guide said 'It has been lovely, and I hope to see you all again soon' Terry couldn't help himself and called out 'Yes love, preferably through Stephen Holbrook!'

Steve used some of his ship board time to sleep and top up his sun tan while I found myself thinking some rather deep and ponderous thoughts... Provoked by the very small groups Steve had been demonstrating to and also, as I've said, by the presence of people like Stephen Smallwood and Emma Elliott.

Steve had not felt happy about working with only thirty or so people in the audience, and yet by his own admission he had felt compelled against his own personal judgement to come on this cruise. It was something, so he said, that spirit had "pushed" him into almost against his will. At the end of his demonstrations he felt that he had aquitted himself reasonably well and was eager to discuss the possibility of doing more work on cruise ships, conditional to there being a larger percentage of English speaking passengers that would at least give him a chance of working to a decent sized audience. He was still slightly perplexed, however, as to the purpose of spirit, pushing him forwards into dealing with such small groups of people when he had become accustomed to working to many hundreds.

By the time the Opera was entering her home port of Genoa I had a half formed theory, and for what it's worth, here it is.

In this first decade of the 21$^{st}$ century it's fairly obvious that the established order of world religions is tearing itself apart and although it has been doing so for a number of years the last half decade in particular has seen a vicious upturn in the nihilistic intensity of this phenomenon. In Britain's own backyard of Northern Ireland, we seem to have a whole load of Protestants and a whole load of Catholics and not very many Christians. The Anglican Church is increasingly at loggerheads with itself with one faction of theology constantly locking horns with another. The Catholic Church lurches from drama to crisis as it seeks to defend the indefensible: mediaeval edicts on birth control do not sit well with the flagrant commercialism of the Vatican's world wide business interests and its protectionism of paedophile priests is totally unforgivable. Add to this an increasing number of Christian sects on both sides of the Atlantic that are now blatantly teaching creativism in their ultra conservative right wing schools while at the same time grooming their pupils to become candidates for high political office (sic. George W. Bush) and there is a recipe for disaster as the Christian right maneuvers into position to launch a world wide holy war against Islam. (As one senior American politician remarked after it was glaringly apparent that Bush's post 9/11 war on terror was not working – "If we'd simply nuked every Islamic city in the world then *that* would have sorted the problem out once and for all!")

And, of course, the Islamic world has much to answer for insofar as true members of the faith have allowed their religion to be hi-jacked by a small minority of mad mullahs and deranged ayatollah's hell bent on the destruction of the west to satisfy their own Satanic blood lust and to satiate their personal quests for power and glory and immortality. How many of these fanatics have actually sat down and read the revered pages of the Holy Koran? Were they to do so they would find gentle words of love and guidance, they would find a code of reverence and respect for the Family of Man, and they would find no mention of Jihad or the callous murder of innocents.

Even within Islam Suni slaughters Shia and the Shi'ite commits equal atrocities of barbarism against his Suni brother. All point the finger of blame at the west, especially at Israel and the United States, and none do anything much to sensibly resolve the ongoing agony between the Jews and the Palastinians.

These people – and I do say "these people" because I totally disassociate myself from this rabble of unholy hooligans – have in turn been egged on, manipulated, used and abused by some of our so called "enlightened" western governments for reasons of political clout, oil revenues, and darker Christian agendas… And in my opinion, within a very short time, the world is going to flip arse over tit and we will see some cataclysmic planetary event that will wipe all of these religions from the face of the earth and put us right back at square one.

And yet Man is a strange beast. It is in his nature to need a God or something to believe in that is greater than himself and greater than the world in which he lives. Thus into this void something must step forwards to fill the gap – something that rises above creed and doctrine, and something which is based on the open vibration of love and understanding.

I am not saying that this will be the spiritualist church but I am saying that it will be a purely spiritual congregation that perhaps holds dear the belief that whatever you do down here on the earthplane reflects what happens to you when you leave this plane of existence for something higher and brighter. Within such a congregation it is people like Steve Holbrook who will be holding the torch and providing the guiding light, and people like pretty young Emma and the old-before-his-years Stephen Smallwood who will be helping to spread the light.

It seems inevitable that in the future Stephen will have no choice other than to teach others how to open themselves up to the will and the world of spirit, and as such, the "small group" demonstrations he has had to deal with on board ship could be seen as the beginning of a prepatory learning curve experience for Steve's future role as a teacher.

Thank you for reading this book. Now I'm going to open a bottle of wine and fill my pipe, and declare this to be the end of part three.

*James Christie*
*Gray Britain, 11th October 2006*

*PS. There's some talk of us going for another cruise around the Greek Islands in the Autumn of 2007, although frankly I'd prefer to go to The Carribean. Quite fancy a few drinks with Johnny Depp and an evening out with Kiera Knightly. Contact Jean at Cruise 365 for details. PPS. Anyone got Kiera's phone number?*

341

# Other MAGE books by the same author

## "The Light In The Darkness"
*Part One of the Stephen Holbrook Trilogy*

## "Out Of This World"
*Part Two of the Stephen Holbrook Trilogy*

## "In The Arms Of The Wind"
*One man's quest to find absolute proof of an afterlife*

## "The Opening"
*A story of love and healing – and sheer bloody horror!*

## www.magepublishing.co.uk